Steps to the Temple, Delights of the Muses, and Other Poems

CAMBRIDGE ENGLISH CLASSICS

Poems

by

Richard Crashaw

RICHARD CRASHAW

Born, 1613 ?
Died, 1649.

RICHARD CRASHAW

STEPS TO THE TEMPLE

DELIGHTS OF THE MUSES

AND OTHER POEMS

THE TEXT EDITED BY

A. R. WALLER

CAMBRIDGE :
at the University Press
1904

London: C. J. CLAY AND SONS,
CAMBRIDGE UNIVERSITY PRESS WAREHOUSE,
AVE MARIA LANE.
Glasgow: 50, WELLINGTON STREET.

Leipzig: F. A. BROCKHAUS.
New York: THE MACMILLAN COMPANY.
Bombay and Calcutta: MACMILLAN AND CO., Ltd.

NOTE.

This edition contains the whole of Crashaw's Poems, English and Latin, now for the first time collected in one volume.

Although not 'English Classics,' it has been thought best to include Crashaw's Latin and Greek poems, for completeness' sake. These are reproduced faithfully from the original issues printed at the Cambridge University Press in 1634 and 1670 and from photographs of the Sancroft MS. No attempt has been made to "improve" Crashaw's spelling or punctuation save in the one or two trifling instances mentioned in the notes, and save in the use of the modern type-forms for *j*, *s*, *u*, *m̃*, etc.

The arrangement of the text is as follows:

I. *Epigrammatum Sacrorum Liber*, from the volume ($5\frac{3}{4} \times 3\frac{1}{2}$ ins.) of 1634. A few additional epigrams that occur in the second edition of 1670 will be found on pp. 299—306.

II. *Steps to the Temple* and *The Delights of the Muses*. The text of 1648 ($5\frac{3}{4} \times 3\frac{3}{8}$ ins.) has been followed, but only those poems have been printed which were not revised at a later date for the volume entitled *Carmen Deo Nostro*, 1652 (see III. below). The text of the first edition of *Steps to the Temple. Sacred Poems, with other Delights of the Muses...Printed and Published according to Order...Printed by T. W. for*

NOTE

Humphrey Moseley,... 1646, has been collated with that of 1648, and both texts with that of *Carmen Deo Nostro*, and the verbal alterations, omissions and additions in these three texts will be found in the Appendix, this course being deemed more satisfactory than to form an eclectic text by guesswork. Certain poems belonging to these three volumes are also in Archbishop Sancroft's MS. (see IV. below) and in the British Museum MSS. (see V. below); variations between these MSS. and the printed volumes will be found in the Appendix. In the text, the latest published form has been printed in each case. For the loan of copies of the texts of 1646 and 1648 I am indebted to the Library of Trinity College, Cambridge.

III. The revised collection of poems entitled *Carmen Deo Nostro* ($6\frac{1}{2} \times 4$ ins.), printed and published in Paris in 1652 and adorned with small plates engraved from Crashaw's own drawings, has been followed from the first page to the last. It bears evidence of having been printed abroad, as its simple errors of the press are numerous. These have been corrected and their places marked by square brackets, and in the Appendix will be found reproductions of the engravings, with indications of their place. Copies of the edition of 1652 are very rare indeed, and it has been thought well to preserve its eccentricities of spacing and its generosity in the matter of titles and half-titles.

IV. The volume of Crashaw's (and other) poems, copied by Archbishop Sancroft and now preserved in the Bodleian, was kindly forwarded from Oxford to the Cambridge University Library, to enable me to collate it. I am much indebted to the authorities at Oxford for this privilege, and to the University Librarian here for making the examination of the MS. as easy as possible.

vi

NOTE

A great many poems in it were first published by Dr Grosart in his *Fuller Worthies'* edition of 1872–3; they were rearranged by him to fall in with the scheme of his edition, but in the following pages they will be found printed in the order in which they occur in the MS., the poems published by Crashaw being, of course, omitted. As indicated above (see II.), verbal differences between MS. and published text will be found in the notes to the latter.

The evidence that some poems other than those indicated in the MS. by the initials R.C. are Crashaw's is mainly based upon Abp Sancroft's table of contents to his volume, a photograph of which I have had made. I regret that in one case the evidence seems clear that a poem printed by Dr Grosart as Crashaw's cannot be his, and it does not therefore find a place in the present text.

Abp Sancroft's table of contents begins thus: ' Mr Crashaw's poëms transcrib'd frõ his own copie, before they were printed ; among w^ch | are some not printed. Latin, on ye Gospels v. p. 7. On other subjects. p. 39. 95. 229. English sacred | poëms p. 111. on other subjects—39. 162. 164. v. 167. v. 196. 202. v. 206. 223. v. Suspetto di Herode. | translat'd frõ Car. Marino. p. 287 v.' The table then gives the titles of poems other than Crashaw's, and amongst these are indexed the two unsigned poems written on p. 205 of the MS., 'On a Freind. On a Cobler': of these, Dr Grosart printed one as Crashaw's and not the other. Dr Grosart took ' 202. v. 206' to mean that all the poems on and between those pages were Crashaw's. If that were so then the verses ' On a Cobler' would be Crashaw's and these he omitted. But, apart from the fact that these two poems are indexed elsewhere among Abp Sancroft's miscellaneous and anonymous collection, they are preceded by a

NOTE

poem to which Abp Sancroft affixed the initials R. Cr.,
are followed by one bearing the same initials, and are
themselves unsigned.

Dr Grosart printed the following seven poems as
Crashaw's: Three 'On ye Gunpowder-Treason' (see
pp. 349–354), two 'Upon the King's Coronation'
(pp. 355–6), 'Upon the birth of the Princesse Elizabeth'
(pp. 357–8) and 'An Elegie on the death of Dr Porter'
(pp. 362–3). The external evidence, however, is not so
strong as Dr Grosart indicated on p. xxii of the Preface
to Vol. I. of his edition of 1872. He says 'All entered
thus 164 v. 167 are by him and so these being entered
under his name in Index as 167 v. 196 must belong to
him.' Of the poems in the MS. on pp. 164–167, the
first, 'Upon a gnatt burnt in a candle,' though lacking
the initials, I take to be Crashaw's, because it is the only
one on that page and that page is credited to him in the
Index. Pp. 165 and 6 contain 'Love's Horoscope,'
signed R. Cr., p. 166 'Ad amicam,' signed T. R.
[Thomas Randolph]. On p. 167 begins the long poem
'Fidicinis et Philomelae' ('Musicks Duell'), signed
R. Cr., which extends to p. 171 and is followed by
other poems, *all* bearing the initials R. Cr., on pp. 171–
179. On pp. 180–187 the five Gunpowder-Treason
and King's Coronation poems are transcribed and they
lack the initials. Pp. 187–190 contain the 'Panegyrick
upon the Birth of the Duke of York,' with the initials
R.Cr., pp. 190–192 the poem 'Upon the birth of the
Princesse Elizabeth,' mentioned above, and again lacking
initials, pp. 192–195 contain poems certainly by other
hands, whose authors are either there given or indexed
by Abp Sancroft, and p. 196 contains 'Ex Euphor-
mione' with the initials R. Cr. again.

The 'Elegie on the death of Dr Porter' is attributed
to Crashaw by Dr Grosart because it is 'entered in Index

NOTE

under Crashaw' (Grosart, ib. p. xxiii). But it will be seen by a reference to Abp Sancroft's contents given above that '229' seems to refer to Latin poems. Now p. 229 contains the Latin 'In Eundem Scazon,' with the initials R. Cr., and the beginning of the Dr Porter poem, which lacks the initials.

Against this negative evidence, which seems to me worthy of consideration, there is the fact that the poems in question are not elsewhere indexed by Abp Sancroft as anonymous or miscellaneous, and the internal evidence of their being from Crashaw's hand is not insignificant. I have therefore decided to print them, after stating the doubts concerning them.

This MS. volume of Abp Sancroft has many interesting poems in it, other than Crashaw's, and my photograph of his table of contents is at the service of other students who may be working at the literature of that period.

V. In 1887–8 Dr Grosart issued a supplement containing a collation of a small MS. volume, recently acquired by the British Museum (Addit. MS. 33,219), considered to be in the handwriting of Crashaw himself. The volume was evidently a transcript of some of his English poems, intended possibly as a gift, since it begins with a few dedicatory lines and a longer dedicatory poem. In his supplement Dr Grosart printed these lines and poem, together with a translation from Grotius and two more poems, as 'hitherto unprinted and unknown.' I have printed the two dedicatory poems and the Grotius, but the other two ('Midst all the darke and knotty snares' and 'Is murther no sin') were already printed by Crashaw in his 'Steps to the Temple,' 1646 and 1648, and will be found in Dr Grosart's own 1872–3 edition on pp. 47 Vol. I. and 144 Vol. II. respectively. In the notes to the various published English poems will be found, as in

NOTE

the case of the Sancroft MS., variations between them and this British Museum MS.

A further acquisition by the British Museum in 1894 (Addit. MS. 34,692) contains a transcript of Crashaw's 'Loe heere a little volume' and 'Upon the Assumption.' It is dated 1642 and seems to have belonged to 'Thom: Lenthall: Pemb: Hall:' in which college Crashaw began his academical career. Its variations are recorded in the notes, as are those of the poems in Harl. MSS. 6917–8, and of the earliest appearances of some of Crashaw's verses in sundry volumes of contemporary verse and prose. Of these, attention may be called to the interesting alternative readings found in the lines under the portrait of Bp Andrewes (see pp. 134 and 372).

For assistance in the collation of the British Museum MSS. I am indebted to Mr Richard Askham, and Mr Albert Ivatt, of Christ's College, has very kindly prepared the indexes for me.

The copy of *Carmen Deo Nostro* used for the purpose of the present edition will rest in future in the library of Peterhouse, of which College Crashaw was made Fellow in 1637 and from which he was ejected, with others, six years later for refusing to accept the Solemn League and Covenant.

A. R. WALLER.

CAMBRIDGE,
May 15, 1904.

x

EPIGRAM-
MATUM
SACRORUM
LIBER.

CANTABRIGIÆ,

Ex Academiæ celeberrimæ
typographeo. 1634.

REVERENDO ADMODUM
VIRO
BENJAMINO LANY
SS. Theologiæ Professori,

Aulæ Pembrochianæ Custodi dignissimo,

ex suorum minimis
minimus
R. C.
custodiam cœlestem
P.

SUus est & florū fructus; quibus fruimur, si non utiliùs, delicatiùs certé. Neque etiam rarum est quòd ad spem veris, de se per flores suos quasi pollicentis, adultioris anni, ipsiúsq; adeò Autumni exigamus fidem. Ignoscas igitur (vir colendissime) properanti sub ora Apollinis sui, primæque adolescentiæ lasciviâ exultanti Musæ. Teneræ ætatis flores adfert, non fructus seræ : quos quidem exigere ad seram illam & sobriam maturitatem, quam in fructibus expectamus meritò, durum fuerit ; forsan & ipsâ hac præcoci importunitate suâ placituros magís : Tibi præsertim quem paternus animus (quod fieri solet) intentum tenet omni suæ spei diluculo, quò tibi de tuorum indole promittas aliquid. Ex more etiam eorum, qui in præmium laboris sui pretiúmque patientiæ festini, ex iis quæ severunt ipsi & excoluerunt, quicquid est flosculi prominulum, primâ quasi verecundiâ auras & apertum Jovem experientis arripiunt avidè, saporémque illi non tam ex ipsius indole & ingenio quàm ex animi sui affectu, foventis in eo curas suas & spes, affingunt. Patere igitur (reverende Custos) hanc tibi ex istiusmodi floribus corollam nedi; convivalem veró: nec aliter passuram Sydus illud oris tui auspicatissimum nisi (quâ est etiam amœnitate) remissiore radio cùm se reclinat, & in tantum de se demit. Neque sanè hoc scriptionis genere (modò partes suas satìs præstiterit) quid esse potuit otio Theologico accommodatius, quo nimirum res ipsa Theologica Poëticâ amœnitate delinita majestatem suam venustate commendat. Hoc demùm quicquid est, amare tamen poteris; & voles, scio: non ut magnum quid, non ut egregium, non ut te dignum denique, sed ut tuum: tuum summo jure; utpote quod è tua gleba, per tuum radium, in manum denique tuam evocatū fuerit. Quod restat hujus libelli fatis, exorandus es igitur (vir spedatissime) ut quem sinu tam facili privatum excepisti, eum jam ore magìs publico allo-quentem te non asperneris. Stes illi in limine, non auspicium modò suum, sed & argumentum. Enimvero Epigramma sacrum tuus ille vultus vel est, vel quid sit docet; ubi nimirum amabili diluitur severum, & sandum suavi demulcetur. Pronum me vides in negatam mihi provinciam; laudum tuarum, intelligo: quas mihi cùm modestia tua abstulerit, reliquum mihi est necessariò ut sim brevis: imò verò longus nimiúm; utpote cui argumentum istud abscissum fuerit, in quo unicè poteram, & sine tædio, prolixus esse. Vale, virorum ornatissime, neque dedigneris quòd colere audeam Genii tui serenitatem supplex tam tenuis, & (quoniam numen quoq; hoc de se non negat) amare etiam. Interim verò da veniam Musæ in tantum sibi non temperanti, quin in hanc saltem laudis tuæ partem, quæ tibi ex rebus sacris apud nos ornatis meritissima est, istiusmodi carmine involare ausa sit, qualicunque,

EPIGRAMMATA SACRA

SALve, alme custos Pierii gregis :
  Per quem erudito exhalat in otio ;
    Seu frigus udi captet antri,
      Sive Jovem nitidósque soles.

Non ipse custos pulchrior invias
Egit sub umbras Æmonios greges ;
    Non ipse Apollo notus illis
      Lege suæ meliore cannæ.

Tu si sereno des oculo frui ;
Sunt rura nobis, sunt juga, sunt aquæ,
    Sunt plectra dulcium sororum ;
      (Non alio mihi nota Phœbo)

Te dante, castos composuit sinus ;
Te dante, mores sumpsit ; & in suo
    Videnda vultu, pulverémque
      Relligio cinerémque nescit.

Stat cincta digná fronde decens caput :
Subsque per te fassa palàm Deos,
    Comìsque, Diva, vestibúsque
      Ingenium dedit ordinémque.

Jámque ecce nobis amplior es modò
Majórque cerni. Quale jubar tremit
    Sub os ! verecundúsque quantâ
      Mole sui Genius laborat !

Jam qui serenas it tibi per genas,
Majore cœlo Sydus habet suum ;
    Majórque circum cuspidatæ
      Ora comit tua flos diei.

Stat causa. Nempe hanc ipse Deus, Deus,
Hanc ara, per te pulchra, diem tibi
    Tuam refundit, obvióque
      It radio tibi se colenti.

RICHARD CRASHAW

Ecce, ecce! sacro in limine, dum pio
Multúmque prono poplite amas humum,
Altaria annuunt ab alto.;
Et refluis tibi plaudit alis

Pulchro incalescens officio, puer
Quicunque crispo sydere crinium,
Vultúque non fatente terram,
Currit ibi roseus satelles.

Et jure. Nam cùm fana tot inviis
Mœrent ruinis, ipsáque (ceu preces
Manúsque, non decora supplex,
Tendat) opem rogat, heu negatam!

Tibi ipsa voti est ara sui rea.
Et solvet. O quàm semper apud Deum
Litabis illum, cujus aræ
Ipse preces priùs audiisti!

EPIGRAMMATA SACRA

Venerabili viro Magistro *Tournay,*
Tutori suo summè observando.

MEssis inauravit Cereri jam quarta capillos,
 Vitis habet Bacchum quarta corona suæ,
Nostra ex quo, primis plumæ vix alba pruinis,
 Ausa tuo Musa est nidificare sinu.
Hîc nemus, hîc soles, & cœlum mitius illi :
 Hîc sua quod Musis umbra vel aura dedit.
Sedit ibi secura malus quid moverit Auster,
 Quæ gravis hybernum vexerit ala Jovem.
Nescio quo interea multùm tibi murmure nota est :
 Nempe sed hoc poteras murmur amare tamen.
Tandem ecce (heu simili de prole puerpera) tandem
 Hôc tenero tenera est pignore faĉta parens.
Jámq́ meam hanc sobolem (rogo) quis sinus alter haberet ?
 Quis mihi tam noti nempe teporis erat ?
Sed quoq; & ipsa Meus *(de te) meus, improba, tutor*
 (*Quàm primùm potuit dicere*) *dixit, erit.*
Has ego legitimæ, nec lævo sydere natæ
 Non puto degeneres indolis esse notas ;
Nempe quòd illa suo patri tam semper apertos,
 Tam semper faciles nôrit adire sinus.
Ergò tuam tibi sume : tuas eat illa sub alas :
 Hoc quoque de nostro, quod tuearis, habe.
Sic quæ Suada tuo fontem sibi fecit in ore,
 Sanĉto & securo melle perennis eat.
Sic tua, sic nullas Siren non mulceat aures,
 Aula cui plausus & sua serta dedit.
Sic tuus ille (precor) Tagus aut eat objice nullo,
 Aut omni (quod adhuc) objice major eat.

RICHARD CRASHAW

Ornatissimo viro Præceptori suo colen-
dissimo, Magistro *Brook*.

O *Mihi qui nunquam nomen non dulce fuisti,*
  Tunc quoque cùm domini fronte timendus eras!
Ille ego pars vestri quondā intactissima regni,
  De nullo virgæ nota labore tuæ,
Do tibi quod de te per secula longa queretur
  Quòd de me nimiùm non metuendus eras:
Quòd tibi turpis ego torpentis inertia sceptri
  Tam ferulæ tulerim mitia jura tuæ.
Scilicet in foliis quicquid peccabitur istis,
  Quod tua virga statim vapulet, illud erit.
Ergò tibi hæc pœnas pro me mea pagina pendat.
  Hîc agitur virgæ res tibi multa tuæ.
In me igitur quicquid nimis illa pepercerit olim,
  Id licet in fœtu vindicet omne meo.
Hîc tuus inveniet satìs in quo sæviat unguis,
  Quôdque veru docto trans obeliscus eat.
Scilicet hæc mea sunt; hæc quæ mala scilicet: ô si
  (Quæ tua nempe forent) hîc meliora forent!
Qualiacunque, suum nôrunt hæc flumina fontem.
  (Nilus ab ignoto fonte superbus eat)
Nec certè nihil est quâ quis sit origine. Fontes
  Esse solent fluvii nomen honôrque sui.
Hic quoque tam parvus (de me mea secula dicant)
  Non parvi soboles hic quoque fontis erat.
Hoc modò & ipse velis de me dixisse, Meorum
  Ille fuit minimus. Sed fuit ille meus.

EPIGRAMMATA SACRA

LECTORI.

SAlve. Jámq; vale. Quid enim quis pergeret ultrâ?
 Quâ jocus & lusus non vocat, ire voles?
Scilicet hîc, Lector, cur noster habebere, non est;
 Delitiis folio non faciente tuis.
Nam nec Acidalios halat mihi pagina rores;
 Nostra Cupidineæ nec favet aura faci.
Frustra hinc ille suis quicquam promiserit alis:
 Frustra hinc illa novo speret abire sinu.
Ille è materna meliùs sibi talia myrto;
 Illa jugis meliùs poscat ab Idaliis.
Quærat ibi suus in quo cespite surgat Adonis,
 Quæ melior teneris patria sit violis.
Illinc totius Floræ, verísque, suíque
 Consilio, ille alas impleat, illa sinus.
Me mea (casta tamen, si sit rudis) herba coronet:
 Me mea (si rudis est, sit rudis) herba juvat.
Nulla meo Circæa tument tibi pocula versu:
 Dulcia, & in furias officiosa tuas.
Nulla latet Lethe, quam fraus tibi florea libat,
 Quam rosa sub falsis dat malè fida genis.
Nulla verecundum mentitur mella venenum:
 Captat ab insidiis linea nulla suis.
Et spleni, & jecori foliis bene parcitur istis.
 Ah malè cum rebus staret utrumque meis.
Rara est quæ ridet; nulla est quæ pagina prurit:
 Nulla salax, si quid nôrit habere salis.
Non nudæ Veneres: nec, si jocus, udus habetur:
 Non nimiùm Bacchus noster Apollo fuit.
Nil cui quis putri sit detorquendus ocello;
 Est nihil obliquo quod velit ore legi.
Hæc coràm, atque oculis legeret Lucretia justis:
 Iret & illæsis hinc pudor ipse genis.
Nam neque candidior voti venit aura pudici
 De matutina virgine thura ferens:
Cùm vestis nive vincta sinus, nive tempora fulgens,
 Dans nive flammeolis frigida jura comis,
Relligiosa pedum sensim vestigia librans,
 Ante aras tandem constitit; & tremuit.

RICHARD CRASHAW

Nec gravis ipsa suo sub numine castior halat
  Quæ pia non puras summovet ara manus.
Tam Venus in nostro non est nimis aurea versu:
  Tam non sunt pueri tela timenda dei.
Sæpe puer dubias circum me moverat alas;
  Fecit & incertas nostra sub ora faces.
Sæpe vel ipse sua calamum mihi blandus ab ala,
  Vel matris cygno de meliore dedit.
Sæpe Dionææ pactus mihi serta coronæ;
  Sæpe, Meus vates tu, mihi dixit, eris.
I procul, i cum matre tua, puer improbe, dixi:
  Non tibi cum numeris res erit ulla meis.
Tu Veronensi cum passere pulchrior ibis:
  Bilbilicísve queas comptiùs esse modis.
Ille tuos finget quocunque sub agmine crines:
  Undique nequitiis par erit ille tuis.
Ille nimis (dixi) patet in tua prælia campus:
  Heu nimis est vates & nimis ille tuus.
Gleba illa (ah tua quam tamen urit adultera messis)
  Esset Idumæo germine quanta parens!
Quantus ibi & quantæ premeret Puer ubera Matris!
  Nec cœlos vultu dissimulante suos.
Ejus in isto oculi satìs essent sydera versu;
  Sydereo matris quàm bene tuta sinu!
Matris ut hic similes in collum mitteret ulnas,
  Inq́ sinus niveos pergeret, ore pari!
Utq́ genis pueri hæc æquis daret oscula labris!
  Et bene cognatis iret in ora rosis!
Quæ Mariæ tam larga meat, quàm disceret illic
  Uvida sub pretio gemma tumere suo!
Staret ibi ante suum lacrymatrix Diva Magistrum:
  Seu levis aura volet, seu gravis unda cadat;
Luminis hæc soboles, & proles pyxidis illa,
  Pulchriùs unda cadat, suaviùs aura volet.
Quicquid in his sordet demum, luceret in illis.
  Improbe, nec satìs est hunc tamen esse tuum?
Improbe cede puer: quid enim mea carmina mulces?
  Carminá de jaculis muta futura tuis.
Cede puer, quà te petulantis fræna puellæ;
  Turpia quà revocant pensa procacis heræ;
Quà miseri malè pulchra nitent mendacia limi;
  Quà cerussatæ, furta decora, genæ;

EPIGRAMMATA SACRA

Quà mirere rosas, alieni sydera veris;
   Quas nivis haud propriæ bruma redempta domat.
Cede puer (dixi, & dico) cede improba mater:
   Altera Cypris habet nos; habet alter Amor.
Scilicet hîc Amor est. Hîc est quoque mater Amoris.
   Sed mater virgo. Sed neque cæcus Amor.
O puer! ô Domine! ô magnæ reverentia matris!
   Alme tui stupor & relligio gremii!
O Amor, innocuæ cui sunt pia jura pharetræ;
   Nec nisi de casto corde sagitta calens!
Me, puer, ô certâ, quem figis, fige sagittâ.
   O tua de me sit facta pharetra levis.
Quodque illinc sitit & bibit, & bibit & sitit usquè;
   Usquè meum sitiat pectus, & usquè bibat.
Fige, puer, corda hæc. Seu spinis exiguus quis,
   Seu clavi aut hastæ cuspide magnus ades;
Seu major cruce cum totâ; seu maximus ipso
   Te corda hæc figis denique. Fige puer.
O metam hanc tuus æternum inclamaverit arcus:
   Stridat in hanc teli densior aura tui.
O tibi si jaculum ferat ala ferocior ullum,
   Hanc habeat triti vulneris ire viam.
Quîque tuæ populus cunque est, quæ turba, pharetræ;
   Hic bene vulnificas nidus habebit aves.
O mihi sis bello semper tam sævus in isto!
   Pectus in hoc nunquam mitior hostis eas.
Quippe ego quàm jaceam pugnâ bene sparsus in illâ!
   Quàm bene sic lacero pectore sanus ero!
Hæc mea vota. Mei sunt hæc quoque vota libelli.
   Hæc tua sint Lector; si meus esse voles.
Si meus esse voles; meus ut sis, lumina (Lector)
   Casta, sed ô nimiùm non tibi sicca precor.
Nam tibi fac madidis meus ille occurrerit alis,
   (Sanguine, seu lacrymâ diffluat ille suâ:)
Stipite totus hians, clavîsque reclusus & hastâ:
   Fons tuus in fluvios desidiosus erit?
Si tibi sanguineo meus hic tener iverit amne,
   Tùne tuas illi, dure, negabis aquas?
Ah durus! quicunque meos, nisi siccus, amores
   Nolit; & hîc lacrymæ rem neget esse suæ.
Sæpe hîc Magdalinas vel aquas vel amaverit undas;
   Credo nec Assyrias mens tua malit opes.

11

RICHARD CRASHAW

Scilicet ille tuos ignis recalescet ad ignes;
Forsan & illa tuis unda natabit aquis.
Hîc eris ad cunas, & odoros funere manes:
Hinc ignes nasci testis, & indè meos.
Hîc mecum, & cum matre sua, mea gaudia quæres:
Maturus Procerum seu stupor esse velit;
Sive per antra sui lateat (tunc templa) sepulchri:
Tertia lux reducem (lenta sed illa) dabit.
Sint fidæ precor ah (dices) facilésque tenebræ;
Lux mea dum noctis (res nova!) poscit opem.
Denique charta meo quicquid mea dicat amori,
Illi quo metuat cunque, flectve, modo,
Læta parùm (dices) hæc, sed neque dulcia non sunt:
Certè & amor (dices) hujus amandus erat.

SI nimium hîc promitti tibi videtur, Lector bone, pro eo cui satisfaciendo libellus iste futurus fuerit; scias me in istis non ad hæc modò spectare quæ hîc habes, sed ea etiam quæ olim (hæc interim fovendo) habere poteris. Nolui enim (si hactenus deesse amicis meis non potui, flagitantibus à me, etiam cum dispendii sui periculo, paterer eos experiri te in tantum favorémque tuum) nolui, inquam, fastidio tuo indulgere. Satìs hîc habes quod vel releges ad ferulam suam (neque enim maturiores sibi annos ex his aliqua vendicant) vel ut pignus plurium adultiorúmque in sinu tuo reponas. Elige tibi ex his utrumvis. Me interim quod attinet, finis meus non fefellit. Maximum meæ ambitionis scopum jamdudum attigi: tunc nimirum cùm qualecunque hoc meum penè infantis Musæ murmur ad aures istas non ingratum sonuit, quibus neque doctiores mihi de publico timere habeo, nec sperare clementiores; adeò ut de tuo jam plausu (dicam ingenuè & breviter) neque securus sim ultrà neque solicitus. Prius tui, quisquis es Lector, apud me reverentia prohibet; de cujus judicio omnia possum magna sperare: posterius illorum reverentia non sinit, de quorum perspicacitate maxima omnia non possum mihi non persuadere. Quanquam ò quàm velim tanti me esse in quo patria mea morem istum suum deponere velit, genio suo tam non dignum; istum scilicet quo, suis omnibus fastiditis, ea exosculatur unicè, quibus trajecisse Alpes & de transmarino esse, in pretium cessit! Sed relictis hisce nimis improbæ spei votis, convertam me ad magistros Acygnianos; quos scio de novissimis meis verbis (quanquam neminem nominárim) iratos me reliquisse: bilem verò componant; & mihi se hoc debere (ambitioso juveni verbum tam magnum ignoscant) debere, inquam, fateantur: quòd nimirum in tam nobili argumento, in quo neque ad fœtida de suis Sanctis figmenta, neque ad putidas de nostris calumnias opus habeant confugere, de tenui hoc meo dederim illorum magnitudini unde emineat. Emineat verò; (serius dico) Sciántque me semper se habituros esse sub ea, quam mihi eorum lux major affuderit, umbrâ, placidissimè acquiescentem.

EPIGRAMMATA
SACRA.

Luc. 18.

Pharisæus & Publicanus.

*E*N *duo Templum adeunt (diversis mentibus ambo :)*
    Ille procul trepido lumine signat humum :
It gravis hic, & in alta ferox penetralia tendit.
    Plus habet hic templi ; *plus habet ille* Dei.

Matth. 21. 7.

In Asinum Christi vectorem.

* *I*Lle *suum didicit quondam objurgare magistrum :*
    Et quid ni discas tu celebrare tuum ?

Mirum non minùs est, te jam potuisse tacere,
    Illum quàm fuerat tum potuisse loqui.

* BALAAMI Asinus.

Luc. 4.

Dominus apud suos vilis.

*E*N *consanguinei ! patriis en exul in oris*
    Christus ! & haud alibi tam peregrinus erat.
Qui socio demum pendebat sanguine latro,
    O consanguineus *quàm fuit ille magìs !*

Joann. 5.

Ad Bethesdæ piscinam positus.

*Q*Uis *novus hic refugis incumbit Tantalus undis,*
    Quem fallit toties tam fugitiva salus ?
Unde hoc naufragium felix ? medicǽ́q procellǽ ?
    Vitáque, tempestas quam pretiosa dedit ?

13

RICHARD CRASHAW

JOANN. 20.

Christus ad Thomam.

SÆva fides! voluisse meos traĉtare dolores?
  Crudeles digiti! sic didicisse Deum?
Vulnera, nè dubites, vis tangere nostra : sed eheu,
  Vulnera, dum dubitas, tu graviora facis.

MATTH. 16. 25.

Quisquis perdiderit animam suam meâ causâ, inveniet eam.

I Vita; I, perdam: mihi mors tua, Christe, reperta est:
  (Mors tua vita mea est; mors tibi, vita mea)
Aut ego te abscondam Christi (mea Vita) sepulchro.
  Non adeò procul est tertius ille dies.

JOANN. 20. 1.

Primo mane venit ad sepulchrum MAGDALENA.

TU matutinos prævertis, sanĉta, rubores,
  Magdala; sed jam tum Sol tuus ortus erat.
Jámque vetus meritò vanos Sol non agit ortus,
  Et tanti radios non putat esse suos.
Quippe aliquo (reor) ille, novus, jam niĉtat in astro,
  Et se noĉturnâ parvus habet faculâ.
Quàm velit ô tantæ vel nuntius esse diei!
  Atque novus Soli Lucifer ire novo!

JOANN. 6.

Quinque panes ad quinque hominum millia.

EN mensæ faciles, rediviváque vulnera cœnæ,
  Quæģ indefessâ provocat ora dape!
Auĉta Ceres stupet arcanâ se crescere messe.
  Denique quid restat? Pascitur ipse cibus.

EPIGRAMMATA SACRA

Act. 8.

Æthiops lotus.

Ille niger *sacris exit (quàm lautus!) ab undis :*
Nec frustra Æthiopem *nempe lavare fuit.*

Mentem quàm niveam piceæ cutis umbra fovebit!
Jam volet & nigros sancta Columba lares.

Luc. 18. 13.

Publicanus procul stans percutiebat pectus suum.

Ecce hic peccator timidus petit advena templum ;
Quòdque audet solum, pectora mœsta ferit.

Fide miser ; pulsáque fores has fortiter : illo
Invenies templo *tu* propiore *Deum.*

Marc. 12. 44.

Obolum Viduæ.

Gutta brevis nummi (vitæ patrona senilis)
E digitis stillat non dubitantis anûs :

Istis multa vagi spumant de gurgite census.
Isti abjecerunt *scilicet ; Illa* dedit.

Luc. 10. 39.

Maria verò assidens ad pedes ejus, audiebat eum.

Aspice (namq̃ novum est) ut ab hospite pendeat hospes
Huic ori parat ; hoc sumit ab ore cibos.

Tûne epulis adeò es (soror) officiosa juvandis,
Et sinis has (inquit) Martha, *perire dapes?*

RICHARD CRASHAW.

Act. 2.

In Spiritûs sancti Descensum.

FErte sinus, ô ferte : cadit vindemia cœli ;
  Sanctáque ab æthereis volvitur uva jugis.
Felices nimiùm, queîs tam bona musta bibuntur ;
  In quorum gremium lucida pergit hyems !
En caput ! en ut nectareo micat & micat astro !
  Gaudet & in roseis viva corona comis !
Illis (ô Superi ! quis sic neget ebrius esse ?)
  Illis, nè titubent, dant sua vina faces.

Luc. 15. 13.

Congestis omnibus peregrè profectus est.

DIc mihi, quò tantos properas, puer auree, nummos ?
  Quorsum festinæ conglomerantur opes ?
Cur tibi tota vagos ructant patrimonia census ?
  Non poterunt siliquæ nempe minoris emi ?

Act. 21. 13.

Non solùm vinciri sed & mori paratus sum.

NOn modò vincla, sed & mortem tibi, Christe, subibo,
  Paulus ait, docti callidus arte doli.
Diceret hoc aliter : Tibi non modò velle ligari,
  Christe, sed & *solvi nempe paratus ero.

    * Phil. 1. 23. τὴν ἐπιθυμίαν ἔχων εἰς τὸ ἀναλῦσαι.

Act. 12. 23.

In Herodem σκωληκόβρωτον.

ILle Deus, Deus : hæc populi vox unica : tantùm
  (Vile genus) vermes credere velle negant.
At citò se miseri, citò nunc errâsse fatentur ;
  Carnes degustant, Ambrosiámque putant.

EPIGRAMMATA SACRA

Matth. 14.

Videns ventum magnum, timuit, & cùm
coepisset demergi, clamavit, &c.

PEtre, cades, ô, si dubitas: ô fide: nec ipsum
(Petre) negat fidis æquor habere fidem.
Pondere *pressa suo subsidunt cætera : solum*
(*Petre*) *tuæ mergit te* levitatis onus.

Act. 8. 18.

Obtulit eis pecunias.

(*Simon ?*
QUorsum hos hîc nummos profers ? quorsum, impie
Non ille hîc Judas, sed tibi Petrus adest.
Vis emisse Deum ? *potiùs (precor) hoc age, Simon,*
Si potes, ipse priùs dæmona vende tuum.

Act. 5. 15.

Umbra S. Petri medetur ægrotis.

COnveniunt alacres (sic, sic juvat ire sub umbras)
Atque umbras *fieri (creditis ?)* umbra *vetat.*
O Petri umbra potens ! quæ non miracula præstat ?
Nunc quoque, Papa, tuum sustinet illa decus.

Marc. 7. 33, 36.

Tetigit linguam ejus, &c.——& loquebatur——
& præcepit illis nè cui dicerent: illi verò
eò magis prædicabant.

CHriste, jubes muta ora loqui; muta ora loquuntur:
Sana tacere jubes ora ; nec illa tacent.
Si digito *tunc usus eras, muta ora resolvens ;*
Nônne opus est totâ *nunc tibi, Christe,* manu ?

RICHARD CRASHAW

Luc. 10. 32.

Sacerdos quidam descendens eâdem viâ,
vidit & præteriit.

SPectásne (ah!) placidísque oculis mea vulnera tractas?
O dolor! ô nostris vulnera vulneribus!
Pax oris quàm torva tui est! quàm triste serenum!
Tranquillus miserum qui videt, ipse facit.

Luc. 17.

Leprosi ingrati.

DUm linquunt Christum (ah morbus!) sanantur euntes:
Ipse etiam morbus sic medicina fuit.

At sani Christum (mens ah malesana!) relinquunt:
Ipsa etiam morbus sic medicina fuit.

Matth. 6. 34.

Nè soliciti estote in crastinum.

I Miser, ínque tuas rape non tua tempora curas:
Et nondum natis perge perire malis.

Mî querulis satìs una dies, satìs angitur horis:
Una dies lacrymis mî satìs uda suis.

Non mihi venturos vacat expectare dolores:
Nolo ego, nolo hodie crastinus esse miser.

Matth. 9. 9.

A telonio Matthæus.

AH satìs, ah nimis est: noli ultrà ferre magistrum,
Et lucro domino turpia colla dare.

Jam fuge; jam (Matthæe) feri fuge regna tyranni:
Inꝗ bonam felix i fugitive *crucem.

* CHRISTI scilicet.

EPIGRAMMATA SACRA

Luc. 7.

Viduæ filius è feretro matri redditur.

EN redeunt, lacrymásq; breves nova gaudia pensant:
Bisq; illa est, uno in pignore, facta parens.
Felix, quæ magìs es nati per funera mater !
Amisisse, iterum cui peperisse fuit.

Matth. 18.

Bonum intrare in cœlos cum uno oculo, &c.

UNo oculo? ah centum potiùs mihi, millia centum :
Nam quis ibi, in cœlo, quis satìs Argus erit?
Aut si oculus mihi tantùm unus conceditur, unus
Iste oculus fiam totus & omnis ego.

Luc. 14.

Hydropicus sanatur.

IPse suum pelagus, morbóque immersus aquoso
Qui fuit, ut lætus nunc micat atque levis !
Quippe in vina iterum Christus (puto) transtulit undas ;
Et nunc iste suis ebrius est ab aquis.

Luc. 2. 7.

Non erat iis in diversorio locus.

ILli non locus est? Illum ergò pellitis? Illum?
Ille Deus, quem sic pellitis ; ille Deus.
O furor ! humani miracula sæva furoris !
Illi non locus est, quo sine nec locus est.

RICHARD CRASHAW

Luc. 16.

In lacrymas Lazari spretas à Divite.

FElix ô! lacrymis (ô Lazare) ditior istis,
Quàm qui purpureas it gravis inter opes!
Illum cùm rutili nova purpura vestiet ignis,
Ille tuas lacrymas quàm volet esse suas!

Matth. 26. 65.

Indignatur Caiphas Christo se confitenti.

TU Christum, Christum quòd non negat esse, lacessis:
Ipsius hoc crimen, quòd fuit ipse, fuit.
Téne Sacerdotem credam? Novus ille Sacerdos,
Per quem impunè Deo non licet esse Deum.

Joann. 12. 37.

Cùm tot signa edidisset, non credebant in eum.

NOn tibi, Christe, fidem tua tot miracula præstant:
(O verbi, ô dextræ dulcia regna tuæ!)
Non præstant? neque te post tot miracula credunt?
Mirac'lum, qui non credidit, ipse fuit.

Marc. 1. 16.

Ad S. Andream piscatorem.

QUippe potes pulchrè captare & fallere pisces!
Centum illîc discis lubricus ire dolis.
Heus bone piscator! tendit sua retia Christus:
Artem inverte, et jam tu quoque disce capi.

EPIGRAMMATA SACRA

JOANN. I. 23.

Ego sum vox, &c.

VOx ego sum, *dicis : tu vox es, sanѱe Joannes ?*
Si vox *es, genitor cur tibi* mutus *erat ?*
Ista tui fuerant quàm mira silentia patris !
Vocem *non habuit tunc quoque cùm genuit.*

ACT. 12.

Vincula sponte decidunt.

QUi ferro *Petrum cumulas, durissime custos,*
A ferro disces mollior esse tuo.
Ecce fluit, nodīsque suis evolvitur ultro :
I fatue, & vinc'lis *vincula pone tuis.*

In diem omnium Sanctorum.

REV. 7. 3.

Nè lædite terram, neque mare, neque arbores,
quousque obsignaverimus servos Dei
nostri in frontibus suis.

NUsquā *immitis agat ventus sua murmura* ; *nusquā*
Sylva tremat, crispis sollicitata comis.
Æqua Thetis placidè allabens ferat oscula Terræ ;
Terra suos Thetidi pandat amica sinus :

Undique Pax effusa piis volet aurea pennis,
Frons bona dum signo est quæque notata suo.

Ah quid in hoc opus est signis aliunde petendis ?
Frons bona sat lacrymis quæque notata suis.

In die Conjurationis sulphureæ.

QUàm bene dispositis *annus dat currere festis !*
Post Omnes Sanѱtos, Omne scelus *sequitur.*

RICHARD CRASHAW

Deus sub utero virginis.

ECce tuus, Natura, pater! pater hic tuus, hic est:
Ille, uterus matris quem tenet, ille pater.

Pellibus exiguis arctatur Filius ingens,
Quem tu non totum (crede) nec ipsa capis.

Quanta uteri, Regina, tui reverentia tecum est,
Dum jacet hîc, cœlo sub breviore, Deus!

Conscia divino gliscunt præcordia motu
(Nec vehit æthereos sanctior aura polos)

Quàm bene sub tecto tibi concipiuntur eodem
Vota, & (vota cui concipienda) Deus!

Quod nubes alia, & tanti super atria cœli
Quærunt, invenient hoc tua vota domi.

O felix anima hæc, quæ tam sua gaudia tangit!
Sub conclave suo cui suus ignis adest.

Corpus amet (licet) illa suum, neque sydera malit:
Quod vinc'lum est aliis, hoc habet illa domum.

Sola jaces, neque sola; toro quocunque recumbis,
Illo estis positi tûque tuúsque toro.

Immo ubi casta tuo posita es cum conjuge conjunx,
(Quod mirum magìs est) es tuus ipsa torus.

Act. 7. 16.

Ad Judæos mactatores Stephani.

FRustra illum increpitant, frustra vaga saxa: nec illi
Grandinis (heu sævæ!) dura procella nocet.

Ista potest tolerare; potest nescire: sed illi,
Quæ sunt in vestro pectore, saxa nocent.

Rev. 1. 9.

D. Joannes in exilio.

EXul, Amor Christi est: Christum tamen invenit exul:
Et solitos illîc invenit ille sinus.

Ah longo, æterno ab terras indicite nobis
Exilio, Christi si sinus exilium est.

EPIGRAMMATA SACRA

MATTH. 2.

Ad Infantes Martyres.

FUndite ridentes animas; effundite cœlo :
 Discet ibi vestra (ô quàm bene!) lingua loqui.

Nec· vos lac vestrum & maternos quærite fontes :
 Quæ vos expectat lactea *tota* via *est.*

LUC. 2.

Quærit Jesum suum beata Virgo.

A*H, redeas miseræ, redeas (puer alme) parenti ;*
 Ah, neque te cœlis tam citò redde tuis.

Cœlum *nostra tuum fuerint ô brachia, si te*
 Nostra suum poterunt brachia ferre Deum.

MATTH. 8.

Non sum dignus ut sub tecta mea venias.

I*N tua tecta Deus veniet : tuus haud sinit illud*
 Et pudor, atque humili in pectore celsa fides.

Illum ergò accipies quoniam non accipis : *ergò*
 In te jam veniet, non tua tecta, *Deus.*

MATTH. 27. 12.

Christus accusatus nihil respondit.

N*Il* ait : *ô sanctæ pretiosa silentia linguæ* !
 Ponderis ô quanti res nihil *illud erat* !

Ille olim, verbum *qui dixit, & omnia* fecit,
 Verbum non dicens *omnia nunc* reficit.

RICHARD CRASHAW

Luc. 2.

Nunc dimittis.

S *Pěsne meas tandem ergò mei tenuere lacerti ?*
   Ergò bibunt oculos lumina nostra tuos ?
Ergò bibant ; possíntque novam sperare juventam :
  O possint senii non meminisse sui !
Immo mihi potiùs mitem mors induat umbram
  (Esse sub his oculis si tamen umbra potest)
Ah satis est. Ego te vidi (puer auree) vidi :
  Nil post te, nisi te (Christe) videre volo.

Luc. 8.

Verbum inter spinas.

S *Æpe Dei verbum sentes cadit inter ; & atrum*
   Miscet spina procax (ah malè juncta !) latus.
Credo quidem : nam sic spinas ab scilicet inter
  Ipse Deus Verbum tu quoque (Christe) cadis.

Luc. 14. 5.

Sabbatum {
  Judaicum,
  &
  Christianum.

R *Es eadem vario quantum distinguitur usu !*
   Nostra hominē servant sabbata ; vestra bovē.
Observent igitur (pacto quid justius isto ?)
  Sabbata nostra homines, sabbata vestra boves.

Matth. 10. 52.

Ad verbum Dei sanatur cæcus.

C *Hriste, loquutus eras (ð sacra licentia verbi !)*
   Jámque novus cæci fluxit in ora dies.
Jam, credo, *Nemo est, sicut Tu, *Christe,* loquutus :
  Auribus ? immo oculis, *Christe, loquutus eras.*

* Joann. 7. 46.

EPIGRAMMATA SACRA

Matth. 11.

Onus meum leve est.

ESse·levis quicunque voles, onus accipe Christi :
    Ala tuis humeris, non onus, illud erit.

Christi onus an quæris quàm [sit] grave? scilicet, audi,
    Tam grave, ut ad summos te premat usque polos.

Joann. 6.

Miraculum quinque panum.

ECce vagi venit unda cibi; venit indole sacrâ
    Fortis, & in dentes fertilis innumeros.

Quando erat inviƐɩæ tam sanƐta licentia cœnæ?
    Illa famem populi pascit, & illa fidem.

Joann. 8. 52.

Nunc scimus te habere dæmonium.

AUt Deus, aut saltem dæmon tibi notior esset,
    (Gens mala) quæ dicis dæmona habere Deum.

Ignorâsse Deum poteras, ô cæca : sed oro,
    Et patrem poteras tam malè nôsse tuum?

In beatæ Virginis verecundiam.

IN gremio, quæris, cur sic sua lumina Virgo
    Ponat? ubi meliùs poneret illa, precor?

O ubi, quàm cœlo, meliùs sua lumina ponat?
    Despicit, at cœlum sic tamen illa videt.

RICHARD·CRASHAW

In vulnera Dei pendentis.

O *Frontis, lateris, manuumq; pedumque cruores !*
O quæ purpureo flumina fonte patent !

In nostram (ut quondam) pes non valet ire salutem,
Sed natat ; in fluviis (ah !) natat ille suis.

Fixa manus ; dat, fixa : pios bona dextera rores
Donat, & in donum solvitur ipsa suum.

O latus, ô torrens ! quis enim torrentior exit
Nilus, ubi pronis præcipitatur aquis ?

Mille & mille simul cadit & cadit undique guttis
Frons : viden' ut sævus purpuret ora pudor ?

Spinæ hôc irriguæ florent crudeliter imbre,
Inq̓ novas sperant protinus ire rosas.

Quisque capillus it exiguo tener alveus amne,
Hôc quasi de rubro rivulus oceano.

O nimiùm vivæ pretiosis amnibus undæ !
Fons vitæ nunquam verior ille fuit.

MATTH. 9. 11.

Quare cum Publicanis manducat Magister vester ?

E *Rgò istis socium se peccatoribus addit ?*
Ergò istis sacrum non negat ille latus ?
Tu, Pharisæe, rogas Jesus cur fecerit istud ?
Næ dicam : Jesus, *non* Pharisæus, *erat.*

MATTH. 28.

Ecce locus ubi jacuit Dominus.

I Psum, Ipsum *(precor) ô potiùs mihi (candide) monstra:*
Ipsi, Ipsi, *ô lacrymis oro sit ire meis.*

Si monstrare locum satìs est, & dicere nobis,
En, Maria, hîc tuus en, hîc jacuit Dominus ;

Ipsa ulnas monstrare meas, & dicere possum,
En, Maria, hîc tuus en, hîc jacuit Dominus.

EPIGRAMMATA SACRA

LUC. 17.

Leprosi ingrati.

*L*Ex jubet ex hominum cœtu procul ire leprosos :
 At mundi *à Christo cur abiêre procul?*

Non abit, at sedes tantùm mutavit in illis ;
 Et lepra, quæ fuerat corpore, mente sedet.

Sic igitur dignâ vice res variatur ; & à se
 Quàm procul antè homines, nunc habuêre Deum.

JOANN. 20.

In cicatrices quas Christus habet in se adhuc superstites.

*Q*Uicquid spina *procax, vel stylo* clavus *acuto,*
 Quicquid purpureâ scripserat hasta *notâ,*

Vivit adhuc tecum : sed jam tua vulnera non sunt :
 Non, sed vulneribus sunt medicina meis.

ACT. 5.

Æger implorat umbram D. Petri.

*P*Etre, *tua lateam paulisper (Petre) sub umbra :*
 Sic mea me quærent fata, nec invenient.

Umbra dabit tua posse meum me cernere solem ;
 Et mea lux umbræ sic erit umbra tuæ.

LUC. 24. 39.

Quid turbati estis? Videte manus meas & pedes, quia ego ipse sum.

*E*N *me, & signa mei, quondam mea vulnera! certè,*
 Vos nisi credetis, vulnera sunt & adhuc.

O nunc ergò fidem sanent mea vulnera vestram :
 O mea nunc sanet vulnera vestra fides.

27

RICHARD CRASHAW

Act. 12.

In vincula Petro sponte delapsa, & apertas fores.

FErri non meminit ferrum : se vincula Petro
Dissimulant : nescit carcer habere fores.

Quàm bene liber erit, carcer quem liberat ! *ipsa*
Vincula quem solvunt, quàm bene tutus erit !

Act. 19. 12.

Deferebantur à corpore ejus sudaria, &c.

IMperiosa premunt morbos, & ferrea fati
Jura ligant, Pauli lintea taEta manu.

Unde hæc felicis laus est & gloria lini ?
Hæc (reor) è Lachesis *pensa fuêre* colo.

Joann. 15.

Christus Vitis ad Vinitorem Patrem.

EN serpit tua, purpureo tua palmite vitis
Serpit, & (ah !) spretis it per humum foliis.

Tu viti succurre tuæ, mi Vinitor ingens :
Da fulcrum ; fulcrum da mihi : quale ? crucem.

Act. 26. 28.

Penè persuades mihi ut fiam Christianus.

PEnè ? quid hoc penè est ? Vicinia sæva salutis !
O quàm tu malus es proximitate boni !

Ah ! portu qui teste perit, bis naufragus ille est ;
Hunc non tam pelagus, quàm sua terra premit.

Quæ nobis spes vix absunt, crudeliùs *absunt :*
Penè fui felix, *Emphasis est miseri.*

EPIGRAMMATA SACRA

JOANN. 3. 19.

Lux venit in mundum, sed dilexerunt homines
magis tenebras quàm lucem.

L Uce suâ venit ecce Deus, mundôque refulget;
  Pergit adhuc tenebras mundus amare suas.
At Stygiis igitur mundus damnabitur umbris:
 Pergit adhuc tenebras mundus amare suas?

LUC. 16.

Dives implorat guttam.

O Mihi si digito tremat & tremat unica summo
  Gutta! ô si flammas mulceat una meas!
Currat opum quocunque volet levis unda mearum:
 Una mihi hæc detur gemmula, Dives ero.

JOANN. 3. 4.

Quomodo potest homo gigni qui est senex?

D Ic, Phœnix unde in nitidos novus emicat annos;
  Plaudit & elusos aurea penna rogos?
Quis colubrum dolus insinuat per secula retro,
 Et jubet emeritum luxuriare latus?
Cur rostro pereunte suam prædata senectam
 Torva ales, rapido plus legit ore diem?
Immo, sed ad nixus quæ stat Lucina secundos?
 Natales seros unde senex habeat.
Ignoras, Pharisæe? sat est: jam credere disces:
 Dimidium fidei, qui bene nescit, habet.

RICHARD CRASHAW

MARC. 11. 13.

Arbor Christi jussu arescens.

ILle jubet : *procul ite mei, mea gloria, rami:*
  Nulla vocet nostras amplius aura comas.

Ite ; nec ô pigeat: nam vos neque fulminis ira,
  Nec trucis ala Noti verberat : Ille jubet.

O vox ! ô Zephyro vel sic quoque dulcior omni !
  Non possum Autumno nobiliore frui.

LUC. 1. 12.

Zacharias minùs credens.

INfantis fore te patrem, res mira videtur ;
  Infans interea faĉlus es ipse pater.

Et dum promissi signum (*nimis anxie*) *quæris,*
  Jam nisi per signum *quærere nulla potes.*

JOANN. 3.

In aquam baptismi Dominici.

Felix ô, sacros cui sic licet ire per artus !
  Felix ! dum lavat hunc, ipsa lavatur aqua.

Gutta quidem sacros quæcunque per ambulat artus,
  Dum manet hîc, gēma est ; dum cadit hinc, lacryma.

LUC. 13. 11.

Mulieri incuivatæ medetur Dominus,
indignante Archisynagogo.

IN *proprios replicata sinus quæ repserat, & jam*
  Dæmonis (*infelix* !) *nil nisi nodus erat,*

Solvitur ad digitum Domini : sed striĉlior illo
  Unicus est nodus ; cor, Pharisæe, tuum.

EPIGRAMMATA SACRA

MATTH. 22. 46.

Neque ausus fuit quisquam ex illo die eum
amplius interrogare.

CHriste, malas fraudes, Pharisaica retia, fallis:
   Et miseros sacro discutis ore dolos.

Ergò tacent tandem, atque invita silentia servant
   Tam bene non aliter te potuêre loqui.

MATTH. 20. 20.

S. Joannes matri suæ.

O Mihi cur dextram, mater, cur, oro, sinistram
   Poscis, ab officio mater iniqua tuo?

Nolo manum Christi dextram mihi, nolo sinistram:
   Tam procul à sacro non libet esse sinu.

MATTH. 4.

Si Filius Dei es, dejice te.

NI se dejiciat Christus de vertice Templi,
   Non credes quòd sit Filius ille Dei.

At mox te humano de pectore dejicit: heus tu,
   Non credes quòd sit Filius ille Dei?

LUC. 19. 41.

Dominus flens ad Judæos.

DIscite vos miseri, venientes discite flammas;
   Nec facite ô lacrymas sic periisse meas.

Nec periisse tamen poterunt: mihi credite, vestras
  -Vel reprimet flammas hæc aqua, vel faciet.

RICHARD CRASHAW

Luc. 18. 11.

Nec velut hic Publicanus.

*I*Stum *? vile caput! quantum mihi gratulor, inquis*
Istum quòd novi tam mihi dissimilem !

Vilis at iste *abiit sacris acceptior aris :*
I nunc, & jactes hunc tibi dissimilem.

Act. 9. 3.

In Saulum fulgore nimio excæcatum.

*Q*U*æ lucis tenebræ? quæ nox est ista diei?*
Nox nova, quam nimii luminis umbra facit !

An Saulus fuerit cæcus, vix dicere possum ;
Hoc scio, quòd captus lumine *Saulus erat.*

Luc. 10. 23.

Beati oculi qui vident.

*C*Um *Christus nostris ibat mitissimus oris,*
Atque novum cæcos jussit habere diem,

Felices, oculus qui tunc habuêre, vocantur ?
Felices, & qui non habuêre, voco.

Luc. 7. 15.

Filius è feretro matri redditur.

*E*Rgòne *tam subitâ potuit vice flebilis horror*
In natalitia candidus ire toga ?

Quos vidi, matris gemitus hos esse dolentis
Credideram ; *gemitus* parturientis *erant.*

32

EPIGRAMMATA SACRA

MATTH. II. 25.

In seculi sapientes.

*E*Rgòne delitias facit, & sibi plaudit ab alto
    Stultitia, ut velit hâc·ambitione peti?
Difficilisne adeò faſta est, & seria tandem?
    Ergò & in hanc etiam quis sapuisse *potest?*
Tantum· erat, ut possit tibi doſtior esse ruina?
    Tanti igitur cerebri res, periisse, fuit?
Nil opus ingenio; nihil hâc opus Arte furoris:
    Simpliciùs poteris scilicet esse miser.

LUC. 4. 29.

In Judæos Christum præcipitare conantes.

*D*Icite, quæ tanta est sceleris fiducia vestri?
    Quod nequiit dæmon, id voluisse scelus?
Quod nequiit dæmon scelus, id voluisse patrare!
    Hoc tentare ipsum dæmona (credo) *fuit.*

REV. 7ɩ 9.

In Draconem præcipitem.

I *Frustra truculente; tuas procul aurea rident*
    Astra minas, cœlo jam bene tuta suo.
Tùne igitur cœlum super ire atque astra parabas?
    Ascensu tanto non opus ad barathrum.

LUC. 2.

Beatæ Virgini credenti.

*M*Iraris (quid enim faceres?) sed & hæc quoq; credis:
    Hæc uteri credis dulcia monstra tui.
En fidei, Regina, tuæ dignissima merce·
    Fida Dei fueras filia; mater eris.

c

RICHARD CRASHAW

MARC. 12.

Licétne Cæsari censum dare?

P*Ost tot Scribarum (Christe) in te prælia, tandem*
Ipse venit Cæsar: Cæsar in arma venit.
Pugnant terribiles non Cæsaris ense, sed ense
Cæsare: quin Cæsar vinceris ipse tamen.
Hoc quoque tu conscribe tuis, Auguste, triumphis.
Sic vinci dignus quis nisi Cæsar erat?

MATTH. 9.

In tibicines & turbam tumultuantem circa defunctam.

V*Ani, quid strepitis? nam, quamvìs* *dormiat *illa,*
Non tamen è somno est sic revocanda suo.
Expectat solos Christi sopor iste susurros:
Dormit; nec dormit omnibus *illa tamen.*

* Vers. 24. Non enim mortua est puella, sed dormit.

MATTH. 6. 19.

Piscatores vocati.

L*Udite jam pisces secura per æquora: pisces*
Nos quoque (sed varia sub ratione) sumus.
Non potuisse capi, vobis spes una salutis:
Una salus nobis est, potuisse capi.

MARC. 12.

Date Cæsari.

C*Uncta Deo debentur: habet tamen & sua Cæsar;*
Nec minus indè Deo est, si sua Cæsar habet.
Non minus indè Deo est, solio si cætera dantur
Cæsareo, Cæsar cùm datur ipse Deo.

34

EPIGRAMMATA SACRA

Matth. 21. 7.

Dominus asino vehitur.

ILle igitur vilem te, te dignatur asellum,
    O non vecturâ non bene digne tuâ?
Heu quibus haud pugnat Christi patientia monstris?
    Hoc, quòd sic fertur, hoc quoque ferre fuit.

Luc. 21. 27.

Videbunt Filium hominis venientem in nube.

IMmo veni: aërios (ô Christe) accingere currus,
    Inq́ triumphali nube coruscus ades.
Nubem quæris? erunt nostra (ah!) suspiria nubes:
    Aut sol in nubem se dabit ipse tuam.

Joann. 20.

Nisi digitum immisero, &c.

IMpius ergò iterum clavos? iterum impius hastam?
    Et totum digitus triste revolvet opus?
Túne igitur Christum (Thoma) quò vivere credas,
    Tu Christum faceres (ah truculente!) mori?

Act. 8.

Ad Judæos mactatores S. Stephani.

QUid datis (ah miseri!) saxis nolentibus iras?
    Quid nimis in tragicum præcipitatis opus?
In mortem Stephani se dant invita: sed illi
    Occiso faciunt sponte suâ tumulum.

Sancto Joanni, dilecto discipulo.

TU fruere; augustôq; sinu caput abde (quod ô tum
    Nollet in æterna se posuisse rosa)
Tu fruere: & sacro dum te sic pectore portat,
    O sat erit tergo me potuisse vehi.

RICHARD CRASHAW

MATTH. 2.
In lactentes Martyres.

VUlnera natorum qui vidit, & ubera matrum,
    Per pueros fluviis (ab!) simul ire suis;
Sic pueros quisquis vidit, dubitavit, an illos
    Lilia cælorum diceret, anne rosas.

MATTH. I. 23.
Deus nobiscum.

NObiscum Deus est? vestrum hoc est (hei mihi!) vestrum:
    Vobiscum Deus est, ô asini atque boves.
Nobiscum non est: nam nos domus aurea sumit:
    Nobiscum Deus est, & jacet in stabulo?
Hoc igitur nostrum ut fiat (dulcissime Jesu)
    Nos dandi stabulis, vel tibi danda domus.

Christus circumcisus ad Patrem.

Has en primitias nostræ (Pater) accipe mortis;
    (Vitam ex quo sumpsi, vivere dedidici)
Ira (Pater) tua de pluviâ gustaverit istâ:
    Olim ibit fluviis hoc latus omne suis.
Tunc sitiat licèt & sitiat, bibet & bibet usquè:
    Tunc poterit toto fonte superba frui.
Nunc hastæ interea possit præludere culter:
    Indolis in pœnas spes erit istâ meæ.

In Epiphaniam Domini.

NOn solitâ contenta dies face lucis Eoæ,
    Ecce micat radiis cæsariata novis.
Persa sagax, propera: discurre per ardua Regum
    Tecta, per auratas marmoreásque domus:
Quære ô, quæ intepuit Reginæ purpura partu;
    Principe vagitu quæ domus insonuit.
Audin' Persa sagax? Qui tanta negotia cœlo
    Fecit, Bethlemiis vagiit in stabulis.

EPIGRAMMATA SACRA

Luc. 2. 49.

Ecce quærebamus te, &c.

TE *quæro misera, & quæro: tu nunc quoque tractas*
Res Patris: Pater *est unica curâ tibi:*
Quippe quòd ad pœnas tantùm & tot nomina mortis,
Ad luctum & lacrymas (hei mihi!) mater ego.

Joann. 2.

Aquæ in vinum versæ.

UNde *rubor vestris, & non sua purpura lymphis?*
Quæ rosa mirantes tam nova mutat aquas?
Numen (convivæ) præsens agnoscite Numen:
Nympha pudica Deum vidit, & erubuit.

Matth. 8. 13.

Absenti Centurionis filio Dominus absens medetur.

QUàm *tacitis inopina salus illabitur alis!*
Alis, quas illi vox tua, Christe, dedit.
Quàm longas vox ista manus habet! hæc medicina
Absens, & præsens *hæc medicina fuit.*

Marc. 4. 40.

Quid timidi estis?

TAnquā illi *insanus faceret sua fulmina ventus!*
Tanquam illi *scopulos nôrit habere fretum!*
Vos vestri scopuli, vos estis ventus & unda:
Naufragium cum illo qui metuit, meruit.

RICHARD CRASHAW

Luc. 2.
Nunc dimittis.

I*Te mei (quid enim ulteriùs, quid vultis?) ocelli :*
Leniter obductis ite superciliis.

Immo & adhuc & adhuc, iterùmq; iterùmq; videte ;
Accipite hæc totis lumina luminibus.

Jámque ite; & tutis ô vos bene claudite vallis :
Servate hæc totis lumina luminibus.

Primum est, quòd potui te (Christe) videre : secundum,
Te viso, rectà jam potuisse mori.

MATTH. 13. 24.
In segetem sacram.

E*Cce suam implorat, demisso vertice, falcem :*
Tu segeti falcem da (Pater alme) suam.

Tu falcem non das? messem tu (Christe) moraris ?
Hoc ipsum falx est : hæc mora messis erit.

Luc. 7. 37.
Cœpit lacrymis rigare pedes ejus, & capillis extergebat.

U*Nda sacras sordes lambit placidissima : flavæ*
Lambit & hanc undam lucida flamma comæ.

Illa per has sordes it purior unda; simùlque
Ille per has lucet purior ignis aquas.

Luc. 18. 41.
Quid vis tibi faciam?

Q*Uid volo (Christe) rogas? quippe ah volo, Christe, videre :*
Quippe ah te (dulcis Christe) videre volo.

At video; fideique oculis te nunc quoque figo :
Est mihi, quæ nunquam est non oculata, fides.

Sed quamvìs videam, tamen ah volo (Christe) videre :
Sed quoniam video (Christe) videre volo.

EPIGRAMMATA SACRA

MATTH. 15. 21.

Christus mulieri Canaaneæ difficilior.

V T *pretium facias dono, donare recusas:*
    Usquè rogat supplex, tu tamen usquè negas.
Hoc etiam donare fuit, donare negare.
    Sæpe dedit, quisquis sæpe negata dedit.

LUC. 11. 27.

Beatus venter & ubera, &c.

E T *quid si biberet Jesus vel ab ubere vestro?*
    Quid facit ad vestram, quòd bibit ille, sitim?
Ubera mox sua & Hic (ô quàm non laĉtea[1]*) pandet:*
    E nato Mater *tum bibet ipsa suo.*

JOANN. 15. 1.

In Christum Vitem.

U L*mum vitis amat (quippe est & in arbore flāma,*
    Quam fovet in viridi peĉtore blandus amor:)
*Illam ex arboribus cunĉtis tu (*Vitis*) amâsti,*
    Illam, quæcunque est, quæ crucis arbor *erat.*

JOANN. 16. 20.

Vos flebitis & lamentabimini.

E R*gò mihi salvete mei, mea gaudia, luĉtus:*
    Quàm charum (ô Deus) est hoc mihi flere meum!
Flerem, ni flerem: Solus tu (dulcis Iefu)
    Lætitiam donas tunc quoque quando negas.

RICHARD CRASHAW

JOANN. 10.

In gregem Christi Pastoris.

O Grex, ô nimiùm tanto Pastore beatus!
  O ubi sunt tanto pascua digna grege?
Nè non digna forent tanto grege pascua, Christus
. Ipse suo est Pastor, pascuum & ipse gregi.

In vulnera pendentis Domini.

SIve oculos, sive ora vocem tua vulnera; certè
  Undique sunt ora (heu!) undique sunt oculi.
Ecce ora! ô nimiùm roseis florentia labris!
  Ecce oculi! sævis ah madidi lacrymis!
Magdala, quæ lacrymas solita es, quæ basia sacro
  Ferre pedi, sacro de pede sume vices.
Ora pedi sua sunt, tua quò tibi basia reddat:
  Quò reddat lacrymas scilicet est oculus.

MARC. 2.

Paralyticus convalescens.

CHristum, quòd misero facilis peccata remittit,
  Scribæ blasphemum dicere non dubitant.
Hoc scelus ut primùm Paralyticus audiit; irâ
  Impatiens, lectum sustulit atque abiit.

JOANN. 8. 59.

Tunc sustulerunt lapides.

SAxa? illi? quid tam fœdi voluêre furores?
  Quid sibi de saxis hi voluêre suis?
Indolem, & antiqui agnosco vestigia patris:
  Panem de saxis hi voluêre suis.

EPIGRAMMATA SACRA

In resurrectionem Domini.

Nasceris, en! tecumque tuus (*Rex auree*) *mundus,*
   Tecum *virgineo *nascitur è tumulo.*
Tecum in natales properat natura secundos,
   Atque novam vitam te novus orbis habet.
Ex vita (*Sol alme*) *tua vitam omnia sumunt:*
   Nil certè, nisi mors, cogitur indè mori.
At certè neque mors: nempe ut queat illa sepulchro
   (*Christe*) *tuo condi, mors volet ipsa mori.*

       * Joann. 19. 41. ἐν ᾧ οὐδέπω οὐδεὶς ἐτέθη.

MATTH. 28. 17.

Aliqui verò dubitabant.

Scilicet & tellus *dubitat tremebunda: sed ipsum hoc,*
   Quòd tellus dubitat, vos dubitare vetat.
Ipsi custodes vobis, si quæritis, illud
   Hoc ipso dicunt, *dicere quòd nequeunt.*

  * Vers. 2. σεισμὸς ἐγένετο μέγας.
  * Vers. 4. ἐσείσθησαν οἱ τηροῦντες καὶ ἐγένοντο ὡσεὶ νεκροί.

JOANN. 20. 20.

In vulnerum vestigia quæ ostendit Dominus,
ad firmandam suorum fidem.

His oculis (*nec adhuc clausis coïêre fenestris*)
   Invigilans nobis est tuus usus amor.
His oculis nos cernit amor tuus: his & amorem
   (*Christe*) *tuum gaudet cernere nostra fides.*

LUC. 17. 19.

Mittit Joannes qui quærant à Christo, an is sit.

Tu qui adeò impatiens properâsti agnoscere Christum,
   Tunc cùm claustra uteri te tenuêre tui,
Tu, quis sit Christus, rogitas? & quæris ab ipso?
   Hoc tibi vel mutus dicere quisque potest.

RICHARD CRASHAW

JOANN. 18. 10.

In Petrum auricîdam.

QUantumcunque ferox tuus hic (Petre) fulminat ensis,
    Tu tibi jam pugnas (ô bone) non Domino.
Scilicet in miseram furis implacidissimus aurem,
    Perfidiæ testis nè queat esse tuæ.

MARC. 3.

Manus arefacta sanatur.

FElix! ergò tuæ spectas natalia dextræ,
    Quæ modò spectanti flebile funus erat.

Quæ nec in externos modò dextera profuit usus,
    Certè erit illa tuæ jam manus & fidei.

MATTH. 27. 24.

In Pontium malè lautum.

ILla manus lavat unda tuas, vanissime Judex:
    Ah tamen illa scelus non lavat unda tuum.

Nulla scelus lavet unda tuum: vel si lavet ulla,
O volet ex oculis illa venire tuis.

MATTH. 17. 27.

In piscem dotatum.

TU piscem si, Christe, velis, venit ecce, suúmque
    Fert pretium: tanti est vel periisse tibi.

Christe, foro tibi non opus est; addicere nummos
Non opus est: ipsum se tibi piscis emet.

EPIGRAMMATA SACRA

Joann. 16. 33.

Ego vici mundum.

TU contra mundum dux es meus, optime Jesu?
 At tu (me miserum!) dux meus ipse jaces.
Si tu, dux meus, ipse jaces, spes ulla salutis?
 Immo, ni jaceas tu, mihi nulla salus.

In ascensionem Dominicam.

VAdit (Io!) per aperta sui penetralia cœli:
 It cœlo, & cœlum fundit ab ore novum.
Spargitur ante pedes, & toto sidere pronus
 Jam propiùs Solis Sol bibit ora sui.
At fratrì debere negans sua lumina Phœbe,
 Aurea de Phœbo jam meliore redit.
Hos, de te victo, *tu das (Pater) ipse* triumphos:
 Unde triumphares, quis satìs alter erat?

In descensum Spiritûs sancti.

JAm cœli circùm tonuit fragor: arma, mindsque
 Turbida cum flammis mista ferebat hyems.
Exclamat Judæus atrox; Venit ecce nefandis,
 Ecce venit meriti fulminis ira memor.
Verùm ubi composito sedit fax blandior astro,
 Flammáque non læsas lambit amica comas;
Judæis, fulmen quia falsum apparuit esse,
 Hoc ipso verum nomine fulmen erat.

Joann. 3. 16.

Sic dilexit mundum Deus, ut Filium morti traderet.

AH nimis est, illum nostræ vel tradere vitæ:
 Guttula quod faceret, cur facit oceanus?
Unde & luxuriare potest, habet hinc mea vita:
 Amplè & magnificè mors habet unde mori.

RICHARD CRASHAW

Luc. 14. 19.

Juga boum emi.

*A*D *cœnam voco te (domini quod jussa volebant)*
    Tu mihi, nescio quos, dicis (inepte) boves.

Imò vale, nobis nec digne nec utilis hospes!
Cœna tuos (credo) malit habere boves.

Act. 14.

D. Paulum, verbo sanantem claudum, pro
    Mercurio Lystres adorant.

*Q*Uis *Tagus hic, quæ Pactoli nova volvitur unda?*
    Non hominis vox est hæc: Deus ille, Deus.

Salve, mortales nimiùm dignate penates!
Digna Deo soboles, digna tonante Deo!

O salve! quid enim (alme) tuos latuisse volebas?
Te dicit certè vel tua lingua Deum.

Laudem hanc haud miror: Meruit facundus haberi,
Qui claudo promptos suasit habere pedes.

In S. Columbam ad Christi caput sedentem.

*C*Ui *sacra* sydereâ *volucris* suspenditur alâ?
    Hunc nive plùs niveum cui dabit illa pedem?

Christe, tuo capiti totis se destinat auris,
    Quà ludit densæ blandior umbra comæ.

Illîc arcano quid non tibi murmure narrat?
    (Murmure mortales non imitante sonos)

Sola avis hæc *nido hoc non est indigna cubare:*
Solus nidus hic *est hâc bene dignus ave.*

44

EPIGRAMMATA SACRA

Act. 12.

In fores Divo Petro sponte apertas.

QUid juvit clausisse fores (*bone janitor*) *istas?*
  Et Petro claves *jam liquet esse suas.*
Dices, Sponte patent: Petri ergò hoc scilicet ipsum
  Est clavis, Petro clave quòd haud opus est.

Luc. 15. 2.

Murmurabant Pharisæi, dicentes, Recipit
peccatores & comedit cum illis.

AH malè, quisquis is est, pereat! qui scilicet istis
  Convivam (*sævus!*) *non sinit esse suum.*
Istis cùm Christus conviva adjungitur, istis
  O non conviva est Christus, at ipse cibus.

Matth. 15.

In trabem Pharisaicam.

CEdant, quæ, rerum si quid tenue atq; minutum est,
  Posse acie certâ figere, vitra dabunt.
Artis opus miræ! Pharisæo en optica trabs *est,*
  Ipsum (*vera loquor*) *quâ videt ille* nihil.

Joann. 9. 22.

Constituerunt ut si quis confiteretur eum esse
Christum, synagogâ moveretur.

INfelix, Christum reus es quicunque colendi!
  O reus infelix! quàm tua culpa gravis!
Tu summis igitur, summis damnabere *cœlis:*
  O reus infelix! quàm tua pœna gravis!

RICHARD CRASHAW

Matth. 20. 20.

De voto filiorum Zebedæi.

Sit tibi (*Joannes*) *tibi sit* (*Jacobe*) *quod optas:*
 Sit tibi dextra *manus;* sit tibi læva *manus.*

Spero, alia in cœlo est, & non incommoda, sedes:
 Si neque læva *manus;* si neque dextra *manus.*

Cœli hanc *aut* illam *nolo mihi quærere partem:*
 O, cœlum, cœlum *da* (*Pater alme*) *mihi.*

Joann. 6.

Ad hospites cœnæ miraculosæ quinque panum.

VEscere pane tuo: sed & (hospes) vescere Christo:
 Est panis pani scilicet ille tuo.

Tunc pane hoc CHRISTI reɛlè satur (hospes) abibis,
 Panem ipsum CHRISTUM si magìs esurias.

Joann. 16. 33.

De Christi contra mundum pugna.

TUne, miser? tu (Mundus ait) mea fulmina contra
 Ferre manus, armis cùm tibi nuda manus?

I liɛlor; manibùsque audacibus injice vinc'la:
 Injecit liɛlor vincula, & arma dedit.

Act. 9. 29.

Græci disputatores Divo Paulo mortem machinantur.

EUge argumentum! sic disputat: *euge sophista!*
 Sic pugnum Logices stringere, sic decuit.

Hoc argumentum in causam quid (Græcule) dicit?
 Dicit, te in causam dicere posse nihil.

46

EPIGRAMMATA SACRA

Luc. 22. 26.

Qui maximus est inter vos, esto sicut qui minimus.

O*Bone, discipulus Christi vis maximus esse?*
At verò fies hâc ratione minor.

Hoc sanctæ ambitionis iter (mihi crede) tenendum est,
Hæc ratio; Tu, nè sis minor, esse velis.

Luc. 19. 41.

In lacrymantem Dominum.

V*Obis (Judæi) vobis hæc volvitur unda;*
Quæ vobis, quoniam spernitis, ignis erit.

Eia faces (Romane) faces! seges illa furoris,
Non nisi ab his undis, ignea messis erit.

Matth. 2.

Christus in Ægypto.

H*Unc tu (Nile) tuis majori flumine monstra:*
Hunc (nimis ignotum) dic caput esse tibi.

Jam tibi (Nile) tumes: jam te quoque multus inunda:
Ipse tuæ jam sis lætitiæ fluvius.

Matth. 9.

In cæcos Christum confitentes, Pharisæos abnegantes.

N*E mihi, tu (Pharisæe ferox) tua lumina jactes:*
En cæcus! Christum cæcus at ille videt.

Tu (Pharisæe) nequis in Christo cernere Christum:
Ille videt cæcus; cæcus es ipse videns.

RICHARD CRASHAW.

MATTH. 16. 24.

Si quis pone me veniet, tollat crucem & sequatur me.

ERgò sequor, sequor en! quippe & mihi crux mea,
 Christe, est:
Parva quidem; sed quam non satìs, ecce, rego.

Non rego? non parvam hanc? ideo neq; parva prenda est.
Crux magna est, parvam non bene ferre crucem.

LUC. 5. 28.

Relictis omnibus sequutus est eum.

QUas Matthæus opes, ad Christi jussa, reliquit,
 Tum primùm verè cœpit habere suas.

Iste malarum est usus opum bonus, unicus iste;
Esse malas homini, quas bene perdat, opes.

MATTH. 25. 29.

Ædificatis sepulchra Prophetarum.

SAnctorum in tumulis quid vult labor ille colendis?
 Sanctorum mortem non sinit ille mori.

Vane, Prophetarum quot ponis saxa sepulchris,
Tot testes lapidum, queis periêre, facis.

MARC. 3.

In manum aridam quâ Christo mota est miseratio.

PRende (miser) Christum; & cum Christo prende salutem:
 At manca est (dices) dextera: prende tamen.

Ipsum hoc, in Christum, manus est: hoc prendere Christum est,
Quâ Christum prendas, non habuisse manum.

EPIGRAMMATA SACRA.

Ad D. Lucam medicum.

NUlla mihi (Luca) de te medicamina posco,
  Ipse licèt medicus sis, licèt æger ego:
Quippe ego in exemplum fidei dum te mihi pono,
  Tu, medice, ipse mihi es tu medicina mea.

Luc. 14. 4.

Hydropicus sanatus, Christum jam sitiens.

PEllitur indè sitis; sed & hinc sitis altera surgit:
  Hinc sitit ille magìs, quò sitit indè minús.

Fælix ô, & mortem poterit qui temnere morbus!
  Cui vitæ ex ipso fonte sititur aqua!

In coetum coelestem omnium Sanctorum.

FElices animæ! quas cœlo debita virtus
  Jam potuit vestris inseruisse polis.

Hoc dedit egregii non parcus sanguinis usus,
  Spèsque per obstantes expatiata vias.

O ver! ô longæ semper seges aurea lucis!
  Nocte nec alternâ dimidiata dies!

O quæ palma manu ridet! quæ fronte corona!
  O nix virgineæ non temeranda togæ!

Pacis inocciduæ vos illîc ora videtis:
  Vos Agni dulcis lumina: vos——Quid ago?

Matth. 8. 13.

Christus absenti medetur.

VOx jam missa suas potuit jam tangere metas?
  O superi! non hoc ire sed îsse fuit.

Mirac'lum fuit ipsa salus (bene credere possis)
  Ipsum, mirac'lum est, quando salutis iter.

D

RICHARD CRASHAW

JOANN. 9.

Cæcus natus.

FElix, qui potuit tantæ post nubila noctis
   (O dignum tantâ nocte!) videre diem:
Felix ille oculus, felix utrinque putandus;
   Quòd videt, & primùm quòd videt ille Deùm.

MATTH. 9.

Et ridebant illum.

LUctibus in tantis, Christum ridere vacabat?
   Vanior iste fuit risus, an iste dolor?
Luctibus in tantis hic vester risus, inepti,
   (Credite mî) meruit maximus esse dolor.

MATTH. 11. 25.

In sapientiam seculi.

NOli altum sapere (hoc veteres voluêre magistri)
   Nè retrahat lassos alta ruina gradus.
Immo mihi dico, Noli sapuisse profundum:
   Non ego ad infernum me sapuisse velim.

In stabulum ubi natus est Dominus.

ILla domus stabulum? non est (Puer auree) non est:
   Illa domus, quâ tu nasceris, est stabulum?
Illa domus toto domus est pulcherrima mundo;
   Vix cœlo dici vult minor illa tuo.
Cernis ut illa suo passim domus ardeat auro?
   Cernis ut effusis rideat illa rosis?
Sive aurum non est, nec quæ rosa rideat illîc;
   Ex oculis facile est esse probare tuis.

EPIGRAMMATA SACRA

Act. 8.

S. Stephanus amicis suis, funus sibi curantibus.

NUlla (precor) busto surgant mihi marmora: bustum
 Hæc mihi sint mortis conscia saxa meæ.

Sic nec opus fuerit, notet ut quis carmine bustum,
 Pro Domino (dicens) occidit ille suo.

Hic mihi sit tumulus, quem mors dedit ipsa; meíque
 Ipse hic martyrii sit mihi martyrium.

In D. Joannem, quem Domitianus ferventi oleo
 (illæsum) indidit.

ILlum (qui, toto currens vaga flammula mundo,
 Non quidem Ioannes, ipse sed audit amor)

Illum ignem extingui, bone Domitiane, laboras?
 Hoc non est oleum, Domitiane, dare.

In tenellos Martyres.

AH qui tam propero cecidit sic funere, vitæ
 Hoc habuit tantùm, possit ut ille mori.

At cujus Deus est sic usus funere, mortis
 Hoc tantùm, ut possit vivere semper, habet.

Matth. 4. 24.

Attulerunt ei omnes malè affectos, dæmoniacos,
 lunaticos——& sanavit eos.

COllige te tibi (torve Draco) furiásque facésque,
 Quásque vocant pestes nox Erebùsque suas:

Fac colubros jam tota suos tua vibret Erinnys;
 Collige, collige te fortiter, ·ut——pereas.

RICHARD CRASHAW

Luc. 2.

Tuam ipsius animam pertransibit gladius.

Quando habeat gladium tua, Christe, tragœdia nullum,
   Quis fuerit gladius, Virgo beata, tuus?

Namq; nec ulla aliàs tibi sunt data vulnera, Virgo,
   Quàm quæ à vulneribus sunt data, Christe, tuis.

Forsan quando senex jam caligantior esset,
   Quod Simeon gladium *credidit,* hasta *fuit.*

Immo neque hasta *fuit, neque* clavus, *sed neq;* spina :
   Hei mihi, spina *tamen,* clavus, *& hasta fuit.*

Nam queiscunq; malis tua, Christe, tragœdia crevit,
   Omnia sunt gladius, *Virgo beata, tuus.*

In sanguinem circumcisionis Dominicæ.

Ad convivas, quos hæc dies apud nos solennes habet.

Heus conviva! bibin'? Maria hæc, Mariǽq, puellus,
   Mittunt de prælo musta bibenda suo.

Una quidem est (toti quæ par tamen unica mundo)
   Unica gutta, suo quæ tremit orbiculo.

O bibite hinc; quale aut quantum vos cunque bibistis,
   (Credite mî) nil tam suave bibistis adhuc.

O bibite & bibite; & restat tamen usquè bibendum:
   Restat, quod poterit nulla domare sitis.

Scilicet hîc, mensura sitis, mensura bibendi est:
   Hæc quantum cupias vina bibisse, bibis.

Luc. 2.

Puer Jesus inter Doctores.

Fallitur, ad mentum qui pendit quemq; profundum,
   Ceu possint læves nil sapuisse genæ.

Scilicet è barba malè mensuratur Apollo;
   Et bene cum capitis stat nive, mentis hyems.

Discat, & à tenero disci quoque posse magistro:
   Canitiem capitis nec putet esse *caput.*

EPIGRAMMATA SACRA

JOANN. 2.

Ad Christum, de aqua in vinum versa.

S^{*Igna tuis tuus hostis habet contraria signis:*}
    In vinum tristes tu mihi vertis aquas.

Ille autem è vino lacrymas & jurgia ducens,
    Vina *iterum in tristes (hei mihi!) mutat* aquas.

LUC. 2.

Christus infans Patri sistitur in templo.

A^{*Gnus eat, ludâtq̄ (licet) sub patre petulco;*}
    Cùmque sua longùm conjuge turtur agat.

Conciliatorem *nihil hìc opus ire per* agnum:
    Nec tener ut volucris non sua fata ferat.

Hactenus exigua hæc, quasi munera, lusimus; hæc quæ
    Multum excusanti sunt capienda manu.

Hoc Donum est; de quo, toto tibi dicimus ore,
    Sume Pater: *meritis hoc tibi sume suis.*

Donum hoc est, hoc est; quod scilicet audeat ipso
    Esse Deo dignum: scilicet ipse Deus.

MATTH. 8.

Leprosus Dominum implorans.

C^{*Redo quòd ista potes, velles modò: sed quia credo,*}
    Christe, quòd ista potes, credo quòd ista voles.

Tu modò, tu faciles mihi, Sol meus, *exere vultus;*
    Non poterit radios nix mea *ferre tuos.*

MATTH. 8.

Christus in tempestate.

Q^{*Uòd fervet tanto circum te, Christe, tumultu,*}
    Non hoc ira maris, Christe, sed ambitio est.

Hæc illa ambitio est, hoc tanto te rogat ore,
    Possit ut ad monitus, Christe, tacere tuos.

RICHARD CRASHAW

ACT. 16. 21.

Annunciant ritus, quos non licet nobis suscipere,
cùm simus Romani.

HOc Cæsar tibi (Roma) tuus dedit, armáq;? solis
   Romanis igitur non licet esse piis?
Ah, meliùs, tragicis nullus tibi Cæsar in armis
   Altus anhelanti detonuisset equo;

Nec domini volucris facies horrenda per orbem
   Sueta tibi in signis torva venire tuis:

Quàm miser ut staret de te tibi (Roma) triumphus,
   Ut tantâ fieres ambitione nihil.

Non tibi, sed sceleri vincis: proh laurea tristis!
   Laurea, Cerbereis aptior umbra comis!

Tam turpi vix ipse pater diademate Pluto,
   Vix sedet ipse suo tam niger in solio.

De tot Cæsareis redit hoc tibi (Roma) triumphis:
   Cæsareè, aut (quod idem est) egregiè misera es.

MATTH. 4.

Hic lapis fiat panis.

ET fuit: ille lapis (quidni sit dicere?) panis,
   Christe, fuit: panis sed tuus ille fuit.
Quippe, Patris cùm sic tulerit suprema voluntas,
   Est panis, panem non habuisse, tuus.

MATTH. 15.

Mulier Canaanitis.

QUicquid Amazoniis dedit olim fama puellis,
   Credite: Amazoniam cernimus ecce fidem.
Fœmina, tam fortis fidei? jam credo fidem esse
   Plus quàm grammaticè fœminei generis.

54

EPIGRAMMATA SACRA

Deus, post expulsum Dæmonem mutum, maledicis
Judæis os obturat.

UNâ penè operâ duplicem tibi Dæmona frangis:
 Iste quidem Dæmon mutus; at ille loquax.

Scilicet in laudes (quæ non tibi laurea surgit?)
 Non magìs hic loquitur, quàm tacet ille tuas.

JOANN. 6.

Dicebant, Verè hic est propheta.

POst tot quæ videant, tot quæ miracula tangant,
 Hæc & quæ gustent (Christe) dabas populo.

Jam Vates, Rex, & quicquid pia nomina possunt,
 Christus erat: vellem dicere, venter erat.

Namque his, quicquid erat Christus, de ventre repleto
 Omne illud vero nomine venter erat.

JOANN. 10. 22.

Christus ambulabat in porticu Solomonis, & hyems erat.

BRuma fuit? non, non: ah non fuit, ore sub isto:
 Si fuit; haud anni, nec sua bruma fuit.

Bruma tibi vernis velit ire decentior horis,
 Per sibi non natas expatiata rosas.

At, tibi nè possit se tam bene bruma negare,
 Sola hæc, quam vibrat gens tua, *grando vetat.

  * Vers. 31. sustulerunt lapides.

RICHARD CRASHAW

MATTH. 28.

Dederunt nummos militibus.

NE miles velit ista loqui, tu munera donas?
    Donas, quod possit, cùm tacet ipse, loqui.

Quæ facis à quoquam, pretio suadente, taceri;
   Clariùs, & dici turpiùs ista facis.

Beatæ Virgini.

De salutatione Angelicâ.

XAῖρε suum neque Cæsareus jam nuntiet ales;
    Xαῖρε tuum pennâ candidiore venit.

Sed taceat, qui Xαῖρε tuum quoque nuntiat, ales;
   Xαῖρε meum pennâ candidiore venit.

Quis dicat mihi Xαῖρε meum magè candidus autor,
   Quàm tibi quæ dicat candidus ille tuum?

Virgo, rogas, quid candidius quàm candidus ille
   Esse potest? Virgo, quæ rogat, esse potest.

Xαῖρε tuum (Virgo) donet tibi candidus ille;
   Donas candidior tu mihi Xαῖρε meum.

Xαῖρε meum de Xαῖρε tuo quid differat, audi:
   Ille tuum dicit, tu paris (ecce) meum.

Pontio lavanti.

NOn satìs est cædes, nisi stuprum hoc insuper addas,
    Et tam virgineæ sis violator aquæ?

Nympha quidem pura hæc & honesti filia fontis
   Luget, adulterio jam temerata tuo.

Casta verecundo properat cum murmure gutta,
   Nec satìs in lacrymam se putat esse suam.

Desine tam nitidos stuprare (ah, desine) rores:
   Aut dic, quæ miseras unda lavabit aquas.

EPIGRAMMATA SACRA

In die Passionis Dominicæ.

TAmne ego sim tetricus? valeant jejunia: vinum
    Est mihi dulce meo (nec pudet esse) cado.

Est mihi quod castis, neque prelum passa, racemis
    Palmite virgineo protulit uva parens.

Hoc mihi (ter denis sat enim maturuit annis)
    Tandem ecce è dolio præbibit hasta suo.

Jámque it; & ô quanto calet aĉtus aromate torrens!
    Acer ut hinc aurâ divite currit odor!

Quæ rosa per cyathos volitat tam viva Falernos?
    Massica quæ tanto sydere vina tremunt?

O ego nescibam; atque ecce est Vinum *illud* amoris:
    Unde ego sim tantis, unde ego par cyathis?

Vincor: & ô istis totus propè misceor auris:
    Non ego sum tantis, non ego par cyathis.

Sed quid ego inviĉti metuo bona robora vini?
    *Ecce est, quæ validum diluit, *unda, merum.*

    * Joh. 19. & continuò exivit sanguis & aqua.

In die Resurreĉtionis Dominicæ.

Venit ad sepulchrum Magdalena ferens aromata.

QUin & tu quoque busta tui Phœnicis adora;
    Tu quoque fer tristes *(mens mea) delitias.*

Si nec aromata sunt, nec quod tibi fragrat amomum;
    (Qualis Magdalinâ est messis odora manu)

Est quod aromatibus præstat, quod præstat amomo:
    Hæc tibi mollicula, hæc gemmea lacrymula.

Et lacryma est aliquid: *neque frustra Magdala flevit:*
    Sentiit hæc, lacrymas non nihil esse suas.

His illa (& tunc cùm Domini caput iret amomo)
    Invidiam capitis fecerat esse pedes.

Nunc quoᵹ cùm sinus huic tanto sub aromate sudet,
    Plus capit ex oculis, quo litet, illa suis.

Christe, decent lacrymæ: decet isto rore *rigari*
    Vitæ *hoc* æternum mane, tuúmque diem.

RICHARD CRASHAW

Luc. 24.

In cicatrices Domini adhuc superstites.

A Rma vides; arcus, pharetrámq;, levésq̄ sagittas,
   Et quocunque fuit nomine miles Amor.

His fuit usus Amor: sed & hæc fuit ipse; suúmque
   Et jaculum, & jaculis ipse pharetra suis.

Nunc splendent tantùm, & deterso pulvere belli
   E memori pendent nomina magna tholo.

Tempus erit tamen, hæc iræ quando arma, pharetrámq̄
   Et sobolem pharetræ spicula tradet Amor.

Heu! quâ tunc animâ, quo stabit conscia vultu,
   Quum scelus agnoscet dextera quæq̄ suum?

Improbe, quæ dederis, cernes ibi vulnera, miles,
   Quâ tibi cunque tuus luserit arte furor.

Seu digito suadente tuo mala Laurus *inibat*
   Temporibus; sacrum seu bibit hasta latus:

Sive tuo clavi sævùm rubuêre sub iĉtu;
   Seu puduit jussis ire flagella tuis.

Improbe, quæ dederis, cernes ibi vulnera, miles:
   Quod dederis vulnus, cernere, vulnus erit.

Plaga sui vindex clavósque *rependet &* hastam :
   Quóque rependet, erit clavus & hasta *sibi.*

Quis tam terribiles, *tam* justas *moverit iras?*
   Vulnera pugnabunt (Christe) vel ipsa tibi.

EPIGRAMMATA SACRA

JOANN. 14.

Pacem meam do vobis.

BElla vocant: arma (ô socii) nostra arma paremus
    Atque enses: nostros scilicet (ah!) jugulos.

Cur ego bella paro, cùm Christus det mihi pacem?
    Quòd Christus pacem dat mihi, bella paro.

Ille dedit (nam quis potuit dare certior autor?)
    Ille dedit pacem: sed dedit ille suam.

ACT. 9.

In D. Paulum illuminatum simul & excæcatum.

QUæ, Christe, ambigua hæc bifidi tibi gloria teli est,
    Quod simul huic oculos abstulit, atq; dedit?

Sancta dies animi, hac oculorum in nocte, latebat;
    Te ut possit Paulus cernere, cæcus erat.

JOANN. 15.

˙Ego sum via. Ad Judæos spretores Christi.

O Sed nec calcanda tamen: pes improbe pergis?
    Improbe pes, ergò hoc cœli erat ire viam?

Ah pereat (Judææ ferox) pes improbus ille,
    Qui cœli tritam sic facit esse viam.

RICHARD CRASHAW

MATTH. 2.

In nocturnum & hyemale iter infantis Domini.

ERgò viatores teneros, cum Prole Parentem,
  Nox habet hos, queîs est digna nec ulla dies?

Nam quid ad hæc Pueri vel labra, genásve Parentis?
 Heu quid ad hæc facient oscula, nox & hyems?

Lilia ad hæc facerent, faceret rosa; quicquid & halat
  Æterna Zephyrus qui tepet in viola.

Hi meruêre, quibus vel nox sit nulla; vel ulla
  Si sit, eat nostrâ puriùs illa die.

Ecce sed hos quoque nox & hyems clausêre tenellos:
  Et quis scit, quid nox, quid meditetur hyems?

Ah nè quid meditetur hyems sævire per Austros!
  Quæq̃ solet nigros nox mala ferre metus!

Ah nè noctis eat currus non mollibus Euris!
  Aspera nè tetricos nuntiet aura Notos!

Heu quot habent tenebræ, quot vera pericula secum!
  Quot noctem dominam, quantáq; monstra colunt!

Quot vaga quæ falsis veniunt ludibria formis!
  Trux oculus! Stygio concolor ala Deo!

Seu veris ea, sive vagis stant monstra figuris;
  Virginei satìs est hinc, satìs indè metûs.

Ergò veni; totòque veni resonantior arcu,
  (Cynthia) prægnantem clange procul pharetram.

Monstra vel ista, vel illa, tuis sint meta sagittis:
  Nec fratris jaculum certior aura vehat.

Ergò veni; totòque veni flagrantior ore,
  Dignáque Apollineas sustinuisse vices.

Scis bene quid deceat Phœbi lucere sororem:
  Ex his, si nescis, (Cynthia) disce genis.

O tua, in his, quantò lampas formosior iret!
  Nox suam, ab his, quantò malit habere diem!

EPIGRAMMATA SACRA

Quantùm ageret tacitos hæc luna modestior ignes!
Atque verecundis sobria staret equis!

Luna, tuæ non est rosa tam pudibunda diei:
Nec tam virgineo fax tua flore tremit.

Ergò veni; sed & astra, tuas age (Cynthia) turmas:
Illa oculos pueri, quos imitentur, habent.

Hinc oculo, hinc astro: at parili face niĉtat utrumque;
Ætheris os, atque os æthereum Pueri.

Aspice, quàm bene res utriusque deceret utrumque!
Quàm bene in alternas mutua regna manus!

Ille oculus cæli hôc si staret in æthere frontis;
Sive astrum hoc Pueri, fronte sub ætherea.

Si Pueri hoc astrum ætherea sub fronte micaret,
Credat & hunc oculum non minùs esse suum.

Ille oculus cæli, hoc si staret in æthere frontis,
Non minùs in cælis se putet esse suis.

Tam pulchras variare vices cum fronte Puelli,
Cùmque Puelli oculis, æther & astra queant.

Astra quidem vellent; vellent æterna pacisci
Fœdera mutatæ sedis inire vicem.

Æther & ipse (licèt numero tam dispare) vellet
Mutatis oculis tam bona paĉta dari.

Quippe iret cælum quantò melioribus astris,
Astra sua hos oculos si modò habere queat!

Quippe astra in cælo quantum meliore micarent,
Si frontem hanc possint cælum habuisse suum.

Æther & astra velint: frustra velit æther, & astra:
Ecce negat Pueri frons, ocullque negant.

Ah neget illa, negent illi: nam quem æthera mallent
Isti oculi? aut frons hæc quæ magìs astra velit?

Quid si aliquod blandâ face lenè renideat astrum?
Laĉlea si cæli tèrque quatèrque via est?

RICHARD CRASHAW

Blandior hic oculus, roseo hôc qui ridet in ore;
Lactea frons hæc est térque quatérque magìs.

Ergò negent, cœlùmque suum sua sydera servent:
Sydera de cœlis non bene danda suis.

Ergò negant: séque ecce sua sub nube recondunt,
Sub tenera occidui nube supercilii:

Nec claudi contenta sui munimine cœli,
Quærunt in gremio Matris ubi lateant.

Non nisi sic tactis ubi nix tepet illa pruinis,
Castàque non gelido frigore vernat hyems.

Scilicet iste dies tam pulchro vespere tingi
Dignus; & hos soles sic decet occidere.

Claudat purpureus qui claudit vesper Olympum;
Puniceo placeas tu tibi (Phœbe) toro;

Dum tibi lascivam Thetis auget adultera noctem,
Pone per Hesperias strata pudenda rosas.

Illas nempe rosas, quas conscia purpura pinxit;
Culpa pudórque suus queîs dedit esse rosas.

Hos soles, niveæ noctes, castùmque cubile,
Quod purum sternet per mare virgo Thetis;

Hos, sancti flores; hos, tam sincera decebant
Lilia; quæǫ̂ sibi non rubuêre rosæ.

Hos, decuit sinus hic; ubi toto sydere proni
Ecce lavant sese lacteo in oceano.

Átque lavent: tandémque suo se mane resolvant,
Ipsa dies ex hoc ut bibat ore diem.

EPIGRAMMATA SACRA

JOANN. 16. 26.

Non dico, me rogaturum Patrem pro vobis.

AH tamen Ipse roga: *tibi scilicet ille roganti*
  Esse nequit durus, nec solet esse, Pater.

Ille suos omni facie te figit amores;
  Inq̃ tuos toto effunditur ore sinus.

Quippe, tuos spectans oculos, se spectat in illis;
  Inq̃ tuo (Jesu) se fovet ipse sinu.

Ex te metitur sese, & sua numina discit:
  Indè repercussus redditur ipse sibi.

Ille tibi se, te ille sibi par nectit utrinque:
  Tam tuus est, ut nec sit magìs ille suus.

Ergò roga: Ipse roga: *tibi scilicet ille roganti*
  Esse nequit durus, nec solet esse, Pater.

Illum ut ego rogitem? Hôc (eheu) non ore rogandum;
  Ore satìs puras non faciente preces.

Illum ego si rogitem, quis scit quibus ille procellis
  Surgat, & in miserum hoc quæ tonet ira caput?

Isto etiam forsan veniet mihi fulmen ab ore:
  (Sæpe isto certè fulmen ab ore venit)

Ille unâ irati forsan me cuspide verbi,
  Uno me nutu figet, & interii:

Non ego, non rogitem: mihi scilicet ille roganti
  Durior esse potest, & solet esse, Pater.

Immo rogabo: nec ore meo tamen: immo rogabo
  Ore meo (Jesu) scilicet ore tuo.

RICHARD CRASHAW

In die Ascensionis Dominicæ.

USq̃ etiam nostros Te (Christe) tenemus amores?
    Heu cœli quantam hinc invidiam patimur!

Invidiam patiamur: habent sua sydera cœli;
    Quæq̃ comunt tremulas crispa tot ora faces;

Phœbènque & Phœbum, & tot piƈtæ vellera nubis;
    Vellera, quæ roseâ Sol variavit acu.

Quantum erat, ut sinerent hâc unâ nos face ferri?
    Una sit hîc: sunt (& sint) ibi mille faces.

Nil agimus: nam tu quia non ascendis ad illum,
    Æther *descendit (Christe) vel ipse tibi.

       * Act. 1. Nubes susceptum eum abstulit.

FINIS.

STEPS

TO THE

TEMPLE,

Sacred Poems.

WITH

The Delights of the Muses.

By RICHARD CRASHAW, *some-times of* Pembroke *Hall, and late fellow of* S. Peters *Coll. in* Cambridge.

The second Edition wherein are added divers pieces not before extant.

LONDON,

Printed for *Humphrey Moseley*, and are to be sold at his Shop at the Princes Armes in St. *Pauls* Church yard.

1 6 4 8.

The Preface to the Reader.

Learned Reader,

THe *Authors friend will not usurpe much upon thy eye:
This is onely for those whom the name of our Divine
Poet hath not yet seized into admiration.* I *dare undertake
that what* Jamblicus (in vita Pythagoræ) *affirmeth of his
Master, at his Contemplations, these Poems can,* viz. *They
shall lift thee, Reader, some yards above the ground*: *and,
as in* Pythagoras *Schoole, every temper was first tuned into
a height by severall proportions of Musick, and spiritualiz'd
for one of his weighty Lectures*; *So maist thou take a Poem
hence, and tune thy soule by it, into a heavenly pitch*; *and
thus refined and borne up upon the wings of meditation, In
these Poems thou maist talke freely of God, and of that other
state.*

Here's Herbert's *second, but equall, who hath retriv'd
Poetry of late, and return'd it up to its Primitive use*; *Let
it bound back to heaven gates, whence it came. Thinke yee,
St.* Augustine *would have steyned his graver Learning
with a booke of Poetry, had he fancied its dearest end to be
the vanity of Love-Sonnets, and Epithalamiums?* *No, no,
he thought with this our Poet, that every foot in a high-borne
verse, might helpe to measure the soule into that better world.*
Divine Poetry, *I dare hold it, in position against* Suarez
on the subject, to be the Language of the Angels; *it is the
Quintessence of Phantasie and discourse center'd in Heaven*;
'tis the very Out-goings of the soule; *'tis what alone our
Author is able to tell you, and that in his owne verse.*

*It were prophane but to mention here in the Preface
those under-headed Poets, Retainers to seven shares and a*

halfe; *Madrigall fellowes, whose onely businesse in verse, is to rime a poore six-penny soule a Suburb sinner into hell;*— *May such arrogant pretenders to Poetry vanish, with their prodigious issue of tumorous heats, and flashes of their adulterate braines, and for ever after, may this our Poet fill up the better roome of man.* Oh! *when the generall arraignment of Poets shall be, to give an accompt of their higher soules, with what a triumphant brow shall our divine Poet sit above, and looke downe upon poore* Homer, Virgil, Horace, Claudian? &c. *who had amongst them the ill lucke to talke out a great part of their gallant Genius, upon Bees, Dung, froggs, and Gnats,* &c. *and not as himself here, upon Scriptures, divine Graces, Martyrs and Angels.*

Reader, we stile his Sacred Poems, Steps to the Temple, *and aptly, for in the Temple of God, under his wing, he led his life, in* St. Maries *Church neere* St. Peters *Colledge: There he lodged under* Tertullian's *roofe of Angels; There he made his nest more gladly than* David's *Swallow neere the house of God, where like a primitive Saint, he offered more prayers in the night, than others usually offer in the day; There he penned these Poems,* Steps *for happy soules to climbe heaven by.* ·

And those other of his pieces, intituled The Delights of the Muses, *(though of a more humane mixture) are as sweet as they are innocent.*

The praises that follow are but few of many that might be conferr'd on him: he was excellent in five Languages (besides his Mother tongue) vid. Hebrew, Greek, Latine, Italian, Spanish, *the two last whereof he had little helpe in, they were of his own acquisition.*

Amongst his other accomplishments in Accademick (as well pious as harmlesse arts) he made his skill in Poetry, Musick, Drawing, Limming, Graving, (exercises of his curious invention and sudden fancy) to be but his subservient recreations for vacant houres, not the grand businesse of his soule.

To the former Qualifications I might adde that which would crowne them all, his rare moderation in diet (almost Lessian temperance) he never created a Muse out of distempers, nor (with our Canary scribblers) cast any strange mists of surfets before the Intelectuall beames of his mind or memory, the latter of which, he was so much a master of, that he had there under locke and key in readinesse, the richest treasures of the best Greek and Latine Poets, some of which Authors hee had more at his command by heart, than others that onely read their works, to retaine little, and understand lesse.

Enough Reader, I intend not a volume of praises larger than his booke, nor need I longer transport thee to think over his vast perfections, I will conclude all that I have impartially writ of this Learned young Gent. (now dead to us) as he himselfe doth, with the last line of his Poem upon Bishop Andrews *Picture before his Sermons*

Verte paginas.

—Look on his following leaves, and see him breath.

The Authors Motto.

Live Jesus, Live, and let it bee
My Life, to dye for love of thee.

The Teare.

1.

WHat bright soft thing is this
   Sweet *Mary* thy faire eyes expence?
   A moist sparke it is,
 A watry Diamond; from whence
The very terme I thinke was found,
The water of a Diamond.

2.

O 'tis not a teare,
 'Tis a star about to drop
   From thine eye its spheare,
 The Sun will stoope and take it up,
Proud will his Sister be to weare
This thine eyes Jewell in her eare.

3.

O 'tis a teare,
 Too true a teare; for no sad eyne
   How sad so e're
 Raine so true a teare as thine;
Each drop leaving a place so deare,
Weeps for it self, is its owne teare.

4.

Such a Pearle as this is
 (Slipt from *Aurora's* dewy Brest)
   The Rose buds sweet lip kisses;
 And such the Rose it self when vext
With ungentle flames, does shed,
Sweating in too warme a bed.

RICHARD CRASHAW

5.

Such the Maiden gem
By the wanton spring put on,
  Peeps from her Parent stem,
And blushes on the watry Sun:
This watry blossome of thy Eyne,
Ripe, will make the richer Wine.

6.

Faire drop, why quak'st thou so?
Cause thou streight must lay thy head
  In the dust? ô no,
The dust shall never be thy bed;
A pillow for thee will I bring,
Stuft with downe of Angels wing.

7.

Thus carried up on high,
(For to heaven thou must goe)
  Sweetly shalt thou lye,
And in soft slumbers bath thy woe,
Till the singing Orbes awake thee,
And one of their bright *Chorus* make the.

8.

There thy selfe shalt bee
An eye, but not a weeping one,
  Yet I doubt of thee,
Whether th' had'st rather there have shone,
An eye of heaven; or still shine here,
In th' Heaven of *Maries* eye a teare.

STEPS TO THE TEMPLE

Divine Epigrams.

On the water of our Lords Baptisme.

EAch blest drop, on each blest limme,
 Is wash't it self, in washing him:
'Tis a gemme while it stayes here,
While it falls hence, 'tis a Teare.

Acts. 8.

On the baptized Æthiopian.

LEt it no longer be a forlorne hope
   To wash an Æthiope:
Hee's washt, his gloomy skin a peacefull shade
   For his white soule is made;
And now, I doubt not, the Eternall Dove,
   A black-fac'd house will love.

On the miracle of multiplyed Loaves.

SEe here an easie Feast that knowes no wound,
 That under Hungers Teeth will needs be found,
A subtle Harvest of unbounded bread,
 What would ye more? Here food it selfe is fed.

Upon the Sepulcher of our Lord.

HEre where our Lord once laid his head
 Now the grave lyes buried.

The Widows Mites.

TWo Mites, two drops, yet all her house and land
 Falls from a steady heart though trembling hand:
The others wanton wealth foams high and brave;
The other cast away, she onely gave.

73

RICHARD CRASHAW

On the Prodigall.

TEll me bright boy, tell me my golden Lad,
  Whither away so frolick? why so glad?
What all thy wealth in counsaile? all thy state?
Are huskes so deare? troth 'tis a mighty rate.

Acts. 5.

The sick implore St. Peters shadow.

UNder thy shadow may I lurke a while,
  Death's busie search I'le easily beguile;
Thy shadow, *Peter*, must shew me the Sun
  My light's thy shadowes shadow, or 'tis done.

On the still surviving marks of our Saviours wounds.

WHat ever storie of their crueltie,
  Or Naile, or Thorne, or Speare have writ in thee.
    Are in another sence,
      Still legible,
    Sweet is the difference,
      Once I did spell
      Every red Letter
      A wound of thine
    Now (what is better)
      Balsome for mine.

Mark. 7.

The dumb healed and the people enjoyned silence.

CHrist bids the dumb tongue speak, it speakes, the sound
  He charges to be quiet, it runs round:
If in the first he us'd his fingers touch,
  His hands whole strength here could not be too much.

STEPS TO THE TEMPLE

Mat. 28.

Come see the place where the Lord lay.

SHew me himself, himself (bright Sir) ô show
    Which way my poor teares to himself may goe;
Were it enough to show the place and say
  Looke *Mary* here, see where thy Lord once lay,
Then could I show these armes of mine, and say
  Looke *Mary* here, see where thy Lord once lay.

T*o* Pontius *washing his hands.*

THy hands are wash't, but ô the water's spilt
    That labour'd to have washt thy guilt;
The flood, if any can, that can suffice,
  Must have its fountaine in thine eyes.

To the infant Martyrs.

GOe smiling soules, your new built Cages breake,
    In heaven you'l learne to sing, ere here to speake:
Nor let the milkie fonts that bath your thirst
            Be your delay,
The place that calls you hence, is at the worst
           Milke all the way.

On the miracle of Loaves.

NOw Lord, or never, they'l beleeve on thee :
  Thou to their teeth hast prov'd thy Deity.

RICHARD CRASHAW

Mark. 4.

Why are ye afraid, O ye of little faith?

A S if the storme meant him,
   Or 'cause heavens face is dim,
     His needs a cloud :
Was ever froward wind
That could be so unkind?
     Or wave so proud?
The wind had need be angry, and the water black,
That to the mighty *Neptune's* self dare threaten wrack.
     There is no storme but this
     Of your owne Cowardise
     That braves you out;
     You are the storme that mocks
     Your selves; you are the rocks
     Of your owne doubt:
Besides this feare of danger, ther's no danger here;
And he that here feares danger, does deserve his feare.

On the B. *Virgins bashfullnesse.*

T Hat on her lap she casts her humble eye,
   'Tis the sweet pride of her humilitie.
The faire starre is well fixt, for where, ô where,
Could she have fixt it on a fairer spheare?
'Tis heaven, 'tis heaven she sees; Heaven's God there lyes,
She can see heaven, and ne're lift up her eyes :
This new guest to her eyes, new lawes hath given,
'Twas once looke up, 'tis now looke downe to heaven.

Upon Lazarus *his teares.*

R Ich *Lazarus*! richer in those Gems thy Teares,
   Then *Dives* in the roabes he weares:
He scorns them now, but ô they'l sute full well
  With th' Purple he must weare in hell.

STEPS TO THE TEMPLE

Two went up into the temple to pray.

TWo went to pray? ô rather say
    One went to brag, th' other to pray:
One stands up close, and treads on high,
Where th' other dares not send his eye;
One neerer to God's Altar trod,
The other to the Altars God.

Upon the asse that bore our Saviour.

HAth only anger an Omnipotence
               in Eloquence?
Within the lips of love and joy doth dwell
               No miracle?
Why else had *Balaams* asse a tongue to chide
               His masters pride?
And thou (heaven burthen'd beast) hast ne're a word
               To praise thy Lord?
That he should find a tongue and vocall thunder
               Was a great wonder,
But ô me thinkes 'tis a farre greater one
               That thou find'st none.

Mat. 8.

I am not worthy that thou should'st come under my roofe.

THy God was making hast into thy roofe,
    Thy humble faith, and feare, keepes him aloofe:
Hee'l be thy guest, because he may not be,
    Hee'l come—into thy house? no, into thee.

RICHARD CRASHAW

I am the Doore.

ANd now th'art set wide ope, the spear's sad art
Lo! hath unlockt thee at the very heart:
He to himselfe (I feare the worst)
And his owne hope
Hath shut these Doores of heaven, that durst
Thus set them ope.

Mat. 10.

The blind cured by the word of our Saviour.

THou speak'st the word (Thy word's a Law)
Thou spak'st and streight the blind man saw:
To speake, and make the blind man see,
Was never man Lord spake like thee!
To speake thus was to speake (say I)
Not to his eare, but to his eye.

Mat. 27.

And he answered them nothing.

O Mighty Nothing! unto thee,
Nothing, we owe all things that bee.
God spake once, when he all things made,
He sav'd all when he Nothing said.
The world was made of Nothing then;
'Tis made by Nothing now againe.

To our Lord, upon the water made Wine.

THou water turn'st to wine (faire friend of life)
Thy foe to crosse the sweet arts of thy reigne
Distills from thence the tears of wrath and strife,
And so turnes wine to water back againe.

STEPS TO THE TEMPLE

Mat. 22.

Neither durst any man from that day, aske him any more questions.

MId'st all the darke and knotty snares,
Black wit or malice can, or dares,
Thy glorious wisedome breaks the Nets,
And treds with uncontrouled steps;
Thy quell'd foes are not onely now
Thy triumphs, but thy Trophies too:
They both at once thy Conquests bee,
And thy Conquests memorie.
Stony amazement makes them stand
Wayting on thy victorious hand,
Like statues fixed to the fame
Of thy renoune, and their own shame,
As if they onely meant to breath
To be the life of their own death.
Twas time to hold their peace, when they
Had ne're another word to say,
Yet is their silence unto thee,
The full sound of thy victorie;
Their silence speaks aloud, and is
Thy well pronounc'd Panegyris.
While they speak nothing, they speak all
Their share in thy Memoriall.
While they speake nothing, they proclame
Thee, with the shrillest trump of fame.
    To hold their peace is all the wayes
    These wretches have to speake thy praise.

Upon our Saviours tombe wherein never man was laid.

HOw life and death in thee
          Agree!
Thou had'st a virgin wombe,
        And tombe,
A *Joseph* did betroth
      Them both.

RICHARD CRASHAW

It is better to goe into heaven with one eye, &c.

ONe eye? a thousand rather, and a thousand more,
   To fix those full-fac't glories, ô hee's poore
   Of eyes that has but *Argus* store.
Yet if thou'lt fil one poor eye, with thy heaven, & thee,
   O grant (sweet goodnesse) that one eye may be
   All and every whit of me.

Luke. 11.

*Upon the dumb Devill cast out, and the slanderous Jewes
put to silence.*

TWo devills at one blow thou hast laid flat,
   A speaking Devill this, a dumbe [one] that.
Was't thy full victories fairer increase,
   That th' one spake, or that th' other held [his] peace?

Luke. 10.

*And a certaine Priest comming that way, looked on him
and passed by.*

WHy doest thou wound my wounds, ô thou that
   passest by,
Handling & turning them with an unwounded eye?
The calme that cooles thine eye does shipwrack mine, for ô,
Unmov'd to see one wretched is to make him so.

Luke. 11.

Blessed be the Paps which thou hast sucked.

SUppose he had been tabled at thy Teates,
   Thy hunger feels not what he eates:
Hee'l have his Teat e're long, a bloody one,
   The mother then must suck the son.

STEPS TO THE TEMPLE

To Pontius *washing his blood-sta[in]ed hands.*

'SMurther no sin? Or a sin so cheape
        That thou did'st heape
A Rape upon't? till thy adult'rous touch
  Taught her these sullied cheeks, this blubber'd face,
She was a Nimph, the meadows knew none such,
  Of honest parentage, of unstain'd race,
The daughter of a faire, and well fam'd fountaine,
As ever Silver-tipt the side of shadie mountaine.

See how she weeps, and weepes, that she appeares
        Nothing but teares,
Each drop's a teare, that weeps for her owne wast;
  Harke how at every touch she does complaine her;
Harke how she bids her frighted drops make hast,
  And with sad murmurs, chides the hands that staine her:
Leave, leave for shame, or else (good judge) decree
What water shal wash this, when this hath washed thee.

Mat. 23.

Yee build the Sepulchres of the Prophets.

THou trim'st a *Prophets* Tombe, and dost bequeath
    The life thou took'st from him unto his death:
Vaine man! the stones that on his Tombe doe lye
Keep but the score of them that made him dye.

Upon the Infant Martyrs.

TO see both blended in one flood,
    The Mothers milke, the Childrens blood,
Makes me doubt if heav'n will gather
Roses hence, or *Lillies* rather.

RICHARD CRASHAW

Joh. 16.

Verily I say unto you, yee shall weep and lament.

WElcome my Grief, my Joy; how deare's?
　　To me my Legacie of Teares!
I'le *weepe*, and *weepe*, and will therefore
Weepe, 'cause I can *weepe* no more:
　Thou, thou (*Deare Lord*) even thou alóne,
　Giv'st joy, even when thou givest none.

John 15.

Upon our Lord's last comfortable discourse with his Disciples.

ALL *Hybla's* honey, all that sweetnesse can,
　　Flowes in thy Song (ô faire, ô dying swan!)
Yet is the joy I take in't small or none;
It is too sweet to be a long-liv'd one.

Luke 16.

Dives *asking a drop.*

A Drop, one drop, how sweetly one faire drop
　　Would tremble on my pearle-tipt fingers top?
My wealth is gone, ô goe it where it will,
　Spare this one jewell; I'le be *Dives* still.

Marke 12.

(*Give to* Cæsar---)
(*And to God*------)

ALL we have is God's, and yet
　　Cæsar challenges a debt,
Nor hath God a thinner share,
What ever *Cæsar's* payments are;
All is God's; and yet 'tis true
All we have is *Cæsar's* too;
All is *Cæsar's*; and what ods,
So long as *Cæsar's* selfe is Gods?

But now they have seen and hated.

SEene? and yet hated thee? they did not see,
 They saw thee not, that saw and hated thee:
No, no, they saw thee not, ô Life, ô Love,
Who saw ought in thee that their hate could move.

Upon the Crowne of thornes taken downe from the
head of our B. Lord bloody.

KNow'st thou this Souldier? 'tis a much chang'd plant,
 which yet
      Thy self did'st set,
O! who so hard a husbandman did ever find,
     A soyle so kind?
Is not the soyle a kind one which returnes
     Roses for Thornes?

Luke 7.

She began to wash his feet with teares, and wipe them
with the haires of her head.

HEr eyes flood lickes his feetes faire staine,
 Her haires flame lickes up that againe:
This flame thus quench't hath brighter beames,
This flood thus stained, fairer streames.

On St. Peter *cutting off* Malchus *his eare.*

WEll *Peter* dost thou wield thy active sword,
 Well for thy selfe (I meane) not for thy Lord:
To strike at eares, is to take heed there be
No witnesse *Peter* of thy perjury.

Joh. 3.

But men loved darknesse rather than light.

THe world's light shines, shine as it will,
 The world will love its *Darkenesse* still:
I doubt though when the World's in Hell,
It will not love its *Darkenesse* halfe so well.

RICHARD CRASHAW

Acts. 21.

I am readie not onely to be bound, but to die.

COme death, come bands, nor do you shrink, my ears,
   At those hard words man's cowardise calls feares:
Save those of feare no other bands feare I;
No other feare than this, the feare to dye.

On St. Peter *casting away his Nets at our Saviours call.*

THou hast the art on't *Peter*, and canst tell
   To cast thy Nets on all occasions well:
When Christ calls, and thy Nets would have thee stay,
To cast them well's to cast them quite away.

Our B. Lord in his Circumcision to his Father.

TO thee these first fruits of my growing death
   (For what else is my life?) lo I bequeath:
Tast this, and as thou lik'st this lesser flood
Expect a Sea, my heart shall make it good.
Thy wrath that wades here now, e're long shall swim,
The floodgate shall be set wide ope for him.
Then let him drinke, and drinke, and doe his worst
To drowne the wantonnesse of his wild thirst.
Now's but the Nonage of my paines, my feares
Are yet both in their hopes, not come to yeares.
The day of my darke woe is yet but morne,
My teares but tender, and my death new borne.
Yet may these unfle[d]g'd griefes give fate some guesse,
These Cradle-torments have their towardnesse.
These purple buds of blooming death may bee,
Erst the full stature of a fatall tree.
And till my riper woes to age are come,
This Knife may be the speares *Præludium.*

STEPS TO THE TEMPLE

On the wounds of our crucified Lord.

O These wakefull wounds of thine!
   Are they Mouthes? or are they eyes?
Be they mouthes, or be they eyne,
   Each bleeding part some one supplies.

Lo, a mouth! whose full bloom'd lips
   At too deare a rate are roses:
Lo, a blood-shot eye! that weeps,
   And many a cruell teare discloses.

O thou that on this foot hast laid
   Many a kisse, and many a teare,
Now thou shalt have all repaid,
   What soe're thy charges were.

This foot hath got a mouth and lips
   To pay the sweet summe of thy kisses,
To pay thy teares, an eye that weeps,
   Instead of teares, such gems as this is.

The difference onely this appeares,
   (Nor can the change offend)
The debt is paid in Ruby-teares
   Which thou in Pearles did'st lend.

On our crucified Lord, naked and bloody.

THey have left thee naked Lord. O that they had;
   This Garment too, I would they had deny'd.
Thee with thy selfe they have too richly clad,
Opening the purple wardrobe of thy side:
   O never could there be garment [too] good
For thee to weare, but this of thine owne blood.

Sampson *to his* Dalilah.

COuld not once blinding mee, cruell suffice?
   When first I look't on thee I lost mine eyes.

RICHARD CRASHAW

HAppy me! O happy sheepe!
Whom my God vouchsafes to keepe;
Even my God, even he it is
That points me to these wayes of blisse;
On whose pastures cheerefull spring,
All the yeare doth sit and sing,
And rejoycing smiles to see
Their green backs weare his liverie:
Pleasure sings my soule to rest,
Plentie weares me at her brest,
Whose sweet temper teaches me
Nor wanton, nor in want to be.
At my feet the blubb'ring Mountaine
Weeping melts into a Fountaine,
Whose soft silver-sweating streames
Make high noone forget his beames:
When my way-ward breath is flying,
He calls home my soule from dying,
Strokes, and tames my rabid griefe,
And does wooe me into life:
When my simple weakenes strayes,
(Tangled in forbidden wayes)
He (my shepheard) is my guide,
Hee's before me, on my side,
And behind me, he beguiles
Craft in all her knottie wiles:
He expounds the giddy wonder
Of my weary steps, and under
Spreads a Path as cleare as Day,
Where no churlish rub says nay
To my joy conducted feet,
Whil'st they gladly goe to meet
Grace and Peace, to meet new laies
Tun'd to my great S[h]epheards praise.
Come now all ye terrors, sally,
Muster forth into the valley,
Where triumphant darknesse hovers

STEPS TO THE TEMPLE

With a sable wing that covers
Brooding horror. Come thou Death
Let the damps of thy dull Breath
Over shadow even the shade,
And make darkenes selfe afraid;
There my feet, even there, shall find
Way for a resolved mind.
Still my Shepheard, still my God
Thou art with me, still thy Rod,
And thy staffe, whose influence
Gives direction, gives defence.
At the whisper of thy word
Crown'd abundance spreads my boord:
While I feast, my foes doe feed
Their ranck malice not their need,
So that with the self same bread
They are starv'd and I am fed.
How my head in ointment swims!
How my cup orelook's her brims!
So, even so still may I move
By the Line of thy deare love;
Still may thy sweet mercy spread
A shady arme above my head,
About my Paths, so shall I find
The faire center of my mind
Thy Temple, and those lovely walls
Bright ever with a beame that falls
Fresh from the pure glance of thine eye,
Lighting to eternity.
There I'le dwell, for ever there
Will I find a purer aire
To feed my life with, there I'le sup
Balme, and *Nectar* in my cup,
And thence my ripe soule will I breath
Warme into the Armes of Death.

RICHARD CRASHAW

Psalme. 137.

ON the proud bankes of great *Euphrates* flood,
    There we sate, and there we wept:
Our Harpes that now no musick understood,
    Nodding on the willowes slept,
      While unhappy captiv'd wee
      Lovely *Sion* thought on thee.
They, they that snatcht us from our countries breast
    Would have a song carv'd to their eares
In *Hebrew* numbers, then (ô cruell jest!)
    When Harpes and Hearts were drown'd in teares:
      Come, they cry'd, come sing and play
      One of *Sions* Songs to day.
Sing? play? to whom (ah) shall we sing or play
    If not *Jerusalem* to thee?
Ah thee *Jerusalem*! ah sooner may
    This hand forget the masterie
      Of Musicks dainty touch, then I
      The Musick of thy memory,
Which when I lose, ô may at once my tongue
    Lose this same busie speaking art,
Unpearch't, her vocall Arteries unstrung,
    No more acquainted with my heart,
      On my dry pallats roof to rest
      A wither'd leaf, an idle guest.
No, no, thy good *Sion* alone must crowne
    The head of all my hope-nurst joyes.
But *Edom* cruell thou! thou cryd'st downe, downe
    Sinke *Sion*, downe and never rise,
      Her falling thou did'st urge, and thrust,
      And haste to dash her into dust,
Dost laugh? proud *Babels* daughter! do, laugh on,
    Till thy ruine teach thee teares,
Even such as these; laugh, till a venging throng
    Of woes, too late doe rouze thy feares.
      Laugh till thy childrens bleeding bones
      Weepe pretious teares upon the stones.

STEPS TO THE TEMPLE

Upon Easter Day.

1.

R Ise heire of fresh eternity
     From thy virgin Tombe,
Rise mighty man of wonders, and thy world with thee,
     Thy Tombe the universall East
     Natures new wombe,
Thy tombe faire immortalities perfumed Nest.

2.

Of all the glories make Noone gay,
     This is the Morne,
This Rock bud's forth the fountaine of the streames of Day,
     In joyes white annalls lives this howre
     When life was borne,
No cloud scoule on his radiant lids, no tempest lower.

3.

Life, by this light's Nativity
     All creatures have,
Death onely by this Dayes just doome is forc't to Dye
     Nor is Death forc't; for may he ly
     Thron'd in thy Grave
Death will on this condition be content to dye.

RICHARD CRASHAW

Sospetto d' Herode.

Libro Primo.

Argomento.

Casting the times with their strong signes,
Death's Master his owne death divines.
Strugling for helpe, his best hope is
Herod's suspition may heale his.
Therefore he sends a fiend to wake,
The sleeping Tyrant's fond mistake;
Who feares (in vaine) that he whose Birth
Meanes Heav'n, should meddle with his Earth.

1.

MUse, now the servant of soft Loves no more,
Hate is thy Theame, and *Herod*, whose unblest
Hand (ô what dares not jealous Greatnesse?) tore
A thousand sweet Babes from their Mothers Brest:
The Bloomes of Martyrdome. O be a Dore
Of language to my infant Lips, yee best
    Of Confessours: whose Throates answering his swords,
    Gave forth your Blood for breath, spoke soules for words.

2.

Great *Anthony*! *Spains* well-beseeming pride,
Thou mighty branch of Emperours and Kings;
The Beauties of whose dawne what eye may bide?
Which With the Sun himselfe weigh's equall wings;
Mappe of Heroick worth! whom farre and wide
To the beleeving world Fame boldly sings:
    Deigne thou to weare this humble Wreath, that bowes
    To be the sacred Honour of thy Browes.

3.

Nor needs my Muse a blush, or these bright Flowers
Other than what their owne blest beauties bring.
They were the smiling sons of those sweet Bowers,
That drinke the deaw of Life, whose deathlesse spring,
Nor *Sirian* flame, nor *Borean* frost deflowers:
From whence Heav'n-labouring Bees with busie wing,
  Suck hidden sweets, which well digested proves
  Immortall Hony for the Hive of Loves.

4.

Thou, whose strong hand with so transcendent worth,
Holds high the reine of faire *Parthenope*,
That neither *Rome*, nor *Athens* can bring forth
A Name in noble deeds Rivall to thee!
Thy Fames full noise, makes proud the patient Earth,
Farre more than matter for my Muse and mee.
  The *Tyrrhene* Seas, and shores sound all the same,
  And in their murmurs keepe thy mighty Name.

5.

Below the Botome of the great Abysse,
There where one Center reconciles all things;
The worlds profound Heart pants; There placed is
Mischiefes old Master, close about him clings
A curl'd knot of embracing Snakes, that kisse
His correspondent cheekes: these loathsome strings
  Hold the perverse Prince in eternall Ties
  Fast bound, since first he forfeited the skies.

6.

The judge of Torments, and the King of Teares,
He fills a burnisht Throne of quenchlesse fire:
And for his old faire Roabes of Light, he weares
A gloomy Mantle of darke flames, the Tire
That crownes his hated head on high appeares;
Where seav'n tall Hornes (his Empires pride) aspire.
  And to make up Hells Majesty, each Horne
  Seav'n crested *Hydra's* horribly adorne.

RICHARD CRASHAW

7.

His Eyes, the sullen dens of Death and Night,
Startle the dull Ayre with a dismall red :
Such his fell glances as the fatall Light
Of staring Comets, that looke Kingdomes dead.
From his black nostrills, and blew lips, in spight
Of Hells owne stinke, a worser stench is spread.
 His breath Hells lightning is : and each deepe groane
 Disdaines to thinke that Heav'n Thunders alone.

8.

His flaming Eyes dire exhalation,
Unto a dreadfull pile gives fiery Breath;
Whose unconsum'd consumption preys upon
That never-dying Life of a long Death.
In this sad House of slow Destruction,
(His shop of flames) hee fryes himself, beneath
 A masse of woes, his Teeth for Torment gnash,
 While his steele sides sound with his Tayles strong lash.

9.

Three Rigourous Virgins waiting still behind,
Assist the Throne of th' Iron-sceptred King.
With whips of Thornes and knotty vipers twin'd
They rouse him, when his ranke thoughts need a sting.
Their lockes are beds of uncomb'd snakes that wind
About their shady browes in wanton Rings.
 Thus reignes the wrathfull King, and while he reignes
 His Scepter and himselfe both he disdaines.

10.

Disdainefull wretch ! how hath one bold sinne cost
Thee all the Beauties of thy once bright Eyes?
How hath one black Eclipse cancell'd, and crost
The glories that did gild thee in thy Rise?
Proud Morning of a perverse Day ! how lost
Art thou unto thy selfe, thou too selfe-wise
 Narcissus ? foolish *Phaeton* ? who for all
 Thy high-aym'd hopes, gaind'st but a flaming fall.

STEPS TO THE TEMPLE

11.

From Death's sad shades, to the Life-breathing Ayre,
This mortall Enemy to mankinds good,
Lifts his Malignant Eyes, wasted with care,
To become beautifull in humane blood.
Where *Jordan* melts his Chrystall, to make faire
The fields of *Palestine*, with so pure a flood,
   There does he fixe his Eyes: and there detect
   New matter, to make good his great suspect.

12.

He calls to mind th' old quarrell, and what sparke
Set the contending Sons of Heav'n on fire:
Oft in his deepe thought he revolves the darke
Sibills divining leaves: he does enquire
Into th' old Prophesies, trembling to marke
How many present prodigies conspire,
   To crowne their past predictions, both he layes
   Together, in his pondrous mind both weighs.

13.

Heavens Golden-winged Herald, late he saw
To a poore *Galilean* virgin sent:
How low the Bright Youth bow'd, and with what awe
Immortall flowers to her faire hand present.
He saw th' old *Hebrewes* wombe, neglect the Law
Of Age and Barennesse, and her Babe prevent
   His Birth, by his Devotion, who began
   Betimes to be a Saint, before a Man.

14.

He saw rich Nectar thawes release the rigour
Of th' Icy North, from frost-bount *Atlas* hands
His Adamantine fetters fall: green vigour
Gladding the *Scythian* Rocks, and *Libian* sands.
He saw a vernall smile, sweetly disfigure
Winters sad face, and through the flowry lands
   Of faire *Engaddi* hony-sweating Fountaines
   With *Manna*, Milk, and Balm, new broach the Mountaines.

93

15.

He saw how in that blest Day-bearing Night,
The Heav'n-rebuked shades made hast away;
How bright a Dawne of Angels with new Light
Amaz'd the midnight world, and made a Day
Of which the Morning knew not: Mad with spight
He markt how the poore Shepheards ran to pay
Their simple Tribute to the Babe, whose Birth
Was the great businesse both of Heav'n and Earth.

16.

He saw a threefold Sun, with rich encrease,
Make proud the Ruby portalls of the East.
He saw the Temple sacred to sweet Peace,
Adore her Princes Birth, flat on her Brest.
He saw the falling Idolls, all confesse
A comming Deity. He saw the Nest
Of pois'nous and unnaturall loves, Earth-nurst;
Toucht with the worlds true *Antidote* to burst.

17.

He saw Heav'n blossome with a new-borne light,
On which, as on a glorious stranger gaz'd
The Golden eyes of Night: whose Beame made bright
The way to *Beth'lem*, and as boldly blaz'd,
(Nor askt leave of the Sun) by Day as Night.
By whom (as Heav'ns illustrious Hand-maid) rais'd
Three Kings (or what is more) three Wise men went
Westward to find the worlds true *Orient*.

18.

Strucke with these great concurrences of things,
Symptomes so deadly, unto Death and him;
Faine would he have forgot what fatall strings,
Eternally bind each rebellious limbe.
He shooke himselfe, and spread his spatious wings:
Which like two Bosom'd sailes embrace the dimme
Aire, with a dismall shade, but all in vaine,
Of sturdy Adamant is his strong chaine.

STEPS TO THE TEMPLE

19

While thus Heav'ns highest counsails, by the low
Foot steps of their Effects, he trac'd too well,
He tost his troubled eyes, Embers that glow
Now with new Rage, and wax too hot for Hell.
With his foule clawes he fenc'd his furrowed Brow,
And gave a gastly shreeke, whose horrid yell
   Ran trembling through the hollow vaults of Night,
   The while his twisted Tayle he gnaw'd for spight.

20.

Yet on the other side, faine would he start
Above his feares, and thinke it cannot be.
He studies Scripture, strives to sound the heart,
And feele the pulse of every Prophecy.
He knows (but knowes not how, or by what Art)
The Heav'n expecting Ages, hope to see
   A mighty Babe, whose pure, unspotted Birth,
   From a chast Virgin wombe, should blesse the Earth.

21.

But these vast Mysteries his senses smother,
And Reason (for what's Faith to him?) devoure.
How she that is a maid should prove a Mother,
Yet keepe inviolate her virgin flower;
How Gods eternall Sonne should be mans Brother,
Poseth his proudest Intellectuall power.
   How a pure Spirit should incarnate bee,
   And life it selfe weare Deaths fraile Livery.

22.

That the Great Angell-blinding light should shrinke
His blaze, to shine in a poore Shepherds eye.
That the unmeasur'd God so low should sinke,
As Pris'ner in a few poore Rags to lye.
That from his Mothers Brest he milke should drinke,
Who feeds with Nectar Heav'ns faire family.
   That a vile Manger his low Bed should prove,
   Who in a Throne of stars Thunders above.

23.

That he whom the Sun serves, should faintly peepe
Through clouds of Infant flesh : that he the old
Eternall Word should be a Child, and weepe.
That he who made the fire, should feare the cold ;
That Heav'ns high Majesty his Court should keepe
In a clay cottage, by each blast control'd.
  That Glories self should serve our Griefs, & feares :
  And free Eternity, submit to yeares.

24.

And further, that the Lawes eternall Giver,
Should bleed in his owne lawes obedience :
And to the circumcising Knife deliver
Himselfe, the forfet of his slaves offence.
That the unblemisht Lambe, blessed for ever,
Should take the marke of sin, and paine of sence.
  These are the knotty Riddles, whose darke doubt
  Intangles his lost Thoughts, past getting out.

25.

While new Thoughts boyl'd in his enraged Brest,
His gloomy Bosomes darkest Character,
Was in his shady forehead seen exprest.
The forehead's shade in Griefes expression there,
Is what in signe of joy among the blest
The faces lightning, or a smile is here.
  Those stings of care that his strong Heart opprest,
  A desperate, *Oh mee*, drew from his deepe Brest.

26.

Oh mee ! (thus bellow'd he) *oh mee* ! what great
Portents before mine eyes their Powers advance ?
And serves my purer sight, onely to beat
Downe my proud Thought, and leave it in a Trance ?
Frowne I ; and can great Nature keep her seat ?
And the gay starrs lead on their Golden dance ?
  Can his attempts above still prosp'rous be,
  Auspicious still, in spight of Hell and me ?

96

STEPS TO THE TEMPLE

27.

Hee has my Heaven (what would he more?) whose bright
And radiant Scepter this bold hand should beare.
And for the never-fading fields of Light,
My faire Inheritance, he confines me here,
To this darke House of shades, horrour, and Night,
To draw a long-liv'd Death, where all my cheere
  Is the solemnity my sorrow weares,
  That Mankinds Torment waits upon my Teares.

28.

Darke, dusky Man, he needs would single forth,
To make the partner of his owne pure ray:
And should we Powers of Heav'n, Spirits of worth,
Bow our bright Heads, before a King of clay?
It shall not be, said I, and clombe the *North*,
Where never wing of *Angell* yet made way.
  What though I mist my blow? yet I strooke high,
  And to dare something, is some victory.

29.

Is he not satisfied? meanes he to wrest
Hell from me too, and sack my Territories?
Vile humane Nature means he not t' invest
(O my despight!) with his divinest Glories?
And rising with rich spoiles upon his Brest,
With his faire Triumphs fill all future stories?
  Must the bright armes of Heav'n, rebuke these eyes?
  Mocke me, and dazle my darke Mysteries?

30.

Art thou not *Lucifer?* he to whom the droves
Of Stars, that gild the Morne in charge were given?
The nimblest of the lightning-winged Loves?
The fairest, and the first-borne smile of Heav'n?
Looke in what Pompe the Mistrisse Planet moves
Rev'rently circled by the lesser seaven,
  Such, and so rich, the flames that from thine eyes,
  Opprest the common-people of the skyes.

31.

Ah ,wretch ! what bootes thee to cast back thy eyes,
Where dawning hope no beame of comfort showes?
While the reflection of thy forepast joyes,
Renders thee double to thy present woes.
Rather make up to thy new miseries,
And meet the mischiefe that upon thee growes.
   If Hell must mourne, Heav'n sure shall sympathize ;
   What force cannot effect, fraud shall devise.

32.

And yet whose force feare I ? have I so lost
My selfe ? my strength too with my innocence ?
Come try who dares, *Heav'n*, *Earth*, what ere dost boast,
A borrowed being, make thy bold defence.
Come thy Creator too, what though it cost
Me yet a second fall ? wee 'd try our strengths.
   Heav'n saw us struggle once, as brave a fight
   Earth now should see, and tremble at the sight.

33.

Thus spoke th' impatient Prince, and made a pause ;
His foule Hags rais'd their heads, & clapt their hands.
And all the Powers of Hell in full applause
Flourisht their Snakes, and tost their flaming brands.
We (said the horrid sisters) wait thy lawes,
Th' obsequious handmaids of thy high commands.
   Be it thy part, Hells mighty Lord, to lay
   On us thy dread commands, ours to obey.

34.

What thy *Alecto*, what these hands can doe,
Thou mad'st bold proofe upon the brow of Heav'n,
Nor should'st thou bate in pride, because that now,
To these thy sooty Kingdomes thou art driven.
Let Heav'ns Lord chide above lowder than thou
In language of his Thunder, thou art even
   With him below : here thou art Lord alone
   Boundlesse and absolute : Hell is thine owne.

35.

If usuall wit, and strength will doe no good,
Vertues of stones, nor herbes: use stronger charmes,
Anger, and love, best hookes of humane blood.
If all faile wee 'l put on our proudest Armes,
And pouring on Heav'ns face the Seas huge flood
Quench his curl'd fires, wee 'l wake with our Alarmes
  Ruine, where e're she sleepes at Natures feet;
  And crush the world till his wide corners meet.

36.

Reply'd the proud King, O my Crownes Defence,
Stay of my strong hopes, you of whose brave worth,
The frighted stars tooke faint experience,
When 'gainst the Thunders mouth we marched forth:
Still you are prodigall of your Love's expence
In our great projects, both 'gainst Heav'n and Earth.
  I thanke you all, but one must single out,
  Cruelty, she alone shall cure my doubt.

37.

Fourth of the cursed knot of Hags is shee,
Or rather all the other three in one;
Hells shop of slaughter shee do's oversee,
And still assist the Execution.
But chiefly there do's she delight to be,
Where Hells capacious Cauldron is set on:
  And while the black soules boile in their own gore,
  To hold them down, and looke that none seeth o're.

38.

Thrice howl'd the Caves of Night, and thrice the sound,
Thundring upon the bankes of those black lakes
Rung, through the hollow vaults of Hell profound:
At last her listning Eares the noise o're takes,
She lifts her sooty lampes, and looking round,
A gen'rall hisse from the whole Tire of snakes
  Rebounding, through Hells inmost Cavernes came,
  In answer to her formidable Name.

RICHARD CRASHAW

39.

'Mongst all the Palaces in Hells command,
No one so mercilesse as this of hers.
The Adamantine Doors, for ever stand
Impenetrable, both to prai'rs and Teares,
The walls inexorable steele, no hand
Of *Time*, or Teeth of hungry *Ruine* feares.
   Their ugly ornaments are the bloody staines,
    Of ragged limbs, torne sculls, & dasht out Braines.

40.

There has the purple *Vengeance* a proud seat,
Whose ever-brandisht Sword is sheath'd in blood.
About her *Hate, Wrath, Warre*, and *Slaughter* sweat;
Bathing their hot limbs in life's pretious flood.
There rude impetuous Rage do's storme, and fret:
And there, as Master of this murd'ring brood,
   Swinging a huge Sith stands impartiall *Death*,
    With endlesse businesse almost out of Breath.

41.

For hangings and for Curtaines, all along
The walls, (abominable ornaments!)
Are tooles of wrath, Anvills of Torments hung;
Fell Executioners of foule intents,
Nailes, hammers, hatchets sharpe, and halters strong,
Swords, Speares, with all the fatall Instruments
   Of sin, and Death, twice dipt in the dire staines
    Of brothers mutuall blood, and Fathers braines.

42.

The Tables furnisht with a cursed Feast,
Which *Harpyes*, with leane *Famine* feed upon,
Unfill'd for ever. Here among the rest,
Inhumane *Erisi-cthon* too makes one;
Tantalus, Atreus, Progne, here are guests:
Wolvish *Lycaon* here a place hath won.
   The cup they drinke in is *Medusa's* scull,
    Which mixt with gall & blood they quaffe brim full.

43.

The foule Queens most abhorred Maids of Honour
Medæa, Jezabell, many a meager Witch,
With Circe, Scylla, stand to wait upon her:
But her best huswifes are the Parcæ, which
Still worke for her, and have their wages from her:
They prick a bleeding heart at every stitch.
  Her cruell cloathes of costly threds they weave,
  Which short-cut lives of murdred Infants leave.

44.

The house is hers'd about with a black wood,
Which nods with many a heavy headed tree.
Each flowers a pregnant poyson, try'd and good,
Each herbe a Plague. The winds sighes timed-bee
By a black Fount, which weeps into a flood.
Through the thick shades obscurely might you see
  Minotaures, Cyclopses, with a darke drove
  Of Dragons, Hydraes, Sphinxes, fill the Grove.

45.

Here Diomed's Horses, Phereus dogs appeare,
With the fierce Lyons of Therodamas.
Busiris ha's his bloody Altar here,
Here Sylla his severest prison has.
The Lestrigonians here their Table reare;
Here strong Procrustes Plants his Bed of Brasse.
  Here cruell Scyron boasts his bloody rockes,
  And hatefull Schinis his so feared Oakes.

46.

What ever Schemes of Blood, fantastick-frames
Of Death Mezentius, or Geryon drew;
Phalaris, Ochus, Ezelinus, names
Mighty in mischiefe, with dread Nero too,
Here are they all, Here all the swords or flames
Assyrian Tyrants, or Egyptian knew.
  Such was the House, so furnisht was the Hall,
  Whence the fourth Fury, answer'd Pluto's call.

RICHARD CRASHAW

47.

Scarce to this Monster could the shady King,
The horrid summe of his intentions tell;
But shee (swift as the momentary wing
Of lightning, or the words he spoke) left Hell.
She rose, and with her to our world did bring,
Pale proofe of her fell presence, Th' aire too well
   With a chang'd countenance witnest the sight,
   And poore fowles intercepted in their flight.

48.

Heav'n saw her rise, and saw Hell in the sight.
The field's faire Eyes saw her, and saw no more,
But shut their flowry lids, for ever Night,
And Winter strow her way; yea, such a sore
Is she to Nature, that a generall fright,
An universall palsie spreading o're
   The face of things, from her dire eyes had run,
   Had not her thick Snakes hid them from the Sun.

49.

Now had the Night's companion from her den,
Where all the busie day she close doth ly,
With her soft wing wipt from the browes of men
Day's sweat, and by a gentle Tyranny,
And sweet oppression, kindly cheating them
Of all their cares, tam'd the rebellious eye
   Of sorrow, with a soft and downy hand,
   Sealing all brests in a *Lethæan* band.

50.

When the *Erinnys* her black pineons spread,
And came to *Bethlem*, where the cruell King
Had now retyr'd himselfe, and borrowed
His Brest a while from care's unquiet sting;
Such as at *Thebes* dire feast she shew'd her head,
Her sulphur-breathed Torches brandishing,
   Such to the frighted Palace now she comes,
   And with soft feet searches the silent roomes.

STEPS TO THE TEMPLE

51.

By *Herod* ———————————— now was borne
The Scepter, which of old great *David* swaid;
Whose right by *David's* image so long worne,
Himselfe a stranger to, his owne had made;
And from the head of *Judahs* house quite torne
The Crowne, for which upon their necks he laid
A sad yoake, under which they sigh'd in vaine,
And looking on their lost state sigh'd againe.

52.

Up, through the spatious Pallace passed she,
To where the Kings proudly-reposed head
(If any can be soft to *Tyranny*
And selfe-tormenting sin) had a soft bed.
She thinkes not fit such he her face should see,
As it is seene by Hell; and seen with dread.
To change her faces stile she doth devise,
And in a pale Ghost's shape to spare his Eyes.

53.

Her selfe a while she layes aside, and makes
Ready to personate a mortall part.
Joseph the Kings dead Brothers shape she takes,
What he by Nature was, is she by Art.
She comes toth' King, and with her cold hand slakes
His Spirits, the Sparkes of Life, and chills his heart,
Lifes forge; fain'd is her voice, and false too, be
Her words; sleep'st thou fond man? sleep'st thou? said she.

54.

So sleeps a Pilot, whose poore Barke is prest
With many a mercylesse o're mastring wave;
For whom (as dead) the wrathfull winds contest,
Which of them deep'st shall digge her watry Grave.
Why dost thou let thy brave soule lye supprest,
In Death-like slumbers; while thy dangers crave
A waking eye and hand? looke up and see
The fates ripe, in their great conspiracy.

55.

Know'st thou not how of th' Hebrewes royall stemme
(That old dry stocke) a despair'd branch is sprung
A most strange Babe! who here conceal'd by them
In a neglected stable lies, among
Beasts and base straw: Already is the streame
Quite turn'd: th' ingratefull Rebells this their young
   Master (with voyce free as the Trumpe of *Fame*)
   Their new King, and thy Successour proclame.

56.

What busy motions; what wild Engines stand
On tiptoe in their giddy Braynes? th' have fire
Already in their Bosomes; and their hand
Already reaches at a sword; They hire
Poysons to speed thee; yet through all the Land
What one comes to reveale what they conspire?
   Goe now, make much of these; wage still their wars
   And bring home on thy Brest more thanklesse scarrs.

57.

Why did I spend my life, and spill my Blood,
That thy firme hand for ever might sustaine
A well-pois'd Scepter? does it now seeme good
Thy brothers blood be-spilt, life spent in vaine?
'Gainst thy owne sons and Brothers thou hast stood
In Armes, when lesser cause was to complaine:
   And now crosse Fates a watch about thee keepe,
   Can'st thou be carelesse now? now can'st thou sleep?

58.

Where art thou man? what cowardly mistake
Of thy great selfe, hath stolne King *Herod* from thee?
O call thy selfe home to thy self, wake, wake,
And fence the hanging sword Heav'n throws upon thee.
Redeeme a worthy wrath rouse thee, and shake
Thy selfe into a shape that may become thee.
   Be *Herod*, and thou shalt not misse from mee
   Immortall stings to thy great thoughts, and thee.

59.

So said, her richest snake, which to her wrist
For a beseeming bracelet she had ty'd
(A speciall Worme it was as ever kist
The foamy lips of *Cerberus*) she apply'd
To the Kings Heart, the Snake no sooner hist,
But vertue heard it, and away she hy'd,
   Dire flames diffuse themselves through every veine,
  This done, Home to her Hell she hy'd amaine.

60.

He wakes, and with him (ne're to sleepe) new feares:
His Sweat-bedewed Bed hath now betrai'd him,
To a vast field of thornes, ten thousand Speares
All pointed in his heart seem'd to invade him:
So mighty were th' amazing Characters
With which his feeling Dreame had thus dismay'd him,
   He his owne fancy-framed foes defies:
  In rage, *My armes, give me my armes*, he cryes.

61.

As when a Pile of food-preparing fire,
The breath of artificiall lungs embraves,
The Caldron-prison'd waters streight conspire,
And beat the hot Brasse with rebellious waves:
He murmurs, and rebukes their bold desire;
Th' impatient liquor, frets, and foames, and raves;
   Till his o're flowing pride suppresse the flame,
  Whence all his high spirits, and hot courage came.

62.

So boyles the fired *Herods* blood-swolne brest,
Not to be slakt but by a Sea of blood.
His faithlesse Crowne he feeles loose on his Crest,
Which on false Tyrants head ne're firmely stood.
The worme of jealous envy and unrest,
To which his gnaw'd heart is the growing food,
   Makes him impatient of the lingring light;
  Hate the sweet peace of all-composing Night.

63.

A Thousand Prophecies that talke strange things,
Had sowne of old these doubts in his deepe brest.
And now of late came tributary Kings,
Bringing him nothing but new feares from th' East,
More deepe suspicions, and more deadly stings,
With which his feav'rous cares their cold increast.
    And now his dream (Hels firebrand) stil-more bright,
    Shew'd him his feares, and kill'd him with the sight.

64.

No sooner therefore shall the Morning see
(Night hangs yet heavy on the lids of Day)
But all his Counsellours must summon'd bee,
To meet their troubled Lord : Without delay
Heralds and Messengers immediately
Are sent about, who poasting every way
    To th'heads and Officers of every band;
    Declare who sends, and what is his command.

65.

Why art thou troubled *Herod*? what vaine feare
Thy blood-revolving Brest to rage doth move?
Heavens King, who doffs himselfe weak flesh to weare,
Comes not to rule in wrath, but serve in love.
Nor would he this thy fear'd Crown from thee Teare,
But give thee a better with himselfe above.
    Poore jealousie! why should he wish to prey
    Upon thy Crowne, who gives his owne away?

66.

Make to thy reason man, and mock thy doubts,
Looke how below thy feares their causes are;
Thou art a Souldier *Herod*; send thy Scouts,
See how hee's furnish't for so fear'd a warre?
What armour does he weare? A few thin clouts.
His Trumpets? tender cries; his men to dare
    So much? rude Shepheards; What his steeds? Alas
    Poore [Beasts]! a slow Oxe, and a simple Asse.

Il fine del primo Libro.

STEPS TO THE TEMPLE

Votiva Domus Petrensis Pro Domo Dei.

U*T magìs in Mundi votis, Avilumq́ querelis*
Jam veniens solet esse Dies, *ubi cuspide primâ*
Palpitat, & roseo Lux prævia *ludit ab* ortu;
Cùm nec abest Phœbus, *nec Eois lætus habenis*
Totus adest, volucrumq́ procul vaga murmura mulcet:

Nos *ità; quos nuper radiis afflavit honestis*
Relligiosa Dies; *nostriq́ per atria Cœli*
(Sacra Domus nostrum *est* Cœlum) *jam* luce tenellâ
Libat adhuc trepidæ *Fax nondum firma* Diei:
Nos *ità jam exercet nimii impatientia* Voti,
Spéq́ *sui* propiore *premit.* ————

———— Quis *pectora tanti*
Tendit amor Cœpti! Desiderio *quàm* longo
Lentæ spes *inhiant!* Domus *ô dulcissima rerum!*
Plena Deo Domus! *Ah,* Quis erit, Quis (*dicimus*) Ille,
(*O Bonus, ô Ingens meritis, ô Proximus* ipsi,
Quem vocat in sua Dona, Deo!) *quo vindice totas*
Excutiant Tenebras *hæc* Sancta Crepuscula? ————

———— Quando,
Quando *erit, ut tremulæ* Flos *heu* tener *ille* Diei,
Qui velut ex Oriente *suo jam* Altaria *circûm*
Lambit, & ambiguo *nobis procul annuit* astro,
Plenis *se pandat* foliis, *&* Lampade totâ
Lætus (ut è medio cûm Sol *micat aureus axe*)
Attonitam *penetrare* Domum *bene possit* adulto
Sidere, *nec dubio* Pia Mœnia *mulceat ore?*
Quando *erit, ut* Convexa *suo quoque pulchra sereno*
Florescant, roseòq́ tremant Laquearia *risu?*
Quæ *nimiùm* informis *tanq[u]am sibi conscia* frontis
Perpetuis jam se lustrant lacrymantia *guttis.*

Quando *erit, ut claris meliori* luce Fenestris
Plurima per vitreos *vivat* Pia Pagina vultus?

Quando *erit, ut* Sacrum *nobis* celebrantibus Hymnum
Organicos *facili, & nunquam fallente susurro*
Nobile murmur agat nervos; *pulmonis iniqui*
Fistula *nec monitus nec faciat male-fida sinistros?*

Denique, *quicquid id est, quod* Res *hîc* Sacra *requirit,*
Fausta . illa, & felix (sitẑ ô Tua) Dextra, *suam cui*
Debeat hæc Aurora Diem. Tibi *supplicat* Ipsa,
Ipsa Tibi *facit* Ara preces. Tu *jam* Illius *audi,*
Audiet Illa tuas. *Dubium est (modò porrige* dextram)
Des *magìs, an* capias : *aude tantùm esse* beatus,
Et danum hoc lucrare Tibi. ————

———— Scis *Ipse volucres*
Quæ Rota *volvat* opes ; *has ergò hîc* fige *perennis*
Fundamenta Domûs Petrensi *in* Rupe ; *suâmẑ*
Fortunæ *sic deme* Rotam. *Scis Ipse procaces*
Divitias *quàm prona vagos vehat* ala *per Euros,*
Divitiis *illas, agè, deme volucribus* alas,
Fdcẑ suus Nostras *illis sit nidus ad* Aras :
Remigii *ut tandem* pennas melioris *adeptæ,*
Se rapiànt Dominúmq; suum *super æthera* secum.

        Felix ô qui sic potuit bene providus uti
Proverb. 23. 5. Fortunæ pennis & opum *levitate* suarum,
        Devitilsque suis Aquilæ sic *addidit* Alas.

EJUSDEM
In cæterorum Operum difficili
Parturitione
GEMITUS.

O *Felix nimis* Illa, *& nostræ nobile Nomen*
Invidiæ Volucris! *facili* q[u]*æ* funere *surgens*
Mater *odora sui* nitidæ *nova fila* juventæ,
Et festinatos *peragit sibi fata per* ignes.
Illa, *haud natales tot* tardis *mensibus horas*
Tam miseris tenuata moris, salutu *velut* uno
In nova secla rapit *sese, &* caput omne *decoras*
Explicat in frondes, roseóq̃ repullulat ortu.
Cinnameos simul Illa *rogos conscenderit,* omnem
Læta bibit Phœbum, *& jam jam victricibus alis*
Plaudit humum, Cinerésque suos.————
————————— Heu! dispare *Fato*
Nos ferimur; Seniorq̃ suo *sub* Apolline Phœnix
Petrensis Mater, dubias *librata per* auras
Pendet adhuc, quæritq̃ sinum *in quo ponat* inertes
Exuvias, *spoliisq̃* suæ Reparata Senectæ
Ore Pari *surgat,* Similíq̃ *per omnia* Vultu.
At nunc heu nixu *secli melioris in* ipso
Deliquium patitur!——
At nunc heu Lentæ longo *in molimine* Vitæ
Interea moritur! Dubio *stant* Mœnia vultu
Parte sui Pulchra, *&* fratres *in fœdera* Muros
Invitant fr[u]*strà, nec respondentia* Saxis
Saxa *suis. Mœrent* Opera *intermissa,* manúsq;
Implorant. ————
————————— *Succurre* Piæ, *succurre* Parenti,
O Quisquis pius *es.* Illi *succurre* Parenti,
Quam *sibi tot sanctæ* Matres *habuere* Parentem.
Quisquis es, ô Tibi, *crede,* Tibi *tot hiantia ruptis*
Mœnibus Ora *loqui!* Matrem Tibi, *crede,* verendam
Muros *tam longo* laceros *senióq̃ sitúque*
Ceu Canos *monstrare suos. Succurre roganti.*
Per Tibi *Plena olim, per jam* Sibi *Sicca precatur*
Ubera, *nè desis* Senio. *Sic* longa Juventus
Te *foveat,* querulæ *nunquam cessura* Senectæ.

RICHARD CRASHAW

On Mr. George Herberts *booke intituled the Temple of
Sacred Poems, sent to a Gentle-woman.*

KNow you faire on what you looke;
  Divinest love lyes in this booke :
Expecting fier from your eyes,
To kindle this his sacrifice.
When your hands untie these strings,
Think yo'have an Angell by the wings.
One that gladly will be nigh,
To waite upon each morning sigh.
To flutter in the balmy aire,
Of your well-perfumed praier ;
These white plumes of his hee'l lend you,
Which every day to heaven will send you :
To take acquaintance of the *spheare*,
And all the smooth-fac'd kindred there.
      And though *Herbert's* name doe owe
      These devotions, fairest, know
      That while I lay them on the shrine
      Of your white hand, they are mine.

STEPS TO THE TEMPLE

On a treatise of Charity.

R Ise then, immortall maid! *Religion* rise!
Put on thy self in thine owne lookes; t' our eyes
Be what thy beauties, not our blots have made thee,
Such as (ere our darke sinnes to dust betrayed thee)
Heav'n set thee down new drest; when thy bright birth
Shot thee like lightning, to th' astonisht earth.
From th' dawn of thy faire eye-lids wipe away,
Dull mists, and melancholy clouds; take day
And thine owne beames about thee, bring the best
Of what so'ere perfum'd thy *Eastern Nest*.
Girt all thy glories to thee : then sit down,
Open thy booke, faire Queen, *and take thy crowne.*
These learned leaves shall vindicate to thee,
Thy holiest, humblest, hand-maid *Charitie.*
She'l dresse thee like thy self, set thee on high,
Where thou shall reach all hearts, command each eye,
Lo where I see thy off'rings wake, and rise,
From the pale dust of that strange sacrifice,
Which they themselves were ; each one putting on
A majestie that may beseeme thy throne.
The Holy youth of Heav'n whose golden rings
Girt round thy awfull altars, with bright wings
Fanning thy faire locks (which the world beleeves,
As much as sees) shall with these sacred leaves
Trick their tall plumes, and in that garbe shall go,
If not more glorious, more conspicuous tho.
——————— Be it enacted then
By the faire lawes of thy firm pointed pen,
God's services no longer shall put on
A *sluttishnesse,* for *pure religion* :
No longer shall our Churches frighted stones
Lie scatter'd like the burnt and martyr'd bones
Of dead *Devotion* ; nor faint marbles weep
In their sad ruines ; nor Religion keep
A melancholy mansion in those cold
Urns. Like God's Sanctuaries they look't of old:

RICHARD CRASHAW

Now seeme they Temples consecrate to *none*,
Or to a *new God desolation.*
No more the *Hypocrite* shall th' *upright* bee
Because he's stiffe, and will confesse no knee :
While others bend their knee, no more shalt thou
(Disdainefull dust and ashes) bend, thy brow ;
Nor on God's Altar cast *two scortching* eyes
Bak't in hot scorn, for *a burnt sacrifice :*
But (for a *Lambe*) thy tame and tender *heart*
New struck by love, still trembling on his dart ;
Or (for two *Turtle Doves*) it shall suffice
To bring a paire of meek and humble *eyes.*
This shall from henceforth be the masculine theme
Pulpits and pens shall sweat in ; to redeeme
Vertue to action, that life-feeding flame
That keepes Religion warme ; not swell a *name*
Of faith, a *mountaine word*, made up of aire,
With those deare spoiles that wont to dresse the faire
And fruitfull Charities full breasts (of old)
Turning her out to tremble in the cold.
What can the poore hope from us, when we bee
Uncharitable ev'n to *Charitie?*

STEPS TO THE TEMPLE.

Fides quæ sola justificat, non est sine Spe & Dilectione.

NAm neq̃ tam sola est. O quis malè censor amarus
   Tam socias negat in mutua sceptra manus?
Deme Fidem; nec aget, nec erit jam nomen Amoris:
   Et vel erit, vel aget quid sine Amore Fides?
Ergò Amor, I, morere; I magnas, Puer alme, per umbras:
   Elysiis non tam numen inane locis.
O bene, quòd pharetra hoc saltem tua præstat & arcus,
   Nè tibi in extremos sit pyra nulla rogos!
O bene, quòd tuus has saltem tibi providet ignis,
   In tu aquas possis funera ferre, faces!
Durus es, ah, quisquis tam dulcia vincula solvis;
   Quæ ligat, & quibus est ipse ligatus Amor.
O bene junctarum divortia sæva sororum,
   Tam penitus mixtas quæ tenuêre manus!
Nam quæ (tam varia) in tam mutua viscera vivunt?
   Aut ubi, quæ duo sunt, tam propè sunt eadem?
Alternis sese circùm amplectuntur in ulnis:
   Extràque & suprà, subter & intus eunt.
Non tam Nympha tenax, Baccho jam mista marito,
   Abdidit in liquidos mascula vina sinus.
Compare jam dempto, saltem sua murmura servat
   Turtur; & in viduos vivit amara modos.
At Fidei sit demptus Amor; non illa dolebit,
   Non erit impatiens, ægráque: jam moritur.
Palma, marem cui tristis hyems procul abstulit umbram,
   Protinus in viridem procubuit faciem?
Undique circumfert caput, omnibus annuit Euris;
   Siqua maritalem misceat aura comam:
Ah misera, expectat longùm, lentùmque expirat,
   Et demum totis excutitur foliis.
At sine Amore Fides, nec tantum vivere perstat
   Quo dici possit vel moritura Fides.
Mortua jam nunc est: nisi demum mortua non est
   Corporea hæc, animâ deficiente, domus.

H

RICHARD CRASHAW

Corpore ab hoc Fidei hanc animam si demis Amoris,
   Jam tua sola *quidem est, sed malè* sola *Fides.*
Hectore ab hoc, currus quem jam nunc sentit Achillis,
   Hectora eum speres quem modò sensit herus?
Tristes exuvias, Oetæi frusta furoris,
   (Vanus) in Alcidæ nomen & acta vocas?
Vel satis in monstra hæc, plùs quàm Nemeæa, malorum
   Hoc Fidei torvum & triste cadaver erit?
Immo, Fidem usquè suos velut ipse Amor ardet amores;
   Sic in Amore fidem comprobat ipsa Fides.

ERGO

Illa Fides vacuâ quæ sola *suberbiet aulâ,*
   Quam Spes desperet, quam nec amabit Amor;
Sola *Fides hæc, tam miserè, tam desolatè*
   Sola, (quod ad nos est) sola *sit usque licet.*
A sociis quæ sola *suis, à se quoque* sola *est.*
   Quæ sibi tam nimia est, sit mihi nulla Fides.

STEPS TO THE TEMPLE

Baptismus non tollit futura peccata.

*Q*Uisquis es ille tener modò quem tua* mater *Achilles*
    In Stygis æthereæ provida tinxit aquis,
Sanus, sed non securus dimitteris illinc :
    In nova non tutus vulnera vivis adhuc.
Mille patent aditus ; & plùs quàm calce petendus
    Ad nigri metues spicula mille dei.
Quòd si est vera salus, veterem meminisse *salutem ;*
    Si nempe hoc verè est esse, fuisse *pium ;*
Illa tibi veteres navis quæ vicerat Austros,
    Si manet in mediis usquè superstes aquis ;
Ac dum tu miseros in littore visis amicos,
    Et peccatorum triste sodalitium,
Illa tibi interea tutis trahet otia velis,
    Expeßans donec tu rediisse queas :
Quin igitur da vina, puer ; da vivere *vitæ ;*
    Mitte suum senibus, mitte supercilium ;
Donemus timidæ, ô socii, sua frigora brumæ :
    Æternæ teneant hîc nova regna rosæ.
Ah non tam tetricos sic elußabimur Euros ;
    Effraßam *non est sic revocare* ratem.

Has undas aliis decet ergò extinguere in undis ;
    Naufragium hoc alio immergere naufragio :
Possit ut ille malis oculus modò naufragus undis,
    Jam lacrymis meliùs naufragus esse suis.

* Ecclesia.

FINIS.

THE

DELIGHTS

OF THE

MUSES.

OR,

Other Poems written on
severall occasions.

By Richard Crashaw, *sometimes of* Pembroke
Hall, and late Fellow of St. Peters *Colledge in* Cambridge.

Mart. *Dic mihi quid melius desidiosus agas.*

LONDON,

Printed by *T.W.* for *H. Moseley*, at
the Princes Armes in S. *Pauls*
Church-yard, 1648.

THE DELIGHTS OF THE MUSES

Musicks Duell.

NOw Westward *Sol* had spent the richest Beams
Of Noons high Glory, when hard by the streams
Of *Tiber*, on the sceane of a greene plat,
Under protection of an Oake; there sate
A sweet Lutes-master : in whose gentle aires
He lost the Dayes heat, and his owne hot cares.
  Close in the covert of the leaves there stood
A Nightingale, come from the neighbouring wood :
(The sweet inhabitant of each glad Tree,
Their Muse, their *Syren*, harmlesse *Syren* she)   10
There stood she listning, and did entertaine
The Musicks soft report : and mold the same
In her owne murmures, that what ever mood
His curious fingers lent, her voyce made good :
The man perceiv'd his Rivall, and her Art,
Dispos'd to give the light-foot Lady sport
Awakes his Lute, and 'gainst the fight to come
Informes it, in a sweet *Præludium*
Of closer straines, and ere the warre begin,
He lightly skirmishes on every string   20
Charg'd with a flying touch : and streightway she
Carves out her dainty voyce as readily,
Into a thousand sweet distinguish'd Tones,
And reckons up in soft divisions,
Quicke volumes of wild Notes; to let him know
By that shrill taste, she could do something too.
  His nimble hands instinct then taught each string
A capring cheerefullnesse; and made them sing
To their owne dance; now negligently rash
He throwes his Arme, and with a long drawne dash   30
Blends all together; then distinctly tripps
From this to that; then quicke returning skipps
And snatches this again, and pauses there.
Shee measures every measure, every where
Meets art with art; sometimes as if in doubt,
Not perfect yet, and fearing to be out,

Trayles her plaine Ditty in one long-spun note,
Through the sleeke passage of her open throat,
A cleare unwrinckled song; then doth shee point it
With tender accents, and severely joynt it   40
By short diminutives, that being rear'd
In controverting warbles evenly shar'd,
With her sweet selfe shee wrangles.   Hee amazed
That from so small a channell should be rais'd
The torrent of a voyce, whose melody
Could melt into such sweet variety,
Straines higher yet; that tickled with rare art
The tatling strings (each breathing in his part)
Most kindly doe fall out; the grumbling Base
In surly groans disdaines the Trebles Grace;   50
The high-perch't treble chirps at this, and chides,
Untill his finger (Moderatour) hides
And closes the sweet quarrell, rowsing all
Hoarce, shrill, at once; as when the Trumpets call
Hot *Mars* to th'Harvest of Deaths field, and woo
Mens hearts into their hands: this lesson too
Shee gives him back; her supple Brest thrills out
Sharpe Aires, and staggers in a warbling doubt
Of dallying sweetnesse, hovers o're her skill,
And folds in wav'd notes with a trembling bill   60
The plyant Series of her slippery song;
Then starts shee suddenly into a Throng
Of short thicke sobs, whose thundring volleyes float,
And roule themselves over her lubrick throat
In panting murmurs, still'd out of her Breast,
That ever-bubling spring; the sugred Nest
Of her delicious soule, that there does lye
Bathing in streames of liquid Melodie;
Musicks best seed-plot, where in ripen'd Aires
A Golden-headed Harvest fairely reares   70
His Honey-dropping tops, plow'd by her breath
Which there reciprocally laboureth
In that sweet soyle, it seemes a holy quire
Founded to th' Name of great *Apollo's* lyre,
Whose silver-roofe rings with the sprightly notes
Of sweet-lipp'd Angell-Imps, that swill their throats

THE DELIGHTS OF THE MUSES

In creame of Morning *Helicon*, and then
Preferre soft-Anthems to the Eares of men,
To woo them from their Beds, still murmuring
That men can sleepe while they their Mattens sing: *80*
(Most divine service) whose so early lay,
Prevents the Eye lidds of the blushing day!
There you might heare her kindle her soft voyce,
In the close murmur of a sparkling noyse,
And lay the ground-worke of her hopefull song,
Still keeping in the forward streame, so long
Till a sweet whirle-wind (striving to get out)
Heaves her soft Bosome, wanders round about,
And makes a pretty Earthquake in her Breast, *70*
Till the fledg'd Notes at length forsake their Nest,
Fluttering in wanton shoales, and to the Sky
Wing'd with their owne wild Eccho's pratling fly.
Shee opes the floodgate, and lets loose a Tide
Of streaming sweetnesse, which in state doth ride
On the wav'd backe of every swelling straine,
Rising and falling in a pompous traine.
And while she thus discharges a shrill peale
Of flashing Aires; she qualifies their zeale
With the coole Epode of a graver Noat, *100*
Thus high, thus low, as if her silver throat
Would reach the brasen voyce of war's hoarce Bird;
Her little soule is ravisht: and so pour'd
Into loose extasies, that shee is plac't
Above her selfe, Musicks *Enthusiast*.

Shame now and anger mixt a double staine
In the Musitians face; yet once againe
(Mistresse) I come; now reach a straine my Lute
Above her mocke, or be for ever mute.
Or tune a song of victory to me, *110*
Or to thy selfe, sing thine owne Obsequie;
So said, his hands sprightly as fire he flings,
And with a quavering coynesse tasts the strings.
The sweet-lip't sisters musically frighted,
Singing their feares are fearefully delighted.
Trembling as when *Appollo's* golden haires
Are fan'd and frizled, in the wanton ayres

121

Of his own breath : which marryed to his lyre
Doth tune the *Sphæares*, and make Heavens selfe looke higher
From this to that, from that to this he flyes   *120*
Feeles Musicks pulse in all her Arteryes,
Caught in a net which there *Apollo* spreads,
His fingers struggle with the vocall threads,
Following those little rills, he sinkes into
A Sea of *Helicon*; his hand does goe
Those parts of sweetnesse which with *Nectar* drop,
Softer then that which pants in *Hebe's* cup.
The humourous strings expound his learned touch,
By various Glosses ; now they seeme to grutch,
And murmur in a buzzing dinne, then gingle   *130*
In shrill tongu'd accents : striving to be single.
Every smooth turne, every delicious stroake
Gives life to some new Grace ; thus doth h'invoke
Sweetnesse by all her Names ; thus, bravely thus
(Fraught with a fury so harmonious)
The Lutes light *Genius* now does proudly rise,
Heav'd on the surges of swolne Rapsodyes.
Whose flourish (Meteor-like) doth curle the aire
With flash of high-borne fancyes : here and there
Dancing in lofty measures, and anon   *140*
Creeps on the soft touch of a tender tone :
Whose trembling murmurs melting in wild aires
Runs to and fro, complaining his sweet cares
Because those pretious mysteryes that dwell,
In musick's ravish't soule he dares not tell,
But whisper to the world : thus doe they vary
Each string his Note, as if they meant to carry
Their Masters blest soule (snatcht out at his Eares
By a strong Extasy) through all the sphæares
Of Musicks heaven ; and seat it there on high   *150*
In th' *Empyræum* of pure Harmony.
At length (after so long, so loud a strife
Of all the strings, still breathing the best life
Of blest variety attending on
His fingers fairest revolution
In many a sweet rise ; many as sweet a fall)
A full-mouth *Diapason* swallowes all.

THE DELIGHTS OF THE MUSES

This done, he lists what she would say to this,
And she although her Breath's late exercise
Had dealt too roughly with her tender throate,   *160*
Yet summons all her sweet powers for a Noate
Alas! in vaine! for while (sweet soule) she tryes
To measure all those wild diversities
Of chatt'ring strings, by the small size of one
Poore simple voyce, rais'd in a naturall Tone;
She failes, and failing grieves; and grieving dyes.
She dyes: and leaves her life the Victors prise,
Falling upon his Lute; ô fit to have
(That liv'd so sweetly) dead, so sweet a Grave!

RICHARD CRASHAW

Ad Reginam.

ET verò jam tempus erat tibi, maxima Mater,
    Dulcibus his oculis accelerare diem :
Tempus erat, nè qua tibi basia blanda vacarent ;
    Sarcina ne collo sit minùs apta tuo.
Scilicet ille tuus, timor & spes ille suorum,
    Quo primum es fælix pignore facta parens,
Ille ferox iras jam nunc meditatur & enses ;
    Jam patris magis est, jam magis ille suus.
Indolis O stimulos ! Vix dum illi transiit infans ;
    Jamque sibi impatiens arripit ille virum.
Improbus ille suis adeò negat ire sub annis :
    Jam nondum puer est, major & est puero.
Si quis in aulæis pictas animatus in iras
    Stat leo, quem doctâ cuspide lusit acus,
Hostis (io !) est ; neq, enim ille alium dignabitur hostem ;
    Nempe decet tantas non minor ira manus.
Tunc hastâ gravis adversùm furit ; hasta bacillum est :
    Mox falsum vero vulnere pectus hiat.
Stat leo, ceu stupeat tali bene fixus ab hoste ;
    Ceu quid in his oculis vel timeat vel amet,
Tam torvum, tam dulce micant : nescire fatetur
    Mars ne sub his oculis esset, an esset Amor.
Quippe illic Mars est, sed qui bene possit amari ;
    Est & Amor certè, sed metuendus Amor :
Talis Amor, talis Mars est ibi cernere ; qualis
    Seu puer hic esset, sive vir ille deus.
Hic tibi jam scitus succedit in oscula fratris,
    Res (ecce !) in lusus non operosa tuos.
Basia jam veniant tua quantacunque caterva ;
    Jam quocunque tuus murmure ludat amor,
En ! Tibi materies tenera & tractabilis hic est :
    Hic ad blanditias est tibi cera satis.
Salve infans, tot basiolis, molle argumentum,
    Maternis labiis dulce negotiolum,
O salve ! Nam te nato, puer aurëe, natus
    Et Carolo & Mariæ tertius est oculus.

THE DELIGHTS OF THE MUSES

Out of Martiall.

FOure Teeth thou had'st thatranck'd in goodly state
Kept thy Mouthes Gate.

The first blast of thy cough left two alone,
The second, none.

This last cough *Ælia*, cought out all thy feare,
Th'hast left the third cough now no businesse here.

RICHARD CRASHAW

Out of Virgil,

In the praise of the Spring.

ALL Trees, all leavy Groves confesse the Spring
   Their gentle friend, then, then the lands begin
To swell with forward pride, and seed desire
To generation; Heavens Almighty Sire
Melts on the Bosome of his Love, and powres
Himselfe into her lap in fruitfull showers.
And by a soft insinuation, mixt
With earths large Masse, doth cherish and assist
Her weake conceptions; No lone shade, but rings
With chatting Birds delicious murmurings.
Then *Venus* mild instinct (at set times) yields
The Herds to kindly meetings, then the fields
(Quick with warme *Zephyres* lively breath) lay forth
Their pregnant Bosomes in a fragrant Birth.
Each body's plump and jucy, all things full
Of supple moisture : no coy twig but will
Trust his beloved bosome to the Sun
(Growne lusty now ;) No Vine so weake and young
That feares the foule-mouth'd Auster or those stormes
That the Southwest-wind hurries in his Armes,
But hasts her forward Blossomes, and layes out
Freely layes out her leaves : Nor doe I doubt
But when the world first out of *Chaos* sprang
So smil'd the Dayes, and so the tenor ran
Of their felicity. A spring was there,
An everlasting spring, the jolly yeare
Led round in his great circle; No winds Breath
As then did smell of Winter, or of Death.
When Lifes sweet Light first shone on Beasts, and when
From their hard Mother Earth, sprang hardy men,
When Beasts tooke up their lodging in the Wood,
Starres in their higher Chambers : never cou'd
The tender growth of things endure the sence
Of such a change, but that the Heav'ns Indulgence
Kindly supplyes sick Nature, and doth mold
A sweetly temper'd meane, nor hot nor cold.

THE DELIGHTS OF THE MUSES

With a Picture sent to a Friend.

I Paint so ill my peece had need to be
    Painted againe by some good Poesie.
I write so ill, my slender Line is scarce
    So much as th' Picture of a well-lim'd verse :
Yet may the love I send be true, though I
    Send nor true Picture, nor true Poesie.
Both which away, I should not need to feare,
    My Love, or *Feign'd* or *painted* should appeare.

The beginning of Helidorus.

THe smiling Morne had newly wak't the Day,
    And tipt the Mountaines with a tender ray :
When on a hill (whose high Imperious brow
Lookes downe, and sees the humble Nile below
Licke his proud feet, and haste into the seas
Through the great mouth that's nam'd from *Hercules*)
A band of men, rough as the Armes they wore
Look't round, first to the sea, then to the shore.
The shore that shewed them what the sea deny'd,
Hope of a prey. There to the maine land ty'd
A ship they saw, no men she had ; yet prest
Appear'd with other lading, for her brest
Deep in the groaning waters wallowĕd
Up to the third Ring ; o're the shore was spread
Death's purple triumph, on the blushing ground
Lifes late forsaken houses all lay drown'd
In their owne bloods deare deluge, some new dead,
Some panting in their yet warme ruines bled :
While their affrighted soules, now wing'd for flight
Lent them the last flash of her glimmering light.
Those yet fresh streames which crawled every where
Shew'd that sterne warre had newly bath'd him there.
Nor did the face of this disaster show
Markes of a fight alone, but feasting too,
A miserable and a monstruous feast,
Where hungry warre had made himself a Guest :
And comming late had eat up Guests and all,
Who prov'd the feast to their owne funerall, &c.

RICHARD CRASHAW

Out of the Greeke
Cupid's *Cryer.*

LOve is lost, nor can his Mother
  Her little fugitive discover :
She seekes, she sighes, but no where spyes him;
Love is lost; and thus shee cryes him.
  O yes ! if any happy eye,
This roaving wanton shall descry;
Let the finder surely know
Mine is the wagge; Tis I that owe
The winged wand'rer; and that none
May thinke his labour vainely gone,
The glad descryer shall not misse,
To tast the *Nectar* of a kisse
From *Venus* lipps; But as for him
That brings him to me, he shall swim
In riper joyes : more shall be his
(*Venus* assures him) than a kisse.
But lest your eye discerning slide,
These markes may be your judgements guide;
His skin as with a fiery blushing
High-colour'd is; His eyes still flushing
With nimble flames, and though his mind
Be ne're so curst, his Tongue is kind :
For never were his words in ought
Found the pure issue of his thought.
The working Bees soft melting Gold,
That which their waxen Mines enfold,
Flow not so sweet as doe the Tones
Of his tun'd accents; but if once
His anger kindle, presently
It boyles out into cruelty,
And fraud : He makes poor mortalls hurts
The objects of his cruell sports.
With dainty curles his froward face
Is crown'd about; But ô what place,
What farthest nooke of lowest Hel!
Feeles not the strength, the reaching spell

THE DELIGHTS OF THE MUSES

Of his small hand? Yet not so small
As 'tis powerfull therewithall.
Though bare his skin, his mind he covers,
And like a saucy Bird he hovers
With wanton wing, now here, now there,
'Bout men and women, nor will spare
Till at length he perching rest,
In the closet of their brest.
His weapon is a little Bow,
Yet such a one as (*Jove* knows how)
Ne're suffred, yet his little Arrow,
Of Heavens high'st Archies to fall narrow.
The Gold that on his Quiver smiles,
Deceives mens feares with flattering wiles.
But ô (too well my wounds can tell)
With bitter shaft's 'tis sauc't too well.
He is all cruell, cruell all;
His Torch Imperious though but small
Makes the Sunne (of flames the fire)
Worse then Sun-burnt in his fire.
Wheresoe're you chance to find him
Cea[z]e him, bring him, (but first bind him)
Pitty not him, but feare thy selfe
Though thou see the crafty Elfe,
Tell down his Silver-drops unto thee,
They'r counterfeit, and will undoe thee.
With baited smiles if he display
His fawning cheeks, looke not that way.
If he offer sugred kisses,
Start, and say, The Serpent hisses.
Draw him, drag him, though he pray
Wooe, intreat, and crying say
Prethee, sweet now let me go,
Here's my Quiver Shafts and Bow,
I'le give thee all, take all, take heed
Lest his kindnesse make thee bleed.
 What e're it be Love offers, still presume
 That though it shines, 'tis fire and will consume.

RICHARD CRASHAW

On Nanus *mounted upon an Ant.*

HIgh mounted on an Ant *Nanus* the tall
   Was thrown alas, and got a deadly fall.
Under th'unruly Beasts proud feet he lies
All torne; with much adoe yet e're he dyes,
Hee straines these words; Base Envy, doe, laugh on.
Thus did I fall, and thus fell *Phaethon.*

Upon Venus *putting on* Mars *his Armes.*

WHat? *Mars* his sword? faire *Cytherea* say,
   Why art thou arm'd so desperately to day?
Mars thou hast beaten naked, and ô then
   What need'st thou put on arms against poore men?

Upon the same.

PAllas saw *Venus* arm'd, and streight she cry'd,
   Come if thou dar'st, thus, thus let us be try'd.
Why foole! saies *Venus*, thus provok'st thou mee,
   That being nak't, thou know'st could conquer thee?

THE DELIGHTS OF THE MUSES

In Se[ren]issimæ Reginæ pa[rt]um hyemalem.

SErta, puer: (quis nunc flores non præbeat hortus?)
   Texe mihi facili pollice serta, puer.
Quid tu nescio quos narras mihi, stulte, Decembres?
   Quid mihi cum nivibus? da mihi serta, puer.
Nix? & hyems? non est nostras quid tale per oras;
   Non est: vel si sit, non tamen esse potest.
Ver agitur: quæcunque trucem dat larva Decembrem,
   Quid fera cunq̃ fremant frigora, ver agitur.
Nonne vides quali se palmite regia vitis
   Prodit, & in sacris quæ sedet uva jugis?
Tam lætis quæ bruma solet ridere racemis?
   Quas hyemis pingit purpura tanta genas?
O Maria! O divum soboles, genitrixque Deorum!
   Siccine nostra tuus tempora ludus erunt?
Siccine tu cum vere tuo nihil horrida brumæ
   Sydera, nil madidos sola morare notos?
Siccine sub mediâ poterunt tua surgere brumâ,
   Atque suas solùm lilia nôsse nives?
Ergò vel invitis nivibus, frendentibus Austris,
   Nostra novis poterunt regna tumere rosis?
O bona turbatrix anni, quæ limite noto
   Tempora sub signis non sinis ire suis!
O pia prædatrix hyemis, quæ tristia mundi
   Murmura tam dulci sub ditione tenes!
Perge precor nostris vim pulchram ferre Calendis:
   Perge precor menses sic numerare tuos.
Perge intempestiva atq̃ importuna videri;
   Inq̃ uteri titulos sic rape cuncta tui.
Sit nobis, sit sæpe hyemes sic cernere nostras
   Exhæredatas floribus ire tuis.
Sæpe sit has vernas hyemes Maiosq̃ Decembres,
   Has per te roseas sæpe videre nives.
Altera gens varium per sydera computet annum,
   Atq̃ suos ducant per vaga signa dies.
Nos deceat nimiis tantum permittere nimbis?
   Tempora tam tetricas ferre Britanna vices?
Quin nostrum tibi nos omnem donabimus annum:
   In partus omnem expende, Maria, tuos.

I 2

RICHARD CRASHAW

Sit tuus ille uterus nostri bonus arbiter anni:
Tempus & in titulos transeat omne tuos.
Nam quæ alia indueret tam dulcia nomina mensis?
Aut quâ tam posset candidus ire togâ?
Hanc laurum Janus sibi vertice vellet utroꝗ,
Hanc sibi vel tota Chloride Maius emet.
Tota suam (vere expulso) respublica florum
Reginam cuperent te, solobêmve tuam.
O bona sors anni, cùm cuncti ex ordine menses
Hic mihi Carolides, *hic* Marianus *erit!*

Epitaphium in Dominum Herrisium.

SIste te paulum (viator) ubi longum sisti
Necesse erit, huc tempe properare te scias
quocunque properas.
Moræ prætium erit
Et Lacrimæ,
Si jacere hic scias ·
Gulielmum
Splendidæ Herrisiorum familiæ
Splendorem maximum:
Quem cum talem vixisse intellexeris,
Et vixisse tantum;
Discas licet
In quantas spes possit
Assurgere mortalitas,
De quantis cadere.
Quem {*Infantem, Essexia——*} *vidit*
    {*Juvenem, Cantabrigia*}
Senem, ah infœlix utraꝗ
Quod non vidit.
Qui
Collegii Christi Alumnus,
Aulæ Pembrokianæ socius,
Utriꝗ, ingens amoris certamen fuit.

THE DELIGHTS OF THE MUSES

Donec
Dulciss. Lites elusit Deus,
Eumque cœlestis Collegii
Cujus semper Alumnus fuit
socium fecit;
Qui & ipse Collegium fuit,
In quo
Musæ omnes & gratiæ,
Nullibi magis sorores,
Sub præcide religione
In tenacissimum sodalitium coaluere.

Quem $\begin{cases} Oratoriæ \\ Poetica \\ Utraque \\ Christianum \end{cases}$ ‐ $\begin{cases} Poetam \\ Oratorem \\ Philosophum \\ Omnes \end{cases}$ *Agnovere.*

Qui $\begin{cases} Fide \\ Spe \\ Charitate \\ Humilitate \end{cases}$ $\begin{cases} Mundum \\ Cœlum \\ Proximum \\ Seipsum \end{cases}$ *Superavit.*

Cujus
Sub verna fronte senilis animus,
Sub morum [f]acilitate, [s]everitas virtutis;
Sub plurima indole, pauci anni;
Sub majore modestia, maxima indoles.
adeo se occuluerunt
ut vitam ejus
Pulchram dixeris & pudicam dissimulationem:
Imo vero & morte,
Ecce enim in ipso funere
Dissimulari se passus est,
Sub tantillo marmore tantum hospitem,
Eo nimerum majore monumento
quo minore tumulo.
Eo ipso die occubuit quo Ecclesia
Anglica nec ad vesperas legit,
Raptus est ne militia mutaret Intellectum ejus;
Scilicet. Id. Octobris, Anno. Sal. 1631.

RICHARD CRASHAW

In Picturam Reverendissimi Episcopi, *D. Andrews.*

HÆc charta monstrat, Fama quem monstrat magis,
Sed & ipsa quem dum fama quem non monstrat satis,
Ille, ille solus totam implevit Tubam,
Tot ora solus domuit & famam quoque
Fecit `modestam : mentis igneæ pater
Agiliq̄ radio Lucis æternæ vigil,
Per alta rerum pondera indomito Vagus
Cucurrit Animo, Quippe naturam ferox
Exhausit ipsam, mille Fœtus artibus,
Et mille Linguis ipse se ingentes procul
Variavit omnes, fuitq̄ toti simul
Cognatus orbi: sic sacrum & solidum jubar
Saturumq̄ cœlo pectus ad patrios Libens
Porrexit `ignes: hac eum (Lector) vides
Hac (ecce) charta: O utinam & audires quoq̄.

Upon Bishop Andrews *Picture before his Sermons.*

THis reverend shadow cast that setting Sun,
  Whose glorious course through our Horrizon run,
Left the dimme face of this du[l]l Hemisphæare,
All one great eye, all drown'd in one great Teare.
Whose faire illustrious soule, led his free thought
Through Learnings Universe, and (vainly) sought
Room for her spatious selfe, untill at length
Shee found the way home, with an holy strength
Snatch't her self hence to Heaven: fill'd a bright place,
'Mongst those immortall fires, and on the face
Of her great Maker fixt her flaming eye,
There still to read true pure divinity.
And now that grave aspect hath deign'd to shrinke
Into this lesse appearance; If you thinke,
'Tis but a dead face, art doth here bequeath:
Looke on the following leaves, and see him breath.

THE DELIGHTS OF THE MUSES

Upon the Death of a Gentleman.

FAithlesse and fond Mortality!
Who will ever credit thee?
Fond and faithlesse thing! that thus,
In our best hopes beguilest us.
What a reckoning hast thou made,
Of the hopes in him we laid?
For Life by volumes lengthened,
A Line or two, to speake him dead.
For the Laurell in his verse,
The sullen Cypresse o're his Herse.
For a silver-crowned Head,
A durty pillow in Death's Bed.
For so deare, so deep a trust,
Sad requitall, thus much dust!
Now though the blow that snatch him hence,
Stopt the Mouth of Eloquence,
Though shee be dumbe e're since his Death,
Not us'd to speake but in his Breath,
Yet if at least shee not denyes,
The sad language of our eyes,
Wee are contented: for then this
Language none more fluent is.
Nothing speakes our Griefe so well
As to speak Nothing. Come then tell
Thy mind in Teares who e're Thou be,
That ow'st a Name to misery.
Eyes are vocall, Teares have Tongues,
And there be words not made with lungs;
Sententious showers, ô let them fall,
Their cadence is Rhetoricall.
Here's a Theame will drinke th'expence,
Of all thy watry Eloquence.
Weepe then, onely be exprest
Thus much, *Hee's Dead*, and weep the rest.

RICHARD CRASHAW

Upon the Death of Mr. Herrys.

A Plant of noble stemme, forward and faire,
  As ever whisper'd to the Morning Aire,
Thriv'd in these happy Grounds, the Earth's just pride,
Whose rising Glories made such haste to hide
His head in Cloudes, as if in him alone
Impatient Nature had taught motion
To start from time, and cheerfully to fly
Before, and seize upon Maturity.
Thus grew this gratious plant, in whose sweet shade,
The Sunne himselfe oft wisht to sit, and made
The Morning Muses perch like Birds, and sing
Among his Branches : yea, and vow'd to bring
His owne delicious Phœnix from the blest
Arabia, there to build her Virgin nest,
To hatch her selfe in ; 'mongst his leaves the Day
Fresh from the Rosie East rejoyc't to play.
To them shee gave the first and fairest Beame
That waited on her Birth: she gave to them
The purest Pearles, that wept her evening Death.
The balmy *Zephirus* got so sweet a Breath
By often kissing them, and now begun
Glad Time to ripen expectation.
The timorous Maiden-Blossomes on each Bough,
Peept forth from their first blushes : so that now
A Thousand ruddy hopes smil'd in each Bud,
And flatter'd every greedy eye that stood
Fixt in Delight, as if already there
Those rare fruits dangled, whence the Golden Yeare
His crowne expected, when (ô Fate, ô Time
That seldome lett'st a blushing youthfull Prime
Hide his hot Beames in shade of silver Age ;
So rare is hoary vertue) the dire rage
Of a mad storme these bloomy joyes all tore,
Ravisht the Maiden Blossoms, and downe bore
The trunke. Yet in this Ground his pretious Root
Still lives, which when weake Time shall be pour'd out

136

Into Eternity, and circular joyes
Dance in an endlesse round, again shall rise
The faire son of an ever-youthfull Spring,
To be a shade for Angels while they sing,
Meane while who e're thou art that passest here,
O doe thou water it with one kind Teare.

In Eundem Scazon.

HUc hospes, oculos flecte, sed lacrimis cæcos,
Legit optime hæc, Quem legere non sinit flectus.
Ars nuper & natura, forma, virtusq;
Æmulatione fervidæ, paciscuntur
Probare in uno juvene quid queant omnes,
Fuere tantæ terra nuper fuit liti
Ergo hic ab ipso Judicem manent cælo.

RICHARD CRASHAW

Upon the Death of the most desired Mr. Herrys.

DEath, what dost? ô hold thy Blow,
   What thou dost, thou dost not know.
Death thou must not here be cruell,
This is Natures choycest Jewell.
This is hee in whose rare frame,
Nature labour'd for a Name,
And meant to leave his pretious feature,
The patterne of a perfect Creature.
Joy of Goodnesse, Love of Art,
Vertue weares him next her heart.
Him the Muses love to follow,
Him they call their vice-*Apollo.*
Apollo golden though thou bee,
Th'art not fairer then is hee.
Nor more lovely lift'st thy head,
Blushing from thine Easterne Bed.
The Glories of thy Youth ne're knew;
Brighter hopes then he can shew.
Why then should it e're be seen,
That his should fade, while thine is Green?
And wilt Thou, (ô cruell boast!)
Put poore Nature to such cost?
O 'twill undoe our common Mother,
To be at charge of such another.
What? thinke we to no other end,
Gracious Heavens do use to send
Earth her best perfection,
But to vanish and be gone?
Therefore onely give to day,
To morrow to be snatcht away?
I've seen indeed the hopefull bud,
Of a ruddy Rose that stood
Blushing, to behold the Ray
Of the new-saluted Day;
(His tender toppe not fully spread)
The sweet dash of a shower now shead,

THE DELIGHTS OF THE MUSES

Invited him no more to hide
Within himselfe the purple pride
Of his forward flower, when lo
While he sweetly 'gan to show
His swelling Gloryes, *Auster* spide him,
Cruell *Auster* thither hy'd him,
And with the rush of one rude blast,
Sham'd not spitefully to wast.
All his leaves, so fresh, so sweet,
And lay them trembling at his feet.
I've seen the Mornings lovely Ray,
Hover o're the new-borne Day,
With rosie wings so richly Bright,
As if he scorn'd to thinke of Night;
When a ruddy storme whose scoule
Made Heavens radiant face looke foule,
Call'd for an untimely Night,
To blot the newly blossom'd Light.
But were the Roses blush so rare,
Were the Mornings smile so faire
As is he, nor cloud, nor wind
But would be courteous, would be kind.
   Spare him Death, ô spare him then,
Spare the sweetest among men.
Let not pitty with her Teares,
Keepe such distance from thine Eares.
But ô thou wilt not, canst not spare,
Haste hath never time to heare.
Therefore if he needs must go,
And the Fates will have it so,
Softly may he be possest,
Of his monumentall rest.
Safe, thou darke home of the dead,
Safe ô hide his loved head.
For Pitties sake ô hide him quite,
From his Mother Natures sight:
Lest for Griefe his losse may move
All her Births abortive prove.

RICHARD CRASHAW

Another.

IF ever Pitty were acquainted
With sterne Death, if e're he fainted,
Or forgot the cruell vigour
Of an Adamantine rigour,
Here, ô here we should have knowne it,
Here or no where hee'd have showne it.
For hee whose pretious memory,
Bathes in Teares of every eye:
Hee to whom our sorrow brings,
All the streames of all her springs:
Was so rich in Grace and Nature,
In all the gifts that blesse a Creature;
The fresh hopes of his lovely Youth,
Flourisht in so faire a growth;
So sweet the Temple was, that shrin'd
The Sacred sweetnesse of his mind;
That could the Fates know to relent,
Could they know what mercy meant;
Or had ever learnt to beare,
The soft tincture of a Teare:
Teares would now have flow'd so deepe,
As might have taught Griefe how to weepe.
Now all their steely operation,
Would quite have lost the cruell fashion.
Sicknesse would have gladly been,
Sick himselfe to have sav'd him:
And his Feaver wish'd to prove,
Burning onely in his Love.
Him when wrath it selfe had seen,
Wrath its selfe had lost his spleen.
Grim Destruction here amaz'd,
In stead of striking would have gaz'd.
Even the Iron-pointed pen,
That notes the Tragick Doomes of men
Wet with teares still'd from the eyes,
Of the flinty Destinies;

THE DELIGHTS OF THE MUSES

Would have learn't a softer style,
And have been asham'd to spoyle
His lives sweet story, by the hast,
Of a cruell stop ill plac't.
In the darke volume of our fate,
Whence each leafe of Life hath date,
Where in sad particulars,
The totall summe of Man appeares.
And the short clause of mortall Breath,
Bound in the period of Death,
In all the Booke if any where
Such a tearme as this, *spare here*
Could have been found 'twould have been read,
Writ in white Letters o're his head :
Or close unto his name annext,
The faire glosse of a fairer Text.
In briefe, if any one were free,
Hee was that one, and onely he.
But he, alas ! even hee is dead,
And our hopes faire harvest spread
In the dust. Pitty now spend
All the teares that griefe can lend.
Sad mortality may hide ;
In his ashes all her pride ;
With this inscription o're his head
All hope of never dying, here lyes dead.

RICHARD CRASHAW

His Epitaph.

PAssenger who e're thou art,
Stay a while, and let thy Heart
Take acquaintance of this stone,
Before thou passest further on.
This stone will tell thee that beneath,
Is entomb'd the Crime of Death;
The ripe endowments of whose mind
Left his Yeares so much behind,
That numbring of his vertues praise,
Death lost the reckoning of his Dayes;
And believing what they told,
Imagin'd him exceeding old.
In him perfection did set forth
The strength of her united worth.
Him his wisdomes pregnant growth
Made so reverend, even in Youth,
That in the Center of his brest
(Sweet as is the Phænix nest)
Every reconciled Grace
Had their Generall meeting place.
In him Goodnesse joy'd to see
Learning learne Humility.
The splendor of his Birth and Blood
Was but the glosse of his owne Good.
The flourish of his sober Youth
Was the Pride of Naked Truth.
In composure of his face,
Liv'd a faire, but manly Grace.
His mouth was Rhetoricks best mold,
His tongue the Touchstone of her Gold.
What word so e're his Breath kept warme,
Was no word now but a charme:
For all persuasive Graces thence
Suck't their sweetest Influence.
His vertue that within had root,
Could not chuse but shine without.
And th'heart-bred lustre of his worth,
At each corner peeping forth,

Pointed him out in all his wayes,
Circled round in his owne Rayes:
That to his sweetnesse, all mens eyes
Were vow'd Loves flaming Sacrifice.
  Him while fresh and fragrant Time
Cherisht in his Golden Prime;
E're *Hebe*'s hand had overlaid
His smooth cheekes with a downy shade;
The rush of Death's unruly wave,
Swept him off into his Grave.
  Enough, now (if thou canst) passe on,
For now (alas) not in this stone
(Passenger who e're thou art)
Is he entomb'd, but in thy Heart.

An Epitaph.

Upon Doctor Brooke.

A *Brooke* whose streame so great, so good,
  Was lov'd, was honour'd, as a flood:
Whose Bankes the Muses dwelt upon,
More than their owne Helicon;
Here at length, hath gladly found
A quiet passage under ground;
Meane while his loved bankes now dry,
The Muses with their teares supply.

Upon Ford's *two Tragedies.*

Loves Sacrifice,

and

The Broken Heart.

THou cheat'st us *Ford*, mak'st one seeme two by Art.
What is *Loves Sacrifice*, but *The broken Heart.*

RICHARD CRASHAW

On a foule Morning, being then to take a journey.

WHere art thou *Sol*, while thus the blind fold Day
    Staggers out of the East, loses her way
Stumbling on night? Rouze thee Illustrious Youth,
And let no dull mists choake the Lights faire growth.
Point here thy beames; ô glance on yonder flocks,
And make their fleeces Golden as thy locks.
Unfold thy faire front, and there shall appeare
Full glory, flaming in her owne free spheare.
Gladnesse shall cloath the Earth, we will instile
The face of things, an universall smile.
Say to the Sullen Morne, thou com'st to court her;
And wilt command proud *Zephirus* to sport her
With wanton gales : his balmy breath shall licke
The tender drops which tremble on her cheeke;
Which rarified, and in a gentle raine
On those delicious bankes distill'd againe,
Shall rise in a sweet Harvest, which discloses
To every blushing Bed of new-borne Roses.
Hee'l fan her bright locks, teaching them to flow,
And friske in curl'd *Mæanders*; Hee will throw
A fragrant Breath suckt from the spicy nest
O'th' pretious *Phœnix*, warme upon her Breast.
Hee with a dainty and soft hand will trim,
And brush her Azure Mantle, which shall swim
In silken Volumes; wheresoe're shee'l tread,
Bright clouds like Golden fleeces shall be spread.
    Rise then (faire blew-ey'd Maid) rise and discover
Thy silver brow, and meet thy Golden lover.
See how hee runs, with what a hasty flight,
Into thy bosome, bath'd with liquid Light.
Fly, fly prophane fogs, farre hence fly away,
Taint not the pure streames of the springing Day,
With your dull influence; it is for you,
To sit and scoule upon Nights heavy brow;
Not on the fresh cheekes of the virgin Morne,
Where nought but smiles, and ruddy joyes are worne.
Fly then, and doe not thinke with her to stay;
Let it suffice, shee'l weare no maske to day.

144

THE DELIGHTS OF THE MUSES

Upon the faire Ethiopian sent to a Gentlewoman.

L O here the faire *Chariclia*! in whom strove
So false a Fortune, and so true a Love.
Now after all her toyles by Sea and Land,
O may she but arrive at your white hand,
Her hopes are crown'd, onely she feares that than,
Shee shall appeare true Ethiopian.

On Marriage.

I Would be married, but I'de have no Wife,
I would be married to a single Life.

RICHARD CRASHAW

To the Morning.

Satisfaction for sleepe.

WHat succour can I hope the Muse will send
   Whose drowsinesse hath wrong'd the Muses friend?
What hope *Aurora* to propitiate thee,
Unlesse the Muse sing my Apologie?
  O in that morning of my shame! when I
Lay folded up in sleepes captivity,
How at the sight did'st Thou draw back thine Eyes,
Into thy modest veyle? how did'st thou rise
Twice dy'd in thine own blushes, and did'st run
To draw the Curtaines, and awake the Sun?
Who rowzing his illustrious tresses came,
And seeing the loath'd object, hid for shame
His head in thy faire Bosome, and still hides
Mee from his Patronage; I pray, he chides:
And pointing to dull *Morpheus,* bids me take
My owne *Apollo,* try if I can make
His *Lethe* be my *Helicon*; and see
If *Morpheus* have a Muse to wait on mee.
Hence 'tis my humble fancie findes no wings,
No nimble rapture starts to Heaven and brings
Enthusiasticke flames, such as can give
Marrow to my plumpe *Genius,* make it live
Drest in the glorious madnesse of a Muse,
Whose feet can walke the milky way, and chuse
Her starry Throne; whose holy heats can warme
The grave, and hold up an exalted arme
To lift me from my lazy Urne, to climbe
Upon the stooping shoulders of old Time,
And trace Eternity — But all is dead,
All these delicious hopes are buried
In the deepe wrinckles of his angry brow,
Where mercy cannot find them: but ô thou

THE DELIGHTS OF THE MUSES

Bright Lady of the Morne, pitty doth lye
So warme in thy soft Brest it cannot dye.
Have mercy then, and when He next shall rise
O meet the angry God, invade his Eyes,
And stroake his radiant Cheekes; one timely kisse
Will kill his anger, and revive my blisse.
So to the treasure of thy pearly deaw,
Thrice will I pay three Teares, to show how true
My griefe is; so my wakefull lay shall knocke
At th'Orientall Gates; and duly mocke
The early Larkes shrill Orizons, to be
An Anthem at the Dayes Nativitie.
And the same rosie-finger'd hand of thine,
That shuts Nights dying eyes, shall open mine.
   But thou, faint God of sleepe, forget that I
Was ever known to be thy votary.
No more my pillow shall thine Altar be,
Nor will I offer any more to thee
My selfe a melting sacrifice; I'me borne
Againe a fresh Child of the Buxome Morne,
Heire of the Suns first Beames; why threat'st thou so?
Why dost thou shake thy leaden Scepter? goe,
Bestow thy Poppy upon wakefull woe,
Sicknesse, and sorrow, whose pale lidds ne're know
Thy downie finger, dwell upon their Eyes,
Shut in their Teares; Shut out their miseries.

Upon the Powder day.

HOw fit our well-rank'd Feasts do follow!
   All mischiefe comes after *All-Hallow*.

RICHARD CRASHAW

Loves Horoscope.

LOve, brave Vertues younger Brother,
    Erst hath made my Heart a Mother,
Shee consults the conscious Spheares,
To calculate her young sons yeares.
Shee askes if sad, or saving powers,
Gave Omen to his infant howers,
Shee askes each starre that then stood by,
If poore Love shall live or dy.

Ah my Heart, is that the way?
    Are these the Beames that rule thy Day?
Thou know'st a Face in whose each looke,
Beauty layes ope Loves Fortune-booke;
On whose faire revolutions wait
The obsequious motions of Loves fate;
Ah my Heart, her eyes and shee,
Have taught thee new Astrologie.
How e're Loves native houres were set,
What ever starry Synod met,
'Tis in the mercy of her eye,
If poore Love shall live or dye.

If those sharpe Rayes putting on
    Points of Death bid Love be gon,
(Though the Heavens in counsell sate,
To crowne an uncontrouled Fate,
Though their best Aspects twin'd upon
The kindest Constellation,
Cast amorous glances on his Birth,
And whisper'd the confederate Earth
To pave his pathes with all the good
That warms the Bed of youth and blood;)
Love ha's no plea against her eye,
Beauty frownes, and Love must dye.

But if her milder influence move,
And gild the hopes of humble Love :
(Though heavens inauspicious eye
Lay blacke on Loves Nativitie ;
Though every Diamond in *Joves* crowne
Fixt his forehead to a frowne,)
Her Eye a strong appeale can give,
Beauty smiles and Love shall live.

O if Love shall live, ô where,
But in her Eye, or in her Eare,
In her Brest, or in her Breath,
Shall I hide poore Love from Death ?
For in the life ought else can give,
Love shall dye, although he live.

Or if Love shall dye, ô where,
But in her Eye, or in her Eare,
In her Breath, or in her Breast,
Shall I Build his funerall Nest ?
While Love shall thus entombed lye,
Love shall live, although he dye.

RICHARD CRASHAW

Principi recèns natæ omen maternæ indolis.

CResce, ò dulcibus imputanda Divis,
O cresce, & propera, puella Princeps,
In matris propera venire partes.
Et cùm par breve fulminum mirorum,
Illinc Carolus, & Jacobus indè,
In patris faciles subire famam,
Ducent fata furoribus decoris;
Cùm terror sacer, Anglicíq̄ magnum
Murmur nominis increpabit omnem
Latè Bosporon, Ottomanicásque
Non picto quatiet tremore Lunas;
Te tunc altera, nec timenda paci,
Poscent prælia. Tu potens pudici
Vibratrix oculi, pios in hostes
Latè dulcia fata dissipabis.
O cùm flos tener ille, qui recenti
Pressus sidere jam sub ora ludit,
Olim fortior omne cuspidatos
Evolvet latus aureum per ignes;
Quíq̄ imbellis adhuc, adultus olim,
Puris expatiabitur genarum
Campis imperiosior Cupido;
O quàm certa superbiore pennâ
Ibunt spicula, melleæque mortes,
Exultantibus hinc & inde turmis,
Quoquò jusseris, impigrè volabunt!
O quot corda calentium deorum
De te vulnera delicata discent!
O quot pectora Principum magistris
Fient molle negotium sagittis!
Nam quæ non poteris per arma ferri,
Cui matris sinus atque utrumque sidus
Magnorum patet officina Amorum?
Hinc sumas licet, ò puella Princeps,
Quantacunque opus est tibi pharetrâ.
Centum sume Cupidines ab uno
Matris lumine, Gratiásque centum,
Et centum Veneres: adhuc manebunt
Centum mille Cupidines; manebunt
Ter centum Venerèsque Gratiæque
Puro fonte superstites per ævum.

THE DELIGHTS OF THE MUSES

Out of the Italian.

A Song.

To thy Lover,
Deere, discover
That sweet blush of thine that shameth
(When those Roses
It discloses)
All the flowers that Nature nameth.

In free Ayre,
Flow thy Haire;
That no more Summers best dresses,
Bee beholden
For their Golden
Locks, to Phœbus flaming Tresses.

O deliver
Love his Quiver,
From thy Eyes he shoots his Arrowes,
Where Apollo
Cannot follow :
Featherd with his Mothers Sparrowes.

O envy not
(That we dye not)
Those deere lips whose doore encloses
All the Graces
In their places,
Brother Pearles, and sister Roses.

From these treasures
Of ripe pleasures
One bright smile to cleere the weather.
Earth and Heaven
Thus made even,
Both will be good friends together.

RICHARD CRASHAW

The aire does wooe thee,
Winds cling to thee;
Might a word once flye from out thee,
Storme and Thunder
Would sit under,
And keepe silence round about thee.

But if Natures
Common Creatures,
So deare Glories dare not borrow :
Yet thy Beauty
Owes a Duty,
To my loving, lingring, sorrow.

When to end mee
Death shall send mee
All his Terrors to affright mee :
Thine eyes Graces
Gild their faces,
And those Terrors shall delight mee.

When my dying
Life is flying,
Those sweet Aires that often slew mee
Shall revive mee,
Or reprive mee,
And to many Deaths renew mee.

THE DELIGHTS OF THE MUSES

Out of the Italian.

LOve now no fire hath left him,
  We two betwixt us have divided it.
Your Eyes the Light hath reft him,
The heat commanding in my *Heart* doth sit.
  O! that poore Love be not for ever spoyled,
  Let my *Heat* to your *Light* be reconciled.

So shall these flames, whose worth
  Now all obscured lyes,
(Drest in those Beames) start forth
  And dance before your eyes.

Or else partake my flames
  (I care not whither)
And so in mutuall Names
  Of Love, burne both together.

Out of the Italian.

WOuld any one the true cause find
  How Love came nak't, a Boy, and blind?
'Tis this; listning one day too long,
To th' Syrens in my Mistris Song,
The extasie of a delight
So much o're-mastring all his might,
To that one Sense, made all else thrall,
  And so he lost his Clothes, eyes, heart and all.

RICHARD CRASHAW.

In faciem Augustiss. Regis à morbillis integram.

MUsa redi; vocat alma parens Academia : Noster
    En redit, ore suo noster Apollo redit.
Vultus adhuc suus, & vultu sua purpura tantùm
    Vivit, & admixtas pergit amare nives.
Tùne illas violare genas ? tùne illa profanis,
    Morbe ferox, tentas ire per ora notis?
Tu Phœbi faciem tentas, vanissime ? Nostra
    Nec Phœbe maculas novit habere suas.
Ipsa sui vindex facies morbum indignatur ;
    Ipsa sedet radiis ô bene tuta suis:
Quippe illîc deus est, cœlùmque & sanĉtius astrum ;
    Quippe sub his totus ridet Apollo genis.
Quòd facie Rex tutus erat, quòd cætera taĉtus :
    Hinc hominem Rex est fassus, & inde deum.

THE DELIGHTS OF THE MUSES

[*On the Frontispiece of* Isaacsons *Chronologie explaned.*

IF with distinctive Eye, and Mind, you looke
Upon the *Front*, you see more than one *Booke*.
Creation is *Gods Booke*, wherein he writ
Each Creature, as a Letter filling it.
History is *Creations* Booke; which showes
To what effects the *Series* of it goes.
Chronologie's the Booke of *Historie*, and beares
The just account of *Dayes*, *Moneths*, and *Yeares*.
But *Resurrection*, in a Later Presse,
And *New Edition*, is the summe of these.
The Language of these Bookes had all been one,
Had not th'*Aspiring Tower of Babylon*
Confus'd the Tongues, and in a distance hurl'd
As farre the speech, as men, o'th' new fill'd world.
   Set then your eyes in method, and behold
Times embleme, *Saturne*; who, when store of Gold
Coyn'd the first age, *Devour'd* that *Birth*, he fear'd;
Till *History*, Times eldest Child appear'd;
And *Phœnix*-like, in spight of *Saturnes* rage,
Forc'd from her *Ashes*, Heyres in every age.
From th'*rising Sunne*, obtaining by just Suit,
A *Springs Ingender*, and an *Autumnes Fruit*.
Who in those *Volumes* at her motion pend,
Unto *Creations Alpha* doth extend.
Againe ascend, and view *Chronology*,
By *Optick Skill* pulling farre *History*
Neerer; whose *Hand* the piercing *Eagles* Eye
Strengthens, to bring remotest Objects nigh.
Under whose *Feet*, you see the *Setting Sunne*,
From the darke *Gnomon*, o're her Volumes runne,
Drown'd in eternall night, never to rise,
Till *Resurrection* show it to the eyes
Of *Earth*-worne men; and her shrill Trumpets sound
Affright the *Bones* of Mortals from the ground.
The *Columnes* both are crown'd with either *Sphere*,
To show *Chronology* and *History* beare,
No other *Culmen* than the double Art,
Astronomy, *Geography*, impart.]

RICHARD CRASHAW

Or Thus.

LEt hoary. *Time*'s vast Bowels be the Grave
To what his Bowels birth and being gave;
Let Nature die, (*Phœnix*-like) from death
Revived Nature takes a second breath;
If on *Times* right hand, sit faire *Historie*,
If, from the seed of emptie Ruine, she
Can raise so faire an *Harvest:* Let Her be
Ne're so farre distant, yet *Chronologie*
(Sharp-sighted as the Eagles eye, that can
Out-stare the broad-beam'd Dayes Meridian)
Will have a *Perspicill* to find her out,
And, through the *Night* of error and dark doubt,
Discerne the *Dawne* of Truth's eternall ray,
As when the rosie *Morne* budds into Day.
  Now that *Time*'s Empire might be amply fill'd,
Babells bold *Artists* strive (below) to build
Ruine a Temple; on whose fruitfull fall
History reares her *Pyramids* more tall
Than were th'*Ægyptian* (by the life these give,
Th'*Egyptian Pyramids* themselves must live :)
On these she lifts the *World*; and on their base
Shewes the two termes and limits of *Time*'s race :
That, the *Creation* is; the *Judgement*, this;
That, the World's *Morning*, this her *Midnight* is.

THE DELIGHTS· OF THE·MUSES

An Epitaph

Upon Mr. Ashton *a conformable Citizen.*

THe modest front of this small floore,
Beleeve me, Reader, can say more
Than many a braver Marble can,
Here lyes a truly honest man.
One whose Conscience was a thing,
That troubled neither Church nor King.
One of those few that in this Towne,
Honour all Preachers, heare their owne.
Sermons he heard, yet not so many
As left no time to practise any.
He heard them reverendly, and then
His practice preach'd them o're agen.
His *Parlour-Sermons* rather were
Those to the Eye, then to the Eare.
His prayers took their price and strength,
Not from the lowdnesse, nor the length.
He was a Protestant at home,
Not onely in despight of *Rome.*
He lov'd his *Father*; yet his zeale
Tore not off his Mothers veile.
To th' Church he did allow her Dresse,
True *Beauty*, to true *Holinesse.*
Peace, which he lov'd in Life, did lend
Her hand to bring him to his end.
When age and death call'd for the score,
No surfets were to reckon for.
Death tore not (therefore) but sans strife
Gently untwin'd his thread of Life.
What remaines then, but that Thou
Write these lines, Reader, in thy Brow,
And by his faire Examples light,
Burne in thy Imitation bright.
So while these Lines can but bequeath
A Life perhaps unto his Death;
His better Epitaph shall bee,
His Life still kept alive in Thee.

RICHARD CRASHAW

Rex Redux.

ILle redit, redit. *Hoc populi bona murmura volvunt ;*
    Publicus hoc (audin'?) plausus ad astra refert :
Hoc omni sedet in vultu commune serenum ;
    Omnibus hinc una est lætitiæ facies.
Rex noster, lux nostra redit ; redeuntis ad ora
    Arridet totis Anglia læta genis :
Quisque suos oculos oculis accendit ab istis ;
    Atque novum sacro sumit ab ore diem.
Fortè roges tanto quæ digna pericula plausu
    Evadat Carolus, quæ mala, quósve metus :
Anne pererrati malè fida volumina ponti
    Ausa illum terris penè negare suis :
Hospitis an nimii rursus sibi conscia, tellus
    Vix bene speratum reddat Ibera Caput.
Nil horum ; nec enim malè fida volumina ponti,
    Aut sacrum tellus vidit Ibera caput.
Verus amor tamen hæc sibi falsa pericula fingit :
    (Falsa peric'la solet fingere verus amor)
At Carolo qui falsa timet, nec vera timeret :
    (Vera peric'la solet temnere verus amor)
Illi falsa timens, sibi vera pericula temnens,
    Non solùm est fidus, sed quoque fortis amor.
Interea nostri satìs ille est causa tri[u]mphi :
    Et satìs (ah !) nostri causa doloris erat.
Causa doloris erat Carolus, sospes licèt esset ;
    Anglia quòd saltem dicere posset, Abest.
Et satìs est nostri Carolus nunc causa triumphi ;
    Dicere quòd saltem possumus, Ille redit.

THE DELIGHTS OF THE MUSES

Out of Catullus.

COme and let us live my Deare,
Let us love and never feare,
What the sowrest Fathers say :
Brightest *Sol* that dyes to day
Lives againe as blith to morrow ;
But if we darke sons of sorrow
Set, ô then, how long a Night
Shuts the Eyes of our short light !
Then let amorous kisses dwell
On our lips, begin and tell
A thousand, and a Hundred score,
An Hundred, and a Thousand more,
Till another Thousand smother
That, and that wipe of[f] another.
Thus at last when we have numbred
Many a Thousand, many a Hundred,
Wee'l confound the reckoning quite,
And lose our selves in wild delight :
While our joyes so multiply,
As shall mocke the envious eye.

Ad Principem nondum natum.

NAscere nunc; ô nunc! quid enim, puer alme, moraris?
Nulla tibi dederit dulcior hora diem.
Ergône tot tardos (ô lente!) morabere menses?
Rex redit. *Ipse veni, & dic bone,* Gratus ades.
Nam quid Ave *nostrum? quid nostri verba triumphi?*
Vagitu meliùs dixeris ista tuo.
At maneas tamen: & nobis nova causa triumphi
Sic demum fueris; nec nova causa tamen:
Nam, quoties Carolo novus aut nova nascitur inf[a]ns,
Revera toties Carolus ipse redit.

RICHARD CRASHAW

Wishes.

To his (supposed) Mistresse.

WHo ere she be,
　　That not impossible she
That shall command my heart and me;

Where ere she lye,
Lock't up from mortall Eye,
In shady leaves of Destiny;

Till that ripe Birth
Of studied fate stand forth,
And teach her faire steps to our Earth;

Till that Divine
Idæa, take a shrine
Of Chrystall flesh, through which to shine;

Meet you her my wishes,
Bespeake her to my blisses,
And be ye call'd my absent kisses.

I wish her Beauty,
That owes not all his Duty
To gaudy Tire, or glistring shoo-ty.

Something more than
Taffata or Tissew can,
Or rampant feather, or rich fan.

More than the spoyle
Of shop, or silkewormes Toyle,
Or a bought blush, or a set smile.

A face thats best
By its owne beauty drest,
And can alone command the rest.

THE DELIGHTS OF THE MUSES

A face made up,
Out of no other shop
Than what natures white hand sets ope.

A cheeke where Youth,
And Blood, with Pen of Truth
Write, what the Reader sweetly ru'th.

A Cheeke where growes
More than a Morning Rose :
Which to no Boxe his being owes.

Lipps, where all Day
A lovers kisse may play,
Yet carry nothing thence away.

Lookes that oppresse
Their richest Tires, but dresse
And cloath their simplest Nakednesse.

Eyes, that displaces
The Neighbour Diamond, and out-faces
That Sunshine, by their own sweet Graces.

Tresses, that weare
Jewells, but to declare
How much themselves more pretious are.

Whose native Ray,
Can tame the wanton Day
Of Gems, that in their bright shades play.

Each Ruby there,
Or Pearle that dare appeare,
Be its own blush, be its own Teare.

A well tam'd Heart,
For whose more noble smart,
Love may be long chusing a Dart.

Eyes, that bestow
Full quivers on loves Bow ;
Yet pay lesse Arrowes than they owe.

Smiles, that can warme
The blood, yet teach a charme,
That Chastity shall take no harme.

Blushes, that bin
The burnish of no sin,
Nor flames of ought too hot within.

Joyes, that confesse,
Vertue their Mistresse,
And have no other head to dresse.

Feares, fond and flight,
As the coy Brides, when Night
First does the longing Lover right.

Teares, quickly fled,
And vaine, as those are shed
For a dying Maydenhead.

Dayes, that need borrow,
No part of their good Morrow,
From a fore spent night of sorrow.

Dayes, that in spight
Of Darkenesse, by the Light
Of a cleere mind are Day all Night.

Nights, sweet as they,
Made short by Lovers play,
Yet long by th' absence of the Day.

Life, that dares send
A challenge to his end,
And when it comes say *Welcome Friend.*

Sydnæan showers
Of sweet discourse, whose powers
Can Crown old Winters head with flowers.

Soft silken Hours,
Open sunnes, shady Bowers;
'Bove all, Nothing within that lowers.

THE DELIGHTS OF THE MUSES

What ere Delight
Can make Dayes forehead bright,
Or give Downe to the Wings of Night.

In her whole frame,
Have Nature all the Name,
Art and ornament the shame.

Her flattery,
Picture and Poesy,
Her counsell her owne vertue be.

I wish, her store
Of worth may leave her poore
Of wishes; And I wish ———— No more.

Now if Time knowes
That her whose radiant Browes
Weave them a Garland of my vowes,

Her whose just Bayes,
My future hopes can raise,
A trophie to her present praise;

Her that dares be,
What these Lines wish to see :
I seeke no further, it is she.

'Tis she, and here
Lo I uncloath and cleare,
My wishes cloudy Character.

May she enjoy it,
Whose merit dare apply it,
But modestly dares still deny it.

Such worth as this is
Shall fixe my flying wishes,
And determine them to kisses.

Let her full Glory,
My fancyes, fly before ye,
Be ye my fictions ; But her story.

RICHARD CRASHAW

Ad Reginam,

Et sibi & Academiæ pa[r]turientem.

Huc ô sacris circumflua cœtibus,
   Huc ô frequentem, Musa, choris pedem
Fer, annuo doctum labore
   Purpureas agitare cunas.
Fœcunditatem provocat, en, tuam
Maria partu nobilis altero,
   Prolêmque Musarum ministram
   Egregius sibi poscit Infans.
Nempe Illa nunquam pignore simplici
Sibive soli facta puerpera est:
   Partu repercusso, vel absens,
   Perpetuos procreat gemellos.
Hos Ipsa partus scilicet efficit,
Inq́ ipsa vires carmina suggerit,
   Quæ spiritum vitâmque donat
   Principibus simul & Camœnis.
Possit Camœnas, non sine Numine,
Lassare nostras Diva puerpera,
   Et gaudiis siccare totam
   Perpetuis Heliconis undam.
Quin experiri pergat, & in vices
Certare sanctis conditionibus.
   Lis dulcis est, nec indecoro
   Pulvere, sic potuisse vinci.

Alternis Natura Diem meditatur & Umbras,
   Hinc atro, hinc albo pignore facta parens.
Tu melior Natura tuas, dulcissima, servas
   (Sed quam dissimili sub ratione!) vices.
Candida Tu, & partu semper Tibi concolor omni:
   Hinc Natam, hinc Natum das; sed utrinque Diem.

THE DELIGHTS OF THE MUSES

To the Queen

An Apologie for the length of the following Panegyrick.

WHen you are Mistresse of the song,
    Mighty Queen, to thinke it long,
Were treason 'gainst that Majesty
Your vertue wears. Your modesty
Yet thinks it so. But ev'n that too
(Infinite, since part of You)
New matter for our Muse supplies,
And so allowes what it denies.
Say then Dread Queen, how may we doe
To mediate 'twixt your self and You?
That so our sweetly temper'd song
Nor be [too] short, nor seeme [too] long.
  Needs must your Noble prayses strength
  That made it long excuse the length.

RICHARD CRASHAW

To the Queen,

Upon her numerous Progenie,

A Panegyrick.

BRitain! the mighty Oceans lovely bride!
Now stretch thy self, fair Isle, and grow; spread wide
Thy bosome, and make roome. Thou art opprest
With thine own glories, and art strangely blest
Beyond thy self: For (lo) the Gods, the Gods
Come fast upon thee; and those glorious ods
Swell thy full honours to a pitch so high
As sits above thy best capacitie.
  Are they not ods? and glorious? that to thee
Those mighty Genii throng, which well might be
Each one an ages labour? that thy dayes
Are gilded with the union of those rayes
Whose each divided beam would be a Sunne
To glad the sphere of any nation?
Sure, if for these thou mean'st to find a seat
Th' hast need, O Britain, to be truly *Great.*
  And so thou art; their presence makes thee so:
They are thy greatnesse. Gods, where-e're they go,
Bring their Heav'n with them: their great footsteps place
An everlasting smile upon the face
Of the glad earth they tread on. While with thee
Those beames that ampliate mortalitie,
And teach it to expatiate, and swell
To majestie and fulnesse, deign to dwell,
Thou by thy self maist sit, blest Isle, and see
How thy great mother Nature dotes on thee.
Thee therefore from the rest apart she hurl'd,
And seem'd to make an Isle, but made a World.
  Time yet hath dropt few plumes since Hope turn'd Joy,
And took into his armes the princely Boy,
Whose birth last blest the bed of his sweet Mother,
And bad us first salute our Prince a brother.

166

THE DELIGHTS OF THE MUSES

The Prince and Duke of York.

Bright *Charles*! thou sweet dawn of a glorious day!
Centre of those thy Grandsires (shall I say,
Henry and *James*? or, *Mars* and *Phœbus* rather?
If this were Wisdomes God, that Wars stern father,
'Tis but the same is said: *Henry* and *James*
Are *Mars* and *Phœbus* under diverse names.)
O thou full mixture of those mighty souls
Whose vast intelligences tun'd the Poles
Of peace and war; thou, for whose manly brow
Both lawrels twine into [one] wreath, and woo
To be thy garland: see, sweet Prince, O see,
Thou, and the lovely hopes that smile in thee,
Art ta'n out and transcrib'd by thy great Mother:
See, see thy reall shadow; see thy Brother,
Thy little self in lesse: trace in these eyne
The beams that dance in those full stars of thine.
From the same snowy Alabaster rock
Those hands and thine were hew'n; those cherries mock
The corall of thy lips: Thou wert of all
This well-wrought *copie* the fair *principall.*

Lady Mary.

Justly, great Nature, didst thou brag, and tell
How ev'n th' hadst drawn that faithfull parallel,
And matcht thy master-piece. O then go on,
Make such another sweet comparison.
Seest thou that *Marie* there? O teach her Mother
To shew her to her self in such another.
Fellow this wonder too; nor let her shine
Alone; light such another star, and twine
Their rosie beams, that so the morn for one
Venus may have a Constellation.

Lady Elizabeth.

These words scarce waken'd Heaven, when (lo) our vows
Sat crown'd upon the noble Infants brows.
Th'art pair'd, sweet Princesse: In this well-writ book
Read o're thy self; peruse each line, each look.

RICHARD CRASHAW

And when th'hast summ'd up all those blooming blisses,
Close up the book, and clasp it with thy kisses.
  So have I seen (to dresse their mistresse May)
Two silken sister-flowers consult, and lay
Their bashfull cheeks together: newly they
Peep't from their buds, show'd like the garden's Eyes
Scarce wak't: like was the crimson of their joyes;
Like were the tears they wept, so like, that one
Seem'd but the others kind reflexion.

The new-borne Prince.

  And now 'twere time to say, Sweet Queen, no more.
Fair source of Princes, is thy pretious store
Not yet exhaust? O no. Heavens have no bound,
But in their infinite and endlesse Round
Embrace themselves. Our measure is not theirs;
Nor may the pov'rtie of mans narrow prayers
Span their immensitie. More Princes come:
Rebellion, stand thou by; Mischief, make room:
War, Bloud, and Death (Names all averse from Joy)
Heare this, We have another bright-ey'd Boy:
That word's a warrant, by whose vertue I
Have full authority to bid you Dy.
  Dy, dy, foul misbegotten Monsters; Dy:
Make haste away, or e'r the world's bright Eye
Blush to a cloud of bloud. O farre from men
Fly hence, and in your Hyperborean den
Hide you for evermore, and murmure there
Where none but Hell may heare, nor our soft aire
Shrink at the hatefull sound. Mean while we bear
High as the brow of Heaven, the noble noise
And name of these our just and righteous joyes,
Where Envie shall not reach them, nor those eares
Whose tune keeps time to ought below the spheres.
  But thou, sweet supernumerary Starre,
Shine forth; nor fear the threats of boyst'rous Warre.
The face of things has therefore frown'd a while
On purpose, that to thee and thy pure smile
The world might ow an universall calm;
While thou, fair Halcyon, on a sea of balm

THE DELIGHTS OF THE MUSES

Shalt flote; where while thou layst thy lovely head,
The angry billows shall but make thy bed:
Storms, when they look on thee, shall straight relent;
And Tempests, when they tast thy breath, repent
To whispers soft as thine own slumbers be,
Or souls of Virgins which shall sigh for thee.
    Shine then, sweet supernumerary Starre;
Nor feare the boysterous names of Bloud and Warre:
Thy Birthday is their Death's Nativitie;
They've here no other businesse but to die.

To the Queen.

    But stay; what glimpse was that? why blusht the day?
Why ran the started aire trembling away?
Who's this that comes circled in rayes that scorn
Acquaintance with the Sun? what second morn
At midday opes a presence which Heavens eye
Stands off and points at? Is't some Deity
Stept from her throne of starres, deignes to be seen?
Is it some Deity? or i'st our Queen?
    'Tis she, 'tis she: Her awfull beauties chase
The Day's abashed glories, and in face
Of noon wear their own Sunshine. O thou bright
Mistresse of wonders! Cynthia's is the night;
But thou at noon dost shine, and art all day
(Nor does thy Sun deny't) our Cynthia.
    Illustrious sweetnesse! in thy faithfull wombe,
That nest of Heroes, all our hopes find room.
Thou art the Mother-Phenix, and thy brest
Chast as that Virgin honour of the East,
But much more fruitfull is; nor does, as she,
Deny to mighty Love a Deitie.
Then let the Eastern world brag and be proud
Of one coy Phenix, while we have a brood,
A brood of Phenixes; while we have Brother
And Sister-Phenixes, and still the Mother.
    And may we long! Long mayst Thou live t'increase
The house and family of Phenixes.
Nor may the life that gives their eye-lids light
E're prove the dismall morning of thy night:

RICHARD CRASHAW

Ne're may a birth of thine be bought so dear
To make his costly cradle of thy beer.
  O mayst thou thus make all the year thine own,
And see such names of joy sit white upon
The brow of every month! And when th'hast done,
Mayst in a son of His find every son
Repeated, and that son still in another,
And so in each child often prove a Mother.
Long mayst Thou, laden with such clusters, lean
Upon thy Royall Elm, fair Vine! And when
The Heav'ns will stay no longer, may thy glory
And name dwell sweet in some Eternall story!

Pardon, bright Excellence, an untun'd string,
That in thy eares thus keeps a murmuring.
O speake a lowly Muses pardon, speake
Her pardon, or her sentence; onely breake
Thy silence. Speake, and she shall take from thence
Numbers, and sweetnesse, and an influence
Confessing Thee. Or if too long I stay,
O speake Thou, and my Pipe hath nought to say:
For see *Apollo* all this while stands mute,
Expecting by thy voice to tune his Lute.

But Gods are gracious; and their Altars make
Pretious the offrings that their Altars take.
Give then this rurall wreath fire from thine eyes,
This rurall wreath dares be thy Sacrifice.

THE DELIGHTS OF THE MUSES

Bulla.

QUid tibi vana suos offert mea bulla tumores?
    Quid facit ad vestrum pondus inane meum?
Expectat nostros humeros toga fortior; ista
    En mea bulla, lares en tua dextra mihi.

    Quid tu? quæ nova machina,
    Quæ tam fortuito globo
    In vitam properas brevem?
    Qualis virgineos adhuc
    Cypris concutiens sinus,
    Cypris jam nova, jam recens,
    Et spumis media in suis,
    Promsit purpureum latus;
    Conchâ de patriâ micas,
    Pulchroq́ exsilis impetu;
    Statim & millibus ebria
    Ducens terga coloribus
    Evolvis tumidos sinus
    Sphærâ plena volubili.
    Cujus per varium latus,
    Cujus per teretem globum
    Iris lubrica cursitans
    Centum per species vagas,
    Et picti facies chori
    Circum regnat, & undiq́
    Et se Diva volatilis
    Jucundo levis impetu
    Et vertigine perfidâ
    Lascivâ sequitur fugâ
    Et pulchrè dubitat; fluit
    Tam fallax toties novis,
    Tot se per reduces vias,
    Errorèsque reciprocos
    Spargit vena Coloribus;
    Et pompâ natat ebriâ.
    Tali militiâ micans
    Agmen se rude dividit;
    Campis quippe volantibus,

Et campi levis æquore
Ordo insanus obambulans
Passim se fugit, & fugat;
Passim perdit, & invenit.
Pulchrum spargitur hîc Chaos.
Hîc viva, hîc vaga flumina
Ripâ non propriâ meant,
Sed miscent socias vias,
Communiá sub alveo
Stipant delicias suas.
Quarum proximitas vaga
Tam discrimine lubrico,
Tam subtilibus arguit
Juncturam tenuem notis,
Pompa ut florida nullibi
Sinceras habeat vias;
Nec vultu niteat suo.
Sed dulcis cumulus novos
Miscens purpureus sinus
Flagrant divitiis suis,
Privatum renuens jubar.
Floris diluvio vagi,
Floris Sydere publico
Latè ver subit aureum,
Atque effunditur in suæ
Vires undique Copiæ.
Nempe omnis quia cernitur,
Nullus cernitur hîc color,
Et vicinia contumax
Allidit species vagas.
Illîc contiguis aquis
Marcent pallidulæ faces.
Undæ hîc vena tenellulæ,
Flammis ebria proximis
Discit purpureas vias,
Et rubro salit alveo.
Ostri Sanguineum jubar
Lambunt lactea flumina;
Suasu cærulei maris
Mansuescit seges aurea;

THE DELIGHTS OF THE MUSES

Et lucis faciles genæ
Vanas ad nebulas stupent;
Subǫ uvis rubicundulis
Flagrant sobria lilia.
Vicinis adeo rosis
Vicinæ invigilant nives,
Ut sint & niveæ rosæ,
Ut sint & rosæ nives;
Accenduntǫ rosæ nives,
Extinguuntǫ nives rosas.
Illîc cum viridi rubet,
Hîc & cum rutilo viret
Lascivi facies chori.
Et quicquid rota lubrica
Caudæ stelligeræ notat,
Pulchrum pergit & in ambitum.
Hîc cæli implicitus labor,
Orbes orbibus obvii;
Hîc grex velleris aurei
Grex pellucidus ætheris;
Qui noctis nigra pascua
Puris morsibus atterit;
Hîc quicquid nitidum et vagum
Cæli vibrat arenula
Dulci pingitur in joco.
Hîc mundus tener impedit
Sese amplexibus in suis.
Succinctiǫ sinu globi
Errat per proprium decus.
Hîc nictant subitæ faces,
Et ludunt tremulum diem.
Mox se surripiunt sui &
Quærunt tecta supercili;
Atǫ abdunt petulans jubar,
Subsiduntǫ proterviter.
Atǫ hæc omnia quam brevis
Sunt mendacia machinæ!
Currunt scilicèt omnia
Sphærâ, non vitreâ quidem,
(Ut quondam siculus globus)

Sed vitro nitidâ magis,
Sed vitro fragili magis,
Et vitro vitreâ magis.

Sum venti ingenium breve
Flos sum, scilicet, aëris,
Sidus scilicet æquoris;
Naturæ jocus aureus,
Naturæ vaga fabula,
Naturæ breve somnium.
Nugarum decus & dolor;
Dulcis, doctaq́ vanitas.
Auræ filia perfidæ;
Et risus facilis parens.
Tantùm gutta superbior,
Fortunatius & lutum.

Sum fluxæ pretium spei;
Una ex Hesperidum insulis.
Formæ pyxis, amantium
Clarè cæcus ocellulus;
Vanæ & cor leve gloriæ.

Sum cæcæ speculum Deæ.
Sum fortunæ ego tessera,
Quam dat militibus suis;
Sum fortunæ ego symbolum,
Quo sancit fragilem fidem
Cum mortalibus Ebriis
Obsignatq́ tabellulas.

Sum blandum, petulans, vagum,
Pulchrum, purpureum, et decens,
Comptum, floridulum, et recens,
Distinctum nivibus, rosis,
Undis, ignibus, aëre,
Pictum, gemmeum, & aureum,
O sum, (scilicet, O nihil.)

Si piget, et longam traxisse in tædia pompam
Vivax, & nimiùm Bulla videtur anus;
Tolle tuos oculos, pensum leve defluet, illam
Parca metet facili non operosa manu.
Vixit adhuc. Cur vixit? adhuc tu nempe legebas;
Tempe fuit tempus tum potuisse mori.

THE DELIGHTS OF THE MUSES

Upon two greene Apricockes sent to Cowley

by Sir Crashaw.

TAke these, times tardy truants, sent by me,
   To be chastis'd (sweet friend) and chide by thee.
Pale sons of our *Pomona*! whose wan cheekes
Have spent the patience of expecting weekes,
Yet are scarce ripe enough at best to show
The redd, but of the blush to thee they ow.
By thy comparrison they shall put on
More summer in their shames reflection,
Than ere the fruitfull *Phœbus* flaming kisses
Kindled on their cold lips. O had my wishes
And the deare merits of your Muse, their due,
The yeare had found some fruit early as you;
Ripe as those rich composures time computes
Blossoms, but our blest tast confesses fruits.
How does thy April-Autumne mocke these cold
Progressions 'twixt whose termes poor time grows old?
With thee alone he weares no beard, thy braine
Gives him the morning worlds fresh gold againe.
'Twas only Paradice, 'tis onely thou,
Whose fruit and blossoms both blesse the same bough.
Proud in the patterne of thy pretious youth,
Nature (methinks) might easily mend her growth.
Could she in all her births but coppie thee,
Into the publick yeares proficiencie,
No fruit should have the face to smile on thee
(Young master of the worlds maturitie)
But such whose sun-borne beauties what they borrow
Of beames to day, pay back againe to morrow,
Nor need be double-gilt. How then must these,
Poore fruites looke pale at thy Hesperides!
Faine would I chide their slownesse, but in their
Defects I draw mine owne dull character.
Take them, and me in them acknowledging,
How much my summer waites upon thy spring.

175

RICHARD CRASHAW

Thesaurus malorum fæmina

QUis deus, O quis erat qui te, mala fæmina, finxit?
　　Proh! Crimen superûm, noxa pudenda deûm!
Quæ divûm manus est adeo non dextera mundo?
　　In nostras clades ingeniosa manus!
Parcite; peccavi: nec enim pia numina possunt
　　Tam crudele semel vel voluisse nefas.
Vestrum opus est pietas; opus est concordia vestrum:
　　Vos equidem tales haud reor artifices.
Heus inferna cohors! fætus cognoscite vestros.
　　Num pudet hanc vestrum vincere posse scelus?
Plaudite Tartarei Proceres, Erebiq́ potentes
　　(Næ mirum est tantum vos potuisse malum)
Jam vestras Laudate manus. Si forte tacetis,
　　Artificum laudes grande loquetur opus.
Quàm bene vos omnes speculo contemplor in isto?
　　Pectus in angustum cogitur omne malum.
Quin dormi Pluto. Rabidas compesce sorores,
　　Jam non poscit opem nostra ruina tuam.
Hæc satis in nostros fabricata est machina muros,
　　Mortal[e]s Furias Tartara nostra dabunt.

In Apollinem depereuntem Daphnen.

S Tulte Cupido,
  Quid tua flamma parat?
Annon sole sub ipso
Accensæ pereunt faces?
Sed fax nostra potentior istis,
Flammas inflammare potest, ipse uritur ignis,
Ecce flammarum potens
Majore sub flammâ gemit.
Eheu! quid hoc est? En Apollo
Lyrâ tacente (ni sonet dolores)
Comâ jacente squallet æternus decor
Oris, en! dominæ quò placeat magis,
Languido tardum jubar igne promit.
Pallente vultu territat æthera.
Mundi oculus lacrymis senescit,
Et solvit pelago debita, quodá hauserat ignibus,
His lacrymis rependit.
Noctis adventu properans se latebris recondit,
Et opacas tenebrarum colit umbras,
Namģ suos odit damnans radios, nocensģ lumen.
An lateat tenebris dubitat, an educat diem,
Hinc suadet hoc luctus furens, inde repugnat amor.

RICHARD CRASHAW

Ænæas Patris sui bajulus.

Mͤnia Troiæ —— Hostis & ignis
  Hostes inter & ignes —— Ænæas spolium pium
At q̊ humeris venerabile pondus
Excipit, & sævæ nunc ô nunc parcite flammæ,
Parcite haud (clamat) mihi,
Sacræ favete sarcinæ,
Quod si negatis, nec licebit
Vitam juvare, sed juvabo funus;
Rogusq̊ fiam patris ac bustum mei.
His dictis acies pervolat hostium,
Gestit, & partis veluti trophæis
Ducit triumphos. Nam furor hostium
Jam stupet & pietate tantâ
Victor vincitur; imò & moritur
Troja libenter Funeribusq̊ gaudet,
Ac faces admittit ovans, ne lateat tenebras
Per opacas opus ingens pietatis.
Debita sic patri solvis tua, sic pari rependis
Officio. Dederat vitam tibi, tu reddis huic,
Felix! parentis qui pater diceris esse tui.

In Pigmaliona.

PÆnitet Artis
Pigmaliona suæ.
Quod felix opus esset
Infelix erat artifex.
Sentit vulnera, nec videt ictum.
Quis credit? gelido veniunt de marmore flammæ.
Marmor ingratum nimis
Incendit autorem suum.
Concepit hic vanos furores;
Opus suum miratur atq; adorat.
Prius creavit, ecce nunc colit manus,
Tentantes digitos molliter applicat;
Decipit molles caro dura tactus.
An virgo vera est, an sit eburnea;
Reddat an oscula quæ dabantur
Nescit. Sed dubitat, Sed metuit, munere supplicat,
Blanditiasq; miscet.
Te, miser, pœnas dare vult, hos Venus, hos triumphos
Capit à te, quòd amorem fugis omnem.
Cur fugis heu vivos? mortua te necat puella.
Non erit innocua hæc, quamvis tuâ fingas manu,
Ipsa heu nocens erit nimis, cujus imago nocet.

RICHARD CRASHAW

Arion.

SQuammea vivæ
Lubrica terga ratis
Jam conscendit Arion.
Merces tam nova solvitur
Navis quàm nova scanditur. Illa
Aërea est merces, hæc est & aquatica navis.
Perdidère illum viri
Mercede magnâ, servat hic
Mercede nullâ piscis: & sic
Salute plus ruina constat illi;
Minoris & servatur hinc quàm perditur.
Hic dum findit aquas, findit hic aëra:
Cursibus, piscis; digitis, Arion:
Et sternit undas, sternit & aëra:
Carminis hoc placido Tridente
Abjurat sua jam murmura, ventusq modestior
Auribus ora mutat:
Ora dediscit, minimos & metuit susurros.
(Sonus alter restat, ut fit sonus illis)
Aura strepens circum muta sit lateri adjacente pennâ,
Ambit & ora viri, nec vela ventis hîc egent;
Attendit hanc ventus ratem: non trahit, at trahitur.

Phænicis { Genethliacon
&
Epicedion.

PHænix alumna mortis,
Quàm mira tu puerpera!
Tu scandis haud nidos, sed ignes.
Non parere sed perire ceu parata:
Mors obstetrix; atq ipsa tu teipsam paris,
Tu Tuiq mater ipsa es,
Tu tuiq filia.
Tu sic odora messis
Surgis tuorum funerum;
Tibiq per tuam ruinam
Reparata, te succedis ipsa. Mors ò
Fœcunda! Sanĉta ò Lucra pretiosæ necis!
Vive (monstrum dulce) vive
Tu tibiq suffice.

THE DELIGHTS OF THE MUSES

Elegia.

I Te meæ lacrymæ (nec enim moror) ite. Sed oro
   Tantùm ne miseræ claudite vocis iter.
O liceat querulos verbis animare dolores,
   Et saltem ah periit dicere noster amor.
Ecce negant tamèn, ecce negant, lacrymæq́ rebelles
   Indomitâ pergunt, præcipitantq́ viâ.
Visne (ô care) igitur Te nostra silentia dicant?
   Vis fleat assiduo murmure mutus amor?
Flebit, & urna suos semper bibet humida rores,
   Et fidas semper, semper habebit aquas.
Interea, quicunq́ estis ne credite mirum
   Si veræ lacrymæ non didicére loqui.

Epitaphium.

QUisquis nectareo serenus ævo;
   Et spe lucidus aureæ juventæ
Nescis purpureos abire soles,
Nescis vincula, ferreamq́ noctem
Imi carceris, horridumq́ Ditem,
Et spectas tremulam procul senectam,
Hinc disces lacrymas, & hinc repones.
Hic, ô scilicet hic brevi sub antro
Spes & gaudia mille, mille longam
(Heu longam nimis) induére noctem.
Flammantem nitidæ facem juventæ,
Submersit Stygiæ paludis unda.
Ergo si lacrymas neges doloris
Huc certe lacrymas feres timoris.

RICHARD CRASHAW

Damno affici sæpe fit lucrum.

DAmna adsunt multis taciti compendia lucri
  Feliciǵ docent plus properare morâ,
Luxuriem annorum positâ sic pelle redemit
Atǵ sagax serpens in nova sæcla subit.
Cernis ut ipsa sibi replicato suppetat ævo,
  Seǵ iteret, multâ morte perennis avis.
Succrescat generosa sibi, facilesǵ per ignes
  Perǵ suos cineres, per sua fata ferax.
Quæ sollers jaɔtura sui? quis funeris usus?
  Flammarumǵ fides, ingeniumǵ rogi?
Siccine fraude subis? pretiosaǵ funera ludis?
  Siccine tu mortem, ne moriaris, adis?
Felix cui mędicæ tanta experientia mortis,
  Cui tam Parcarum est officiosa manus.

Humanæ vitæ descriptio.

O Vita, tantum lubricus quidam furor
  Spoliumǵ vitæ! scilicet longi brevis
Erroris hospes! Error ô mortalium!
O certus error! qui sub incerto vagum
Suspendit ævum, mille per dolos viæ
Fugacis, & proterva per volumina
Fluidi laboris, ebrios laɔtat gradus;
Et irretitos ducit in nihilum dies.
O fata! quantum perfidæ vitæ fugit
Umbris quod imputemus atǵ auris, ibi
Et umbra & aura serias partes agunt
Miscentǵ scenam, vòlvimur ludibrio
Procacis æstus, ut per incertum mare
Fragilis protervo cymba com nutat freto.
Et ipsa vitæ, fila, quêis nentes Deæ
Ævi severa texta producunt manu,
Hæc ipsa nobis implicant vestigia
Retrahunt trahuntǵ donec everso gradu
Ruina lassos alta deducat pedes.
Felix, fugaces quisquis excipiens dies
Gressus serenos fixit, insidiis sui
Nec servit ævi, vita inoffensis huic
Feretur auris, atǵ claudâ rariùs
Titubabit horâ : vortices anni vagi
Hic extricabit, sanus Assertor sui.

THE DELIGHTS OF THE MUSES

Tranquillitas animi, similitudine ductâ ab ave
captivâ & canorâ tamen.

UT cùm delicias leves, loquacem
Convivam nemoris, vagamq́ musam
Observans dubiâ viator arte
Prendit desuper: horridusve ruris
Eversor, malè persido paratu
(Heu durus!) rapit, atq́ io triumphans
Vadit; protinus & sagace nisu
Evolvens digitos, opus tenellum
Ducens pollice lenis erudito,
Virgarum implicat ordinem severum,
Angustam meditans domum volucri.
Illa autem, hospitium licet vetustum
Mentem sollicitet nimis nimisq́
Et suetum nemus, hinc opaca mitis
Umbræ frigora, & hinc aprica puri
Solis fulgura, Patriæq́ sylvæ
Nunquam muta quies; ubi illa dudum
Totum per nemus, arborem per omnem,
Hospes libera liberis querelis
Cognatum benè provocabat agmen:
Quanquam ipsum nemus, arboresq́ alumnam
Implorant profugam, atq́ amata multùm
Quærant murmura, lubricumq́ carmen
Blandi gutturis & melos serenum:
Illa autem, tamen, illa jam relictæ
(Simplex!) haud meminit domus, nec ultrà
Sylvas cogitat; at brevi sub antro,
Ah pennâ nimium brevis recisâ,
Ah ritu viduo, sibiq́ sola,
Privata heu fidicen! canit, vagoq́
Exercens querulam domum susurro
Fallit vincula, carceremq́ mulcet;
Nec pugnans placidæ procax quieti
Luctatur gravis, orbe sed reducto

RICHARD CRASHAW

Discursu vaga saltitans tenello,
Metitur spatia invidæ cavernæ.
Sic in se pia mens reposta, secum
Altè tuta sedet, nec ardet extrà,
Aut ullo solet æstuare fato:
Quamvis cuncta tumultuentur, atræ
Sortis turbine non movetur illa:
Fortunæ furias onusq̃ triste
Non tergo minus accipit quieto,
Quàm vectrix Veneris columba blando
Admittit juga delicata collo.
Torvæ si quid inhorruit procellæ,
Si quid sæviat & minetur, illa
Spernit, nescit, & obviis furorem
Fallit blanditiis, amatq̃ & ambit
Ipsum, quo malè vulneratur, ictum.
Curas murmure non fatetur ullo;
Non lambit lacrymas dolor, nec atræ
Mentis nubila frons iniqua prodit.
Quod si lacryma pervicax rebelli
Erumpit tamen evolatq̃ guttâ,
Invitis lacrymis, negante luctu,
Ludunt perspicui per ora risus.

184

CARMEN
DEO NOSTRO,
TE DECET HYMNUS
SACRED POEMS,
COLLECTED,
CORRECTED,
AUGMENTED,

Most humbly Presented.

TO
MY LADY
THE COUNTSSE OF
DENBIGH

BY

Her most devoted Servant.

R. C.

IN hea[r]ty acknowledgment of his immortall
obligation to her Goodnes & Charity.

AT PARIS,

By PETER TARGA, Printer to the Arch-
bishope [o]f Paris, in S. Victors streete at
the golden sunne.

M. DC. LII.

CRASHAWE,

THE

ANAGRAMME.

HE WAS CAR.

WAs Car then Crashawe; or Was Crashawe Car,
 Since both within one name combined are?
Yes, Car's Crashawe, he Car; t'is love alone
Which melts two harts, of both composing one.
So Crashawe's still the same: so much desired
By strongest witts; so honor'd so admired
Car Was but He that enter'd as afriend
With whom he shar'd his thoughtes, and did commend
(While yet he liv'd) this worke; they lov'd each other:
Sweete Crashawe was his friend; he Crashawes brother.
So Car hath Title then; t'was his intent
That what his riches pen'd, poore Car should print.
Nor feares he checke praysing that happie one
Who was belov'd by all; dispraysed by none.
To witt, being pleas'd with all things, he pleas'd all.
Nor would he give, nor take offence; befall
What might; he would possesse himselfe: and live
As deade (devoyde of interest) t'all might give
Desease t'his well composed mynd; forestal'd
With heavenly riches: which had wholy call'd
His thoughtes from earth, to live above in'th aire
A very bird of paradice. No care
Had he of earthly trashe. What might suffice
To fitt his soule to heavenly exercise.
Sufficed him: and may we guesse his hart
By what his lipps brings forth, his onely part
Is God and godly thoughtes. Leaves doubt to none
But that to whom one God is all; all's one.

RICHARD CRASHAW

What he might eate or weare he tooke no thought.
His needfull foode he rather found then sought.
He seekes no downes, no sheetes, his bed's still made
If he can find, a chaire or stoole, he's layd,
When day peepes in, he quitts his restlesse rest.
And still, poore soule, before he's up he's dres't.
Thus dying did he live, yet lived to dye
In th-virgines lappe, to whom he did applye
His virgine thoughtes and words, and thence was styld
By foes, the chaplaine of the virgine myld
While yet he lived without: His modestie
Imparted this to some, and they to me.
Live happie then, deare soule; injoy the rest
Eternally by paynes thou purchacedest,
While Car must live in care, who was thy friend
Nor cares he how he live, so in the end,
He may injoy his dearest Lord and thee;
And sitt and singe more skilfull songs eternally.

CARMEN DEO NOSTRO

AN

EPIGRAMME

Upon the pictures in the following Poemes which the Authour first made with his owne hand, admirably well, as may be seene in his Manuscript dedicated to the right Honorable Lady the L. Denbigh.

Twixt pen and pensill rose a holy strife
   Which might draw vertue better to the life.
Best witts gave votes to that: but painters swore
They never saw peeces so sweete before
As thes: fruites of pure nature; where no art
Did lead the untaught pensill, nor had part
In th'-worke.
The hand growne bold, with witt will needes contest.
Doth it prevayle? ah wo: say each is best.
This to the eare speakes wonders; that will trye
To speake the same, yet lowder, to the eye.
Both their aymes are holy, both conspire
To wound, to burne the hart with heavenly fire.
This then's the Doome, to doe both parties right:
This, to the eare speakes best; that, to the sight.

THOMAS CAR.

189

RICHARD CRASHAW

NON VI.

'Tis not the work of force but skill
To find the way into man's will.
'Tis love alone can hearts unlock.
Who knowes the WORD, he needs not knock.

TO THE
Noblest & best of Ladyes, the Countesse of Denbigh.

Perswading her to Resolution in Religion,
& to render her selfe without further
delay into the Communion of
the Catholick Church.

WHat heav'n-intreated HEART is This?
Stands trembling at the gate of blisse;
Holds fast the door, yet dares not venture
Fairly to open it, and enter.
Whose DEFINITION is à doubt
Twixt life & death, twixt in & out.
Say, lingring fair! why comes the birth
Of your brave soul so slowly forth?
Plead your pretences (o you strong
In weaknes!) why you choose so long
In labor of your selfe to ly,
Nor daring quite to live nor dy?
Ah linger not, lov'd soul! à slow
And late consent was a long no,
Who grants at last, long time tryd
And did his best to have deny'd,
What magick bolts, what mystick Barres
Maintain the will in these strange warres!

190

CARMEN DEO NOSTRO

What fatall, yet fantastick, bands
Keep The free Heart from it's own hands!
So when the year takes cold, we see
Poor waters their owne prisoners be.
Fetter'd, & lockt up fast they ly
In a sad selfe-captivity.
The' astonisht nymphs their flood's strange fate deplore,
To see themselves their own severer shore.
Thou that alone canst thaw this cold,
And fetch the heart from it's strong Hold;
Allmighty Love! end this long warr,
And of a meteor make a starr.
O fix this fair Indefinite.
And 'mongst thy shafts of soveraign light
Choose out that sure decisive dart
Which has the Key of this close heart,
Knowes all the corners of't, & can controul
The self-shutt cabinet of an unsearcht soul.
O let it be at last, love's houre.
Raise this tall Trophee of thy Powre;
Come once the conquering way; not to confute
But kill this rebell-wo[r]d, Irresolute
That so, in spite of all this peevish strength
Of weaknes, she may write Resolv'd at Length,
Unfold at length, unfold fair flowre
And use the season of love's showre,
Meet his well-meaning Wounds, wise heart!
And hast to drink the wholsome dart.
That healing shaft, which heavn till now
Hath in love's quiver hid for you.
O Dart of love! arrow of light!
O happy you, if it hitt right,
It must not fall in vain, it must
Not mark the dry regardles dust.
Fair one, it is your fate; and brings
Æternall worlds upon it's wings.
Meet it with wide-spread armes; & see
It's seat your soul's just center be.
Disband dull feares; give faith the day.
To save your life, kill your delay

RICHARD CRASHAW

It is love's seege; and sure to be
Your triumph, though his victory.
'Tis cowardise that keeps this feild
And want of courage not to yeild.
Yeild then, ô yeild. that love may win
The Fort at last, and let life in.
Yeild quickly. Lest perhaps you prove
Death's prey, before the prize of love.
This Fort of your fair selfe, if't be not won,
He is repulst indeed; But you'are vndone.

CARMEN DEO NOSTRO

TO

THE NAME

ABOVE EVERY NAME,

THE

NAME OF

JESUS

A HYMN.

I Sing the NAME which None can say
But touch't with An interiour RAY:
The Name of our New PEACE; our Good:
Our Blisse: & Supernaturall Blood:
The Name of All our Lives & Loves.   ·
Hearken, And Help, ye holy Doves!
The high-born Brood of Day; you bright
Candidates of blissefull Light,
The HEIRS Eleƈt of Love; whose Names belong
Unto The everlasting life of Song;
All ye wise SOULES, who in the wealthy Brest
Of This unbounded NAME build your warm Nest.
Awake, MY glory. SOUL, (if such thou be,
And That fair WORD at all referr to Thee)
          Awake & sing
          And be All Wing;
Bring hither thy whole SELF; & let me see
What of thy Parent HEAVN yet speakes in thee.
          O thou art Poore
          Of noble POWRES, I see,
And full of nothing else but empty ME,
Narrow, & low, & infinitely lesse
Then this GREAT mornings mighty Busynes.
          One little WORLD or two
          (Alas) will never doe.

We must have store.
Goe, SOUL, out of thy Self, & seek for More.
Goe & request
Great NATURE for the KEY of her huge Chest
Of Heavns, the self involving Sett of Sphears
(Which dull mortality more Feeles then heares)
Then rouse the nest
Of nimble ART, & traverse round
The Aiery Shop of soul-appeasing Sound:
And beat a summons in the Same
All-soveraign Name
To warn each severall kind
And shape of sweetnes, Be they such
As sigh with supple wind
Or answer Artfull Touch,
That they convene & come away
To wait at the love-crowned Doores of
Th[i]s Illustrious DAY.
Shall we dare This, my Soul? we'l doe't and bring
No Other note for't, but the Name we sing.
Wake LUTE & HARP
And every sweet-lipp't Thing
That talkes with tunefull string;
Start into life, And leap with me
Into a hasty Fitt-tun'd Harmony.
Nor must you think it much
T'obey my bolder touch;
I have Authority in LOVE's name to take you
And to the worke of Love this morning wake you;
Wake; In the Name
Of HIM who never sleeps, All Things that Are,
Or, what's the same,
Are Musicall;
Answer my Call
And come along;
Help me to meditate mine Immortall Song.
Come, ye soft ministers of sweet sad mirth,
Bring All your houshold stuffe of Heavn on earth;
O you, my Soul's most certain Wings,
Complaining Pipes, & prattling Strings,

CARMEN DEO NOSTRO

     Bring All the store
Of SWEETS you have ; And murmur that you have no more.
     Come, nére to part,
     NATURE & ART!
     Come; & come strong,
To the conspiracy of our Spatious song.
     Bring All the Powres of Praise
Your Provinces of well-united WORLDS can raise;
Bring All [your] LUTES & HARPS of HEAVN & EARTH;
What ére cooperates to The common mirthe
     Vessells of vocall Joyes,
Or You, more noble Architects of Intellectuall Noise,
Cymballs of Heav'n, or Humane sphears,
Solliciters of SOULES or EARES;
     And when you'are come, with All
That you can bring or we can call;
     O may you fix
     For ever here, & mix
     Your selves into the long
And everlasting series of a deathlesse SONG;
Mix All your many WORLDS, Above,
And loose them into ONE of Love.
     Chear thee my HEART!
     For Thou too hast thy Part
     And Place in the Great Throng
Of This unbounded All-imbracing SONG.
     Powres of my Soul, be Proud!
     And speake lowd
To All the dear-bought Nations This Redeeming Name,
And in the wealth of one Rich WORD proclaim
New Similes to Nature.
     May it be no wrong
Blest Heavns, to you, & your Superiour song,
That we, dark Sons of Dust & Sorrow,
     A while Dare borrow
The Name of Your Dilights & our Desires,
And fitt it to so farr inferior LYRES.
Our Murmurs have their Musick too,
Ye mighty ORBES, as well as you,
     Nor yeilds the noblest Nest

RICHARD CRASHAW

Of warbling SERAPHIM to the eares of Love,
A choicer Lesson then the joyfull BREST
  Of a poor panting Turtle-Dove.
And we, low Wormes have leave to doe
The Same bright Busynes (ye Third HEAVENS) with you.
Gentle SPIRITS, doe not complain.
  We will have care
  To keep it fair,
And send it back to you again.
Come, lovely NAME! Appeare from forth the Bright
  Regions of peacefull Light,
Look from thine own Illustrious Home,
Fair KING of NAMES, & come.
Leave All thy native Glories in their Georgeous Nest,
And give thy Self a while The gracious Guest
Of humble Soules, that seek to find
  The hidden Sweets
  Which man's heart meets
When Thou art Master of the Mind.
Come, lovely Name; life of our hope!
Lo we hold our HEARTS wide ope!
Unlock thy Cabinet of DAY
Dearest Sweet, & come away.
  Lo how the thirsty Lands
Gasp for thy Golden Showres! with longstretch't Hands.
  Lo how the laboring EARTH
  That hopes to be
  All Heaven by THEE,
  Leapes at thy Birth.
The' attending WORLD, to wait thy Rise,
  First turn'd to eyes;
And then, not knowing what to doe;
Turn'd Them to TEARES, & spent Them too.
Come ROYALL Name, & pay the expence
Of All this Pretious Patience.
  O come away
And kill the DEATH of This Delay.
O see, so many WORLDS of barren yeares
Melted & measur'd out in Seas of TEARES.
O see, The WEARY liddes of wakefull Hope

196

CARMEN DEO NOSTRO

(LOVE'S Eastern windowes) All wide ope
      With Curtains drawn,
To catch The Day-break of Thy DAWN.
O dawn, at last, long look't for Day!
Take thine own wings, & come away.
Lo, where Aloft it comes! It comes, Among
The Conduct of Adoring SPIRITS, that throng
Like diligent Bees, And swarm about it.
      O they are wise;
And know what SWEETES are suck't from out it.
      It is the Hive,
      By which they thrive,
Where All their Hoard of Hony lyes.
Lo where it comes, upon 'The snowy DOVE's
Soft Back; And brings a Bosom big with Loves.
WELCOME to our dark world, Thou
      Womb of Day!
Unfold, thy fair Conceptions; And display
The Birth of our Bright Joyes.
      O thou compacted
Body of Blessings: spirit of Soules extracted!
O dissipate thy spicy Powres
(Clowd of condensed sweets) & break upon us
      In balmy showrs;
O fill our senses, And take from us
All force of so Prophane a Fallacy
To think ought sweet but that which smells of Thee.
Fair, flowry Name; In none but Thee
And Thy Nectareall Fragrancy,
      Hourly there meetes
An universall SYNOD of All sweets;
By whom it is defined Thus
      That no Perfume
      For ever shall presume
To passe for Odoriferous,
But such alone whose sacred Pedigree
Can prove it Self some kin (sweet name) to Thee.
SWEET NAME, in Thy each Syllable
A Thousand Blest ARABIAS dwell;
A Thousand Hills of Frankincense;

RICHARD CRASHAW

Mountains of myrrh, & Beds of species,
And ten Thousand PARADISES,
The soul that tasts thee takes from thence
How many unknown WORLDS there are
Of Comforts, which Thou hast in keeping!
How many Thousand Mercyes there
In Pitty's soft lap ly a sleeping!
Happy he who has the art
   To awake them,
   And to take them
Home, & lodge them in his HEART.
O that it were as it was wont to be!
When thy old Freinds of Fire, All full of Thee,
Fought against Frowns with smiles; gave Glorious chase
To Persecutions; And against the Face
Of DEATH & feircest Dangers, durst with Brave
And sober pace march on to meet A GRAVE.
On their Bold BRESTS about the world they bore thee
And to the Teeth of Hell stood up to teach thee,
In Center of their inmost Soules they wore thee,
Where Rackes & Torments striv'd, in vain, to reach thee.
   Little, alas, thought They
Who tore the Fair Brests of thy Freinds,
   Their Fury but made way
For Thee; And serv'd them in Thy glorious ends.
What did Their weapons but with wider pores
Inlarge thy flaming-brested Lovers
   More freely to transpire
   That impatient Fire
The Heart that hides Thee hardly covers.
What did their Weapons but sett wide the Doores
For Thee: Fair, purple Doores, of love's devising;
The Ruby windowes which inrich't the EAST
Of Thy so oft repeated Rising.
Each wound of Theirs was Thy new Morning;
And reinthron'd thee in thy Rosy Nest,
With blush of thine own Blood thy day adorning,
It was the witt of love óreflowd the Bounds
Of WRATH, & made thee way through All Those WOUNDS.
Wellcome dear, All-Adored Name!

198

CARMEN DEO NOSTRO

For sure there is no Knee
That knowes not THEE.
Or if there be such sonns of shame,
    Alas what will they doe
    When stubborn Rocks shall bow
And Hills hang down their Heavn-saluting Heads
    To seek for humble Beds
Of Dust, where in the Bashfull shades of night
Next to their own low NOTHING they may ly,
And couch before the dazeling light of thy dread majesty.
They that by Love's mild Dictate now
    Will not adore thee,
Shall Then with Just Confusion, bow
    And break before thee.

IN
THE HOLY
NATIVITY
OF
OUR LORD GOD
A
HYMN
SUNG AS BY THE
SHEPHEARDS.

200

CARMEN DEO NOSTRO

THE

HYMN.

CHORUS.

COme we shepheards whose blest Sight
  Hath mett love's Noon in Nature's night;
Come lift we up our loftyer Song
And wake the SUN that lyes too long.

To all our world of well-stoln joy
He slept; and dream't of no such thing.
While we found out Heavn's fairer ey
And Kis't the Cradle of our KING.
Tell him He rises now, too late
To show us ought worth looking at.

Tell him we now can show Him more
Then He e're show'd to mortall Sight;
Then he Himselfe e're saw before;
Which to be seen needes not His light.
Tell him, Tityrus, where th'hast been
Tell him, Thy[r]sis, what th-hast seen.

Tityrus. Gloomy night embrac't the Place
Where The Noble Infant lay.
The BABE look't up & shew'd his Face;
In spite of Darknes, it was DAY.
It was THY day, SWEET! & did rise
Not from the EAST, but from thine EYES.

    Chorus   It was THY day, Sweet

Thyrs. WINTER chidde aloud; & sent
The angry North to wage his warres.
The North forgott his feirce Intent;
And left perfumes in stead of scarres.
By those sweet eye[s'] persuasive powrs
Where he mean't frost, he scatter'd flowrs.

    Chorus   By those sweet eyes'

RICHARD CRASHAW

Both. We saw thee in thy baulmy Nest,
Young dawn of our æternall DAY!
We saw thine eyes break from their EA[s]TE
And chase the trembling shades away.
We saw thee; & we blest the sight,
We saw thee by thine own sweet light.

Tity. Poor WORLD (said I.) what wilt thou doe
To entertain this starry STRANGER?
Is this the best thou canst bestow?
A cold, and not too cleanly, manger?
Contend, the powres of heav'n & earth.
To fitt à bed for this huge birthe.

   Cho. Contend the powers

Thy[r]. Proud world, said I; cease your contest
And let the MIGHTY BABE alone.
The Phænix builds the Phænix' nest.
Lov's architecture is his own.
The BABE whose birth embraves this morn,
Made his own bed e're he was born.

   Cho. The BABE whose.

Ti[t]. I saw the curl'd drops, soft & slow,
Come hovering o're the place's head;
Offring their whitest sheets of snow
To furnish the fair INFANT's bed :
Forbear, said I; be not too bold.
Your fleece is white But t'is too cold.

   Cho. Forbear, sayd I

Thyr. I saw the obsequious SERAPHIMS
Their rosy fleece of fire bestow.
For well they now can spare their wing.
Since HEAVN it self lyes here below.
Well done, said I: but are you sure
Your down so warm, will passe for pure?

   Cho. Well done sayd I

CARMEN DEO NOSTRO

Tit. No no, your KING's not yet to seeke
Where to repose his Royall HEAD
See see, how soon his new-bloom'd CHEEK
Twixt's mother's brests is gone to bed.
Sweet choise, said we! no way but so
Not to ly cold, yet slep in snow.

   Cho. Sweet choise, said we.

Both. We saw thee in thy baulmy nest,
Bright dawn of our æternall Day!
We saw thine eyes break from thir EAST
And chase the trembling shades away.
We saw thee: & we blest the sight.
We saw thee, by thine own sweet light.

   Cho. We saw thee, &c.

FULL CHORUS.

Wellcome, all WONDERs in one sight!
Æternity shutt in a span.
Sommer in Winter. Day in Night.
Heaven in earth, & GOD in MAN.
Great little one! whose all-embracing birth
Lifts earth to heaven, stoopes heav'n to earth.

WELLCOME. Though nor to gold nor silk,
To more then Cæsar's birth right is;
Two sister-seas of Virgin-Milk,
With many a rarely-temper'd kisse
That brea[t]hes at once both MAID & MOTHER,
Warmes in the one, cooles in the other.

WELCOME, though not to those gay flyes
Guilded ith' Beames of earthly kings;
Slippery soules in smiling eyes;
But to poor Shepheards, home-spun things:
Whose Wealth's their flock; whose witt, to be
Well read in their simplicity.

203

RICHARD CRASHAW

Yet when young April's husband showrs
Shall blesse the fruitfull Maia's bed
We'l bring the First-born of her flowrs
To kisse thy FEET & crown thy HEAD.
To thee, dread lamb! whose love must keep
The shepheards, more then they the sheep.
To THEE, meek Majesty! soft KING
Of simple GRACES & sweet LOVES.
Each of us his lamb will bring
Each his pair of sylver Doves;
Till burnt at last in fire of Thy fair eyes,
Our selves become our own best SACRIFICE.

CARMEN DEO NOSTRO

NEW YEAR'S

DAY.

R Ise, thou best & brightest morning!
   Rosy with a double Red;
  With thine own blush thy cheeks adorning
And the dear drops this day were shed.

All the purple pride that laces
The crimson curtains of thy bed,
  Guilds thee not with so sweet graces
Nor setts thee in so rich a red.

Of all the fair-cheek't flowrs that fill thee
None so fair thy bosom strowes,
  As this modest maiden lilly
Our sins have sham'd into a rose.

Bid thy golden GOD, the Sun,
Burnisht in his best beames rise,
  Put all his red-ey'd Rubies on;
These Rubies shall putt out their eyes.

Let him make poor the purple east,
Search what the world's close cabinets keep,
  Rob the rich births of each bright nest
That flaming in their fair beds sleep,

Let him embrave his own bright tresses
With a new morning made of gemmes;
  And wear, in those his wealthy dresses,
Another Day of Diadems.

When he hath done all he may
To make himselfe rich in his rise,
  All will be darknes to the Day
That breakes from one of these bright eyes.

RICHARD CRASHAW

And soon this sweet truth shall appear
Dear BABE, ere many dayes be done,
The morn shall come to meet thee here,
And leave her own neglected Sun.

Here are Beautyes shall bereave him
Of all his eastern Paramours.
His Persian Lovers all shall leave him,
And swear faith to thy sweeter Powres.

IN
THE GLORIOUS
EPIP·HANIE
OF OUR LORD
GOD,
A HYMN.

SUNG AS BY THE
THREE KINGS

RICHARD CRASHAW

(1. *KINGE*.)

BRight BABE ! Whose awfull beautyes make
The morn incurr a sweet mistake ;
(2.) For whom the'officious heavns devise
To disinheritt the sun's rise,
(3.) Delicately to displace
The Day, & plant it fairer in thy face ;
[1.] O thou born KING of loves,
    [2.] Of lights,
    [3.] Of joyes!
(C*ho*.) Look up, sweet BABE, look up & see
    For love of Thee
    Thus farr from home
    . The EAST is come
To seek her self in thy sweet Eyes.
(1.) We, who strangely went astray,
    Lost in a bright
    Meridian night,
(2.) A Darkenes made of too much day,
    (3.) Becken'd from farr
    By thy fair starr,
Lo at last have found our way.
(C*ho*.) To THEE, thou DAY of night ! thou east of west !
Lo we at last have found the way.
To thee, the world's great universal east,
The Generall & indifferent DAY.
(1.) All-circling point. All centring sphear.
The world's one, round, Æternall year.
(2.) Whose full & all-unwrinkled face
Nor sinks nor swells with time or place ;
(3.) But every where & every while
Is One Consistent solid smile ;
      (1.) Not vext & tost
      (2.) 'Twixt spring & frost,
(3.) Nor by alternate shredds of light
Sordidly shifting hands with shades & night.
(C*ho*.) O little all! in thy embrace
The world lyes warm, & likes his place.

CARMEN DEO NOSTRO

Nor does his full Globe fail to be
Kist on Both his cheeks by Thee.
Time is too narrow for thy YEAR
Nor makes the whole WORLD thy half-sp[h]ear.
  (1.) To Thee, to Thee
   From him we flee
(2.) From HIM, whom by a more illustrious ly,
The blindnes of the world did call the eye;
(3.) To HIM, who by These mortall clouds hast made
 Thy self our sun, though thine own shade.
(1.) Farewell, the wo[r]ld's false light.
   Farewell, the white
   Ægypt! a long farewell to thee
   Bright IDOL; black IDOLATRY.
The dire face of inferior DARKNES, kis't
And courted in the pompus mask of a more specious mist.
  (2.) Farewell, farewell
   The proud & misplac't gates of hell,
   Pertch't, in the morning's way
And double-guilded as the doores of DAY.
The deep hypocrisy of DEATH & NIGHT
More desperately dark, Because more bright.
  (3.) Welcome, the world's sure Way!
   HEAVN's wholsom ray.
  (Cho.) Wellcome to us; and we
  (SWEET) to our selves, in THEE.
(1.) The deathles HEIR of all thy FATHER's day!
  (2.) Decently Born.
Embosom'd in a much more Rosy MORN,
The Blushes of thy All-unblemish't mother.
  (3.) No more that other
   Aurora shall sett ope
Her ruby casements, or hereafter hope
   From mortall eyes
To meet Religious welcomes at her rise.
(Cho.) We (Pretious ones!) in you have won
A gentler MORN, a juster sun.
(1.) His superficiall Beames sun-burn't our skin;
  (2.) But left within
(3.) The night & winter still of death & sin.

(*Cho.*) Thy softer yet more certaine DARTS
Spare our eyes, but peirce our HARTS.
(1.) Therfore with HIS proud persian spoiles
(2.) We court thy more concerning smiles.
     (3.) Therfore with his Disgrace
We guild the humble cheek of this chast place;
(*Cho.*) And at thy FEET powr forth his FACE.
(1.) The doating nations now no more
Shall any day but THINE adore.
(2.) Nor (much lesse) shall they leave these eyes
For cheap Ægyptian Deityes.
(3.) In whatsoe're more Sacred shape
Of Ram, He-goat, or reverend ape,
Those beauteous ravishers opprest so sore
The too-hard-tempted nations.
     (1.) Never more
By wanton heyfer shall be worn
(2.) A Garland, or a guilded horn.
The altar-stall'd ox, fatt OSYRIS now
     With his fair sister cow,
(3.) Shall kick the clouds no more; But lean & tame,
(*Cho.*) See his horn'd face, & dy for shame.
And MITHRA now shall be no name.
(1.) No longer shall the immodest lust
Of Adulterous GODLES dust
(2.) Fly in the face of heav'n; As if it were
The poor world's Fault that he is fair.
(3.] Nor with perverse loves & Religious RAPES
Revenge thy Bountyes in their beauteous shapes;
And punish Best Things worst; Because they stood
Guilty of being much for them too Good.
[1.] Proud sons of death! that durst compell
Heav'n it self to find them hell;
[2.] And by strange witt of madnes wrest
From this world's EAST the other's WEST.
[3.] All-Idolizing wormes! that thus could crowd
And urge Their sun into thy cloud;
Forcing his sometimes eclips'd face to be
A long deliquium to the light of thee.
[*Cho.*] Alas with how much heavyer shade

CARMEN DEO NOSTRO

The shamefac't lamp hung down his head
       For that one eclipse he made
       Then all those he suffered!
[1.] For this he look't so bigg; & every morn
With a red face confes't this scorn.
Or hiding his vex't cheeks in a hir'd mist
Kept them from being so unkindly kis't.
[2.] It was for this the day did rise
       So oft with blubber'd eyes.
For this the evening wept; and we ne're knew
       But call'd it deaw.
       [3.] This dayly wrong
Silenc't the morning-sons, & damp't their song;
[*Cho.*] Nor was't our deafnes, but our sins, that thus
Long made th'Harmonious orbes all mute to us.
       [1.] Time has a day in store
       When this so proudly poor
And self-oppressed spark, that has so long
By the love-sick world bin made
Not so much their sun as SHADE,
Weary of this Glorious wrong
From them & from himself shall flee
For shelter to the shadow of thy TREE;
[*Cho.*] Proud to have gain'd this pretious losse
And chang'd his false crown for thy CROSSE.
[2.] That dark Day's clear doom shall define
Whose is the Master FIRE, which sun should shine.
That sable [j]udgment-seat shall by new lawes
Decide & settle the Great cause
       Of controverted light,
[*Cho.*] And natur's wrongs rejoyce to doe thee Right.
[3.] That forfeiture of noon to night shall pay
All the idolatrous thefts done by this night of day;
And the Great Penitent presse his own pale lipps
With an elaborate love-eclipse
       To which the low world's lawes
       Shall lend no cause
[*Cho.*] Save those domestick which he borrowes
From our sins & his own sorrowes.
[1.] Three sad hour[s'] sackcloth then shall show to us

RICHARD CRASHAW

His penance, as our fault, conspicuous.
[2.] And he more needfully & nobly prove
The nation's terror now then erst their love.
[3.] Their hated loves changd into wholsom feares,
[Cho.] The shutting of his eye shall open Theirs.
[1.] As by a fair-ey'd fallacy of day
Miss-ledde before they lost their way,
So shall they, by the seasonable fright
Of an unseasonable night,
Loosing it once again, stumble'on true LIGHT.
[2.] And as before his too-bright eye
Was Their more blind idolatry,
So his officious blindines now shall be
Their black, but faithfull perspective of thee;
    [3.] His new prodigious night,
Their new & admirable light;
The supernaturall DAWN of Thy pure day.
    While wondring they
(The happy converts now of him
Whom they compell'd before to be their sin)
    Shall henceforth see
To kisse him only as their rod
Whom they so long courted as GOD,
[Cho.] And their best use of him they worship't be
To learn, of Him at lest, to worship Thee.
[1.] It was their Weaknes woo'd his beauty;
    But it shall be
Their wisdome now, as well as duty,
To'injoy his Blott; & as a large black letter
Use it to spell Thy beautyes better;
And make the night i[t] self their [t]orch to thee.
[2.] By the oblique ambush of this close night
    Couch't in that conscious shade
The right-ey'd Areopagite
Shall with a vigorous guesse invade
And catche thy quick reflex; and sharply see
    On this dark Grou[n]d
    To d[e]scant THEE.
[3.] O prize of the rich SPIRIT! with that feirce chase
    Of this strong soul, shall he

CARMEN DEO NOSTRO

Leap at thy lofty FACE,
And s[e]ize the swift Flash, in rebound
From this o[b]sequious cloud;
    Once call'd a sun;
    Till dearly thus undone,
[*Cho.*] Till thus triumphantly tam'd (o ye two
Twinne SUNNES!) & taught now to negotiate you.
[1.] Thus shall that reverend child of light,
[2.] By being scholler first of that new night,
Come forth Great master of the mystick day;
[3.] And teach obscure MANKIND a more close way
By the frugall negati[v]e light
Of a most wise & well-abused Night
To read more legible thine originall Ray,
[*Cho.*] And make our Darknes serve THY day;
Maintaining t'wixt thy world & ours
A commerce of contrary powres,
    A mutuall trade
    'Twixt sun & SHADE,
By confederat BLACK & WHITE
Borrowing day & lending night.
[1.] Thus we, who when with all the noble powres
That (at thy cost) are call'd, not vainly, ours
    We vow to make brave way
Upwards, & presse on for, the pure intelligentiall Prey;
    [2.] At lest to play
    The amorous Spyes
And peep & proffer at thy sparkling Throne;
[3.] In stead of bringing in the blissfull PRIZE
    And fastening on Thine eyes,
    Forfeit our own
    And nothing gain
But more Ambitious losse, at lest of brain;
[*Cho.*] Now by abased liddes shall learn to be
Eagles; and shutt our eyes that we may see.

RICHARD CRASHAW

The Close.

Therfore to THEE & thine Auspitious ray
    (Dread sweet!) lo thus
      At lest by us,
The delegated EYE of DAY
Does first his Scepter, then HIMSELF in solemne Tribute pay.
      Thus he undresses
      His sacred unshorn treses;
At thy adored FEET, thus, he layes down
      [1.] His gorgeous tire
      Of flame & fire,
[2.] His glittering ROBE, [3.] his sparkling CROWN,
[1.] His GOLD, [2.] his MIRRH, [3.] his FRANKINCENCE,
[Cho.] To which He now has no pretence.
For being show'd by this day's light, how farr
He is from sun enough to make THY starr,
His best ambition now, is but to be
Somthing a brighter SHADOW (sweet) of thee.
Or on heavn's azure forhead high to stand
Thy golden index; with a duteous Hand
Pointing us Home to our own sun
The world's & his HYPERION.

CARMEN DEO NOSTRO

TO THE
QUEEN'S
MAJESTY.

M ADAME.

'Mongst those long rowes of c[r]ownes that guild your race,
These Royall sages sue for decent place.
The day-break of the nations; their first ray;
When the Dark WORLD dawn'd into Christian DAY.
And smil'd i'th' BABE's bright face, the purpling Bud
And Rosy dawn of the right Royall blood;
Fair first-fruits of the LAMB. Sure KINGS in this;
They took a kingdom while they gave a kisse.
But the world's Homage, scarse in These well blown,
We read in you (Rare Queen) ripe & full-grown.
For from this day's rich seed of Diadems
Does rise a radiant croppe of Royalle stemms,
A Golden harvest of crown'd heads, that meet
And crowd for kisses from the LAMB's white feet.
In this Illustrious throng, your lofty floud
Swells high, fair Confluence of all highborn Bloud!
With your bright head whose groves of scepters bend
Their wealthy tops; & for these feet contend.
So swore the LAMB's dread fire. And so we see't.
Crownes, & the HEADS they kisse, must court these FEET.
Fix here, fair Majesty! May your Heart ne're misse
To reap new CROWNES & KINGDOMS from that kisse.
Nor may we misse the joy to meet in you
The aged honors of this day still new.
May the great time, in you, still greater be
While all the YEAR is your EPIPHANY,
While your each day's devotion duly brings
Three KINGDOMES to supply this day's three KINGS.

THE OFFICE OF THE HO L Y CROSSE

CARMEN DEO NOSTRO

THE

HOWRES

FOR THE HOUR OF

MATINES.

The Versicle.

Lord, by thy Sweet & Saving Sign,

The Responsory.

Defend us from our foes & Thine.
℣. Thou shallt open my lippes, O Lord.
℟. And my mouth shall shew forth thy Prayse.
℣. O God make speed to save me.
℟. O Lord make hast to help me.
Glory be to the Father,
                    and to the Son,
                    and to the H. Ghost.
As it was in the beginning, is now, & ever shall be, world
without end.   Amen.

THE HYMN.

The wakefull Matines hast to sing,
    The unknown sorrows of our king,
The Father'[s] word & wisdom, made
Man, for man, by man's betraid;
The world's price sett to sale, & by the bold
Merchants of Death & sin, is bought & sold.
Of his Best Freinds (yea of himself) forsaken,
By his worst foes (because he would) beseig'd & taken.

RICHARD CRASHAW

The Antiphona.

All hail, fair TREE.
Whose Fruit we be.
What song shall raise
Thy seemly praise.
Who broughtst to light
Life out of death, Day out of night.

The Versicle.

Lo, we adore thee,
Dread LAMB! And bow thus low before thee,

The Responsor.

'Cause, by the covenant of thy CROSSE,
Thou'hast sav'd at once the whole world's losse.

The Prayer.

O Lord JESU-CHRIST, son of the living GOD! interpose,
I pray thee, thine own pretious death, thy CROSSE &
Passion, betwixt my soul & thy judgment, now & in the hour
of my death. And vouchsafe to graunt unto me thy grace &
mercy; unto all quick & dead, remission & rest; to thy church
peace & concord; to us sinners life & glory everlasting. Who
livest and reignest with the FATHER, in the unity of the HOLY
GHOST, one GOD, world without end.   Amen.

CARMEN DEO NOSTRO

FOR THE HOUR OF

PRIME.

The Versicle.

Lord by thy sweet & saving Sign.

The Responsor.

Defend us from our foes & thine.
℣. Thou shalt open.
℟. And my mouth.
℣. O God make speed.
℟. O Lord make hast.
    Glory be to.
    As it was in.

THE HYMN.

THe early Prime blushes to say
    She could not rise so soon, as they
Call'd Pilat up; to try if He
Could lend them any cruelty.
  Their hands with lashes arm'd, their toungs with lyes.
And loathsom spittle, blott those beauteous eyes,
The blissfull springs of joy; from whose all-chearing Ray
The fair starrs fill their wakefull fires the sun himselfe drinks
    Day.

The Antipho[n]a.

Victorious Sign
That now dost shine,
Transcrib'd above
Into the land of light & love;

RICHARD CRASHAW

O let us twine
Our rootes with thine,
That we may rise
Upon thy wings, & reach the skyes.

The Versicle.

Lo we adore thee
Dread LAMB! and fall
Thus low before thee

The Responsor.

'Cause by the Convenant of thy CROSSE
Thou'hast sav'd at once the whole world's losse.

The Pray[e]r.

O L[or]d JESU-CHRIST son of the living [G]OD! interpose,
I pray thee, thine own pretious death, thy CROSSE &
Passion, betwixt my soul & thy judgment, now & in the hour
of my death. And vouchsafe to graunt unto me thy grace &
mercy; unto all quick & dead, remission & rest; to thy church
peace & concord; to us sinners life & glory everlasting. Who
livest and reignest with the FATHER, in the unity of the HOLY
GHOST, one GOD, world without end. Amen.

CARMEN DEO NOSTRO

THE THIRD.

The Versicle.

Lord, by thy sweet & saving SIGN

The Responsor.

Defend us from our foes & thine.
℣. Thou shalt open.
℞. And my mouth.
℣. O GOD make speed.
℞. O LORD make hast.
℣. Glory be to.
℞. As it was in the.

THE HYMN.

THe Third hour's deafen'd with the cry
Of crucify him, crucify.
So goes the vote (nor ask them, Why?)
Live Barabbas! & let GOD dy.
But there is witt in wrath, and they will try
A HAIL more cruell the[n] their crucify.
For while in sport he weares a spitefull crown,
The serious showres along his decent
Face run sadly down.

The Antiphona.

CHRIST when he dy'd
Deceivd [t]he CROSSE;
And on death's side
Threw all the losse.
The captive world awak't, & found
The prisoners loose, the Ja[yl]or bound.

The Versicle.

Lo we adore thee
Dread LAMB, & fall
thus low before thee

The Responsor.

'Cause by the convenant of thy CROSSE
Thou'hast sav'd at once the whole wor[l]d's losse.

RICHARD CRASHAW

The Prayer.

O Lord Jesu-Christ, son of the living God! interpose,
I pray thee, thine own pretious death, thy Crosse &
Passion, betwixt my soul & thy judgment, now & in the hour
of my death. And vouchsafe to graunt unto me thy grace &
mercy; unto all quick & dead, remission & rest; to thy church
peace & concord; to us sinners life & glory everlasting. Who
livest and reignest with the Father, in the unity of the Holy
Ghost, one God, [w]orld without end.   Amen.

THE SIXT.

The Versicle.

Lord by thy sweet & saving SIGN,

The Responsor.

Defend us from our foes & thine.

℣. Thou shalt open.
℟. And my mouth.
℣. O GOD make speed.
℟. O LORD make hast.
℣. Glory be
℟. As it was in

THE HIMN.

NOw is The noon of sorrow's night;
High in his patience, as their spite.
Lo the faint LAMB, with weary limb
Beares that huge tree which must bear Him.
That fatall plant, so great of fame
For fruit of sorrow & of shame,
Shall swell with both for HIM; & mix
All woes into one CRUCIFIX.
Is tortur'd Thirst, it selfe, too sweet a cup?
GALL, & more bitter mocks, shall make it up.
Are NAILES blunt pens of superficiall smart?
Contempt & scorn can send sure wounds to search the inmost
    Heart.

The Antiphona.

O deare & sweet Dispute
'Twixt death's & Love's farr different FRUIT!
Different as farr
As antidotes & poysons are.
By that first fatall TREE
Both life & liberty
Were sold and slain;
By this they both look up, & live again.

223

RICHARD CRASHAW

The Versicle.

Lo we adore thee
Dread LAMB! & bow thus low before thee;

The Responsor.

'Cause by the convenant of thy CROSSE
Thou'hast sav'd the world from certain losse.

The Prayer.

O Lord JESU-CHRIST, son of the living GOD! interpose, I pray thee, thine own pretious death, thy CROSSE & Passion, betwixt my soul & thy judgment, now & in the hour of my death. And vouchsafe to graunt unto me thy grace & mercy; unto all quick & dead, remission & rest; to thy church peace & concord; to us sinners life & glory everlasting. Who livest and reignest with the FATHER, in the unity of the HOLY GHOST, one GOD, world without end. Amen.

CARMEN DEO NOSTRO

THE NINTH.

The Versicle.

Lord by thy sweet & saving SIGN.

The Responsor.

Defend us from our foes &' thine.
℣. Thou shalt open.
℞. And my mouth.
℣. O GOD make speed.
℞. O LORD make hast.
Glory be to.
As it was in.

THE HYMN.

THe ninth with awfull horror hearkened to those groanes
Which taught attention ev'n to ro[c]ks & stones.
Hear, FATHER, hear! thy LAMB (at last) complaines.
Of some more painfull thing then all his paines.
Then bowes his all-obedient head, & dyes
His own lov's, & our sin's GREAT SACRIFICE.
The sun saw That; And would have seen no more
The center shook. Her uselesse veil th'inglorious Temple
  tore.

The Antiphona.

O strange mysterious strife
Of open DEATH & hidden LIFE!
When on the crosse my king did bleed,
LIFE seem'd to dy, DEATH dy'd indeed.

The Versicle.

Lo we adore thee
D[rea]d LAMB! and fall
  thus low before thee

The Responsor.

'Cause by the convenant of thy CROSSE
Thou'hast sav'd at once the whole wor[l]d's losse.

P   225

RICHARD CRASHAW

The Prayer.

O Lord JESU-CHRIST, son of the living GOD! interpose, I pray thee, thine own pretious death, thy CROSSE & Passion, betwixt my soul & thy judgment, now & in the hour of my death. And vouchsafe to graunt unto me thy grace & mercy; unto all quick & dead, remission & rest; to thy church peace & concord; to us sinners life & glory everlasting. Who livest and reignest with the FATHER, in the unity of the HOLY GHOST, one GOD, world without end. Amen.

EVENSONG.

The Versicle.

Lord, by thy sweet & saving SIGN

The Responsor.

Defend us from our foes & thine.
℣. Thou shalt open.
℟. And my mouth.
℣. O GOD make speed.
℟. O LORD make hast.
℣. Glory be to.
℟. As it was in the.

THE HYMN.

BUt there were Rocks would not relent at This.
Lo, for their own hearts, they rend his.
Their deadly hate lives still; & hath
A wild reserve of wanton wrath;
Superfluous SPEAR! But there's à HEART stands by
Will look no wounds be lost, no deaths shall dy.
Gather now thy Greif's ripe FRUIT. Great mother-maid!
Then sitt thee down, & sing thine Ev'nsong in the sad
    TREE's shade.

The Antiphona.

O sad, sweet TREE!
Wofull & joyfull we
Both weep & sing in shade of thee.
When the dear NAILES did lock
And graft into thy gracious Stock
        The hope; the health,
        The worth, the wealth
Of all the ransom'd WORLD, thou hadst the power
        (In that propitious Hour)
        To poise each pretious limb,
And prove how light the World was, when it weighd with
    HIM.

RICHARD CRASHAW

Wide maist thou spred
Thine Armes; And with thy bright & blisfull head
O'relook all Libanus. Thy lofty crown
The king himself is; Thou his humble THRONE.
Where yeilding & yet conquering he
Prov'd a new path of patient Victory.
When wondring death by death was slain,
And our Captivity his Captive ta'ne.

The Versicle.

Lo we adore thee
Dread LAMB! & bow thus low before thee;

The Responsor.

'Cause by the convenant of thy CROSSE.
Thou'hast sav'd the world from certain losse.

The Prayer.

O lord JESU-CHRIST, son of the living, &c.

COMPLINE.

The Versicle.
Lord by thy sweet & saving SIGN,
The Responsor.
Defend us from our foes & thine.
℣. Thou shalt open.
℟. And my mouth.
℣. O GOD make speed.
℟. O LORD make hast.
℣. Glory be
℟. As it was in

THE HIMN.

THe Complin hour comes last, to call
Us to our own LIVE's funerall.
Ah hartlesse task! yet hope takes head;
And lives in Him that here lyes dead.
Run, MARY, run! Bring hither all the BLEST
ARABIA, for thy Royall Phœnix'nest;
Pour on thy noblest sweets, Which, when they touch
This sweeter BODY, shall indeed be such.
But must thy bed, lord, be a borow'd grave
Who lend'st to all things All the LIFE they have.
O rather use this HEART, thus farr a fitter STONE,
'Cause, though a hard & cold one, yet it is thine owne.
    Amen.

The Antiphona.
    O save us then
    Mercyfull KING of men!
    Since thou wouldst needs be thus
A SAVIOUR, & at such à rate, for us;
    Save us, o save us, lord.
We now will own no shorter wish, nor name a narrower word.
    Thy blood bids us be bold.
    Thy Wounds give us fair hold.
    Thy Sorrows chide our shame.
Thy Crosse, thy Nature, & thy name
    Advance our claim
    And cry with one accord
    Save them, o save them, lord.

RICHARD CRASHAW

THE
RECOMMENDATION.

THese Houres, & that which hover's o're my END,
Into thy hands, and hart, lord, I, commend.

Take Both to Thine Account, that I & mine
In that Hour, & in these, may be all thine.

That as I dedicate my devoutest BREATH
To make a kind of LIFE for my lord's DEATH,

So from his living, & life-giving DEATH,
My dying LIFE may draw a new, & never fleeting BREATH.

UPON
THE
H. SEPULCHER.

Here where our LORD once lay'd his Head,
Now the grave lyes Buryed.

CARMEN DEO NOSTRO

VEXILLA REGIS,

THE

HYMN

OF THE HOLY

CROSSE.

I.

Look up, languisting Soul! Lo where the fair
  BADG of thy faith calls back thy care,
      And biddes thee ne're forget
      Thy life is one long Debt
Of love to Him, who on this painfull TREE
Paid back the flesh he took for thee.

II.

Lo, how the streames of life, from that full nest
Of loves, thy lord's too liberall brest,
      Flow in an amorous floud
      Of WATER wedding BLOOD.
With these he wash't thy stain, transfer'd thy smart,
And took it home to his own heart.

III.

But though great LOVE, greedy of such sad gain
Usurp't the Portion of THY pain,
      And from the nailes & spear
      Turn'd the steel point of fear,
Their use is chang'd, not lost; and now they move.
Not stings of w[ra]th, but wounds of love.

231

IV.

Tall TREE of life! thy truth makes good
What was till now ne're understood,
  Though the prophetick king
  Struck lowd his faithfull string.
It was thy wood he meant should make the T[HR]ONE
For a more then SALOMON.

V.

Larg throne of love! Royally spred
With purple of too Rich a red.
  Thy crime is too much duty;
  Thy Burthen, too much beauty;
Glorious, or Greivous more? thus to make good
Thy costly excellence with thy KING's own BLOOD.

VI.

Even ballance of both worlds! our world of sin,
And that of grace heavn way'd in HIM,
  Us with our price thou weighed'st;
  Our price for us thou payed'st;
Soon as the right-hand scale rejoyc't to prove
How much Death weigh'd more light then love.

VII.

Hail, our alone hope! let thy fair head shoot
Aloft; and fill the nations with thy noble fruit.
  The while our hearts & we
  Thus graft our selves on thee;
Grow thou & they. And be thy fair increase
The sinner's pardon & the just man's peace.

Live, o for ever live & reign
The LAMB whom his own love hath slain!
And let thy lost sheep live to'inherit
That KINGDOM which this CROSSE did merit.
  A M E N.

TO OUR B. LORD

UPON THE CHOISE OF HIS

Sepulcher.

How life & death in Thee
Agree!
Thou hadst a virgin womb,
And tomb.
A JOSEPH did betroth
Them both.

RICHARD CRASHAW

CHARITAS NIMIA.
OR
THE
DEAR BARGAIN.

L Ord, what is man? why should he coste thee
   So dear? what had his ruin lost thee?
Lord what is man? that thou hast overbought
So much a thing of nought?

Love is too kind, I see; & can
Make but à simple merchant man.
'Twas for such sorry merchandise,
Bold Painters have putt out his Eyes.

Alas, sweet lord, what wer't to thee
If there were no such wormes as we?
Heav'n ne're the lesse still heavn would be,
        Should Mankind dwell
        In the deep hell.
What have his woes to doe with thee?

        Let him goe weep
        O're his own wounds;
        SERAPHIMS will not sleep
Nor spheares let fall their faithfull rounds.

Still would The youthfull SPIRITS sing;
And still thy spatious Palace ring.
Still would those beauteous ministers of light
        Burn all as bright,

And bow their flaming heads before thee
Still thrones & Dominations would adore thee
Still would those ever-wakefull sons of fire
        Keep warm thy prayse
        Both nights & dayes,
And teach thy lov'd name to their noble lyre.

CARMEN DEO NOSTRO

Le[t] froward Dust then doe it's kind;
And give it self for sport to the proud wind.
Why should a peice of peevish clay plead shares
In the Æternity of thy old cares?
Why shouldst you bow thy awfull Brest to see
What mine own madnesses have done with me?

Should not the king still keepe his throne
Because some desperate Fool's undone?
Or will the world's Illustrious eyes
Weep for every worm that dyes;
   Will the gallant sun
   E're the lesse glorious run?
Will he hang down his golden head
Or e're the sooner seek his western bed,
   Because some foolish fly
   Growes wanton, & will dy?

If I were lost in misery,
What was it to thy heavn & thee?
What was it to thy pretious blood
If my foul Heart call'd for a floud?

  What if my faithlesse soul & I
   Would needs fall in
   With guilt & sin,
What did the Lamb, that he should dy?
What did the lamb, that he should need?
When the wolf sins, himself to bleed?

   If my base lust,
Bargain'd with Death & well-beseeming dust
   Why should the white
   Lamb's bosom write
   The purple name
   Of my sin's shame?

Why should his unstaind brest make good
My blushes with his own heart-blood?

O my SAVIOUR, make me see
How dearly thou hast payd for me

That lost again my LIFE may prove
As then in DEATH, so now in love.

SANCTA MARIA

DOLORUM

OR
THE MOTHER
OF
SORROWS.

A
Patheticall descant upon the
devout Plainsong

OF

*STABAT MATER
DOLOROSA.*

236

SANCTA MARIA

DOLORUM.

I.

IN shade of death's sad TREE
  Stood Dolefull SHEE.
Ah SHE! now by none other
Name to be known, alas, but SORROW's [M]OTHER.
  Before her eyes
Her's, & the whole world's joyes,
Hanging all torn she sees; and in his woes
And Paines, her Pangs & throes.
Each wound of His, from every Part,
All, more at home in her one heart.

II.

  What kind of marble than
  Is that cold man
  Who can look on & see, .
Nor keep such noble sorrowes company?
  Sure ev'en from you
  (My Flints) some drops are due
To see so many unkind swords contest
  So fast for one soft Brest.
While with à faithfull, mutuall, floud
Her eyes bleed TEARES, his wounds weep BLOOD.

III.

  O costly intercourse
  Of deaths, & worse
  Divided loves. While son & mother
Discourse alternate wounds to one another;
  Quick Deaths that grow
  And gather, as they come & goe:
His Nailes write swords in her, which soon her heart
  Payes back, with more then their own smart;
Her SWORDS, still growin[g] with his pain,
Turn SPEARES, & straight come home again.

237

RICHARD CRASHAW

IV.

She sees her son, her GOD,
Bow with à load
Of borrowd sins; And swimme
In woes that were not made for Him.
Ah hard command
Of love! Here must she stand
Charg'd to look on, & with à stedfast ey
See her life dy:
Leaving her only so much Breath
As serves to keep alive her death.

V.

O Mother turtle-dove!
Soft sourse of love
That these dry lidds might borrow
Something from thy full Seas of sorrow!
O in that brest
Of thine (the nob[l]est nest
Both of love's fires & flouds) might I recline
This hard, cold, Heart of mine!
The chill lump would relent, & prove
Soft subject for the seige of love.

VI.

O teach those wounds to bleed
In me; me, so to read
This book of loves, thus writ
In lines of death, my life may coppy it
With loyall cares.
O let me, here, claim shares;
Yeild somthing in thy sad prærogative
(Great Queen of greifes) & give
Me too my teares; who, though all stone,
Think much that thou shouldst mourn alone.

CARMEN DEO NOSTRO

VII.

Yea let my life & me
Fix here with thee,
And at the Humble foot
Of this fair TREE take our eter[n]all root.
That so we may
At least be in loves way;
And in these chast warres while the wing'd wounds flee
So fast'twixt him & thee,
My brest may catch the kisse of some kind dart,
Though as at second hand, from either heart.

VIII.

O you, your own best Darts
Dear, dolefull hearts!
Hail; & strike home & make me see
That wounded bosomes their own weapons be.
Come wounds! come darts!
Nail'd hands! & peirced hearts!
Come your whole selves, sorrow's great son & mother!
Nor grudge à yonger-Brother
Of greifes his portion, who (had all their due)
One single wound should not have left for you.

IX.

Shall I, sett there
So deep a share
(Dear wounds) & onely now
In sorrows draw no Dividend with you?
O be more wise
I[f] not more soft, mine eyes!
Flow, tardy founts! & into decent showres
Dissolve my Dayes & Howres.
And if thou yet (faint soul!) deferr
To bleed with him, fail not to weep with her.

RICHARD CRASHAW

X.

Rich Queen, lend some releife;
At least an almes of greif
To'a heart who by sad right of sin
Could prove the whole summe (too sure) due to him.
By all those stings
Of love, sweet bitter things,
Which these torn hands transcrib'd on thy true heart
O teach mine too the art
To study him so, till we mix
Wounds; and become one crucifix.

XI.

O let me suck the wine
So long of this chast vine
Till drunk of the dear wounds, I be
A lost Thing to the world, as it to me.
O faithfull freind
Of me & of my end!
Fold up my life in love; and lay't beneath
My dear lord's vitall death.
Lo, heart, thy hope's whole Plea! Her pretious Breath
Powr'd out in prayrs for thee; thy lord's in death.

CARMEN DEO NOSTRO

UPON

THE

BLEEDING

CRUCIFIX

A

SONG.

I.

JEsu, no more! It is full tide.
From thy head & from thy feet,
From thy hands & from thy side
All the purple Rivers meet.

II.

What need thy fair head bear a part
In showres, as if thine eyes had none?
What need They help to drown thy heart,
That strives in torrents of it's own?

III.

Thy restlesse feet now cannot goe
For us & our eternall good.
As they were ever wont. What though?
They swimme. Alas, in their own floud.

IV.

Thy hands to give, thou canst not lift;
Yet will thy hand still giving be.
It gives but ô, it self's the gift.
It gives though bound; though bound 'tis free.

RICHARD CRASHAW

V.

But ô thy side, thy deep-digg'd side!
That hath a double Nilus going.
Nor ever was the pharian tide
Half so fruitfull, half so flowing.

VI.

No hair so small, but payes his river
To this red sea of thy blood
Their little channells can deliver
Somthing to the Generall floud.

VII.

But while I speak, whither are run
All the rivers nam'd before?
I counted wrong. There is but one;
But ô that one is one all ore.

VIII.

Rain-swoln rivers may rise proud,
Bent all to drown & overflow.
But when indeed all's overflow'd
They themselves are drowned too.

IX.

This thy blood's deluge, a dire chance
Dear Lord to thee, to us is found
A deluge of Deliverance;
A deluge least we should be drown'd.

N'ere wast thou in a sense so sadly true,
The WELL of living WATERS, Lord, till now.

UPON

THE CROWNE OF THORNS

TAKEN DOWNE

From the head of our Bl. LORD, all Bloody.

KNow'st thou This, Souldier? 'Tis à much-chang'd plant
    which yet
    Thy selfe didst sett.

O who so hard a Husbandman did ever find;
    A soile so kind?

Is not the soile a kind one, which returnes
    Roses for Th[or]nes?

UPON

THE BODY OF OUR

BL. LORD,

NAKED

AND

BLOODY.

They 'have left thee naked, LORD, O that they had!
This garment too I would they had deny'd.

Thee with thy self they have too richly clad;
Opening the purple wardrobe in thy side.

O never could there be garment too good
For thee to wear, But this, of thine own Blood.

THE
HYMN
OF
SANITE THOMAS
IN
ADORATION OF
THE
BLESSED
SACRAMENT.

RICHARD CRASHAW

ADORO

TE

With all the powres my poor Heart hath
Of humble love & loyall Faith,
Thus lowe (my hidden life!) I bow to thee
Whom too much love hath bow'd more low for me.
Down down, proud sense! Discourses dy.
Keep close, my soul's inquiring ey!
Nor touch nor tast must look for more
But each sitt still in his own Dore.

Your ports are all superfluous here,
Save That which lets in faith, the eare.
Faith is my skill. Faith can beleive
As fast as love new lawes can give.
Faith is my force. Faith strength affords
To keep pace with those powrfull words.
And words more sure, more sweet, then they
Love could not think, truth could not say.

O let thy wretch find that releife
Thou didst afford the faithfull theife.
Plead for me, love! Alleage & show
That faith has farther, here, to goe
And lesse to lean on. Because than
Though hidd as GOD, wounds writt thee man,
Thomas might touch; None but might see
At least the suffring side of thee;
And that too was thy self which thee did cover,
But here ev'n That's hid too which hides the other.

Sweet, consider then, that I
Though allow'd nor hand nor eye
To reach at thy lov'd Face; nor can
Tast thee GOD, or touch thee MAN
Both yet beleive; And wittnesse thee
My LORD too & my GOD, as lowd as He.

246

CARMEN DEO NOSTRO

Help, lord, my Hope increase ;
And fill my portion in thy peace.
Give love for life ; nor let my dayes
Grow, but in new powres to thy name & praise.

O dear memoriall of that Death
Which lives still, & allowes us breath !
Rich, Royall food ! Bountyfull BREAD !
Whose use denyes us to the dead ;
Whose vitall gust alone can give
The same leave both to eat & live ;
Live ever Bread of loves, & be
My life, my soul, my surer selfe to mee.

O soft self-wounding Pelican !
Whose brest weepes Balm for wounded man.
Ah this way bend thy benign floud
To'a bleeding Heart that gaspes for blood.
That blood, whose least drops soveraign be
To wash my worlds of sins from me.
Come love ! Come LORD ! & that long day
For which I languish, come away.
When this dry soul those eyes shall see,
And drink the unseal'd sourse of thee.
When Glory's sun faith's shades shall chase,
And for thy veil give me thy FACE.

A M E N.

RICHARD CRASHAW

LAUDA SION SALVATOREM.
THE HYMN.
FOR
THE BL.
SACRAMENT.

I.

Rise, Royall Sion! rise & sing
  Thy soul's kind shepheard, thy hart's King.
Stretch all thy powres; call if thou can
Harpes of heavn to hands of man.
This soveraign subject sitts above
The best ambition of thy love.

II.

Lo the Bread of Li[f]e, this day's
Triumphant Text, provokes thy prayse.
The living & life-giving bread,
To the great twelve distributed
When Life, himself, at point to dy
Of love, was his own Legacy.

III.

Come, love! & let us work a song
Lowd & pleasant, sweet & long;
Let lippes & Hearts lift high the noise
Of so just & solemn joyes,
Which on his white browes this bright day
Shall hence for ever bear away.

IV.

Lo the new Law of a new Lord.
With a new Lamb blesses the Board.
The aged Pascha pleads not yeares
But spyes love's dawn, & disappeares.
Types yeild to Truthes; shades shrink away;
And their Night dyes into our Day.

248

CARMEN DEO NOSTRO

V.

But lest THAT dy too, we are bid.
Ever to doe what he once did.
And by à mindfull, mystick breath
That we may live, revive his DEATH;
With a well-bles't bread & wine.
Transsum'd, & taught to turn divine.

VI.

The Heavn-instructed house of FAITH
Here a holy Dictate hath
That they but lend their Form & face,
Themselves with reverence leave their place
Nature, & name, to be made good.
By' a nobler Bread, more needfull BLOOD.

VII.

Where nature's lawes no leave will give,
Bold FAITH takes heart, & dares beleive
In different species, name not things,
Himself to me my SAVIOUR brings,
As meat in That, as Drink in this;
But still in Both one CHRIST he is.

VIII.

The Receiving Mouth here makes
Non wound nor breach in what he takes.
Let one, or one THOUSAND be
Here Dividers, single he
Beares home no lesse, all they no more,
Nor leave they both lesse then before.

IX.

Though in it self this SOVERAIN FEAST
Be all the same to every Guest,
Yet on the same (life-meaning) Bread
The child of Death eates himself Dead.
Nor is't love's fault, but sin's dire skill
That thus from LIFE can DEATH distill.

RICHARD CRASHAW

X.

When the blest signes thou broke shall see,
Hold but thy Faith intire as he
Who, howsoe're clad, cannot come
Lesse then whole CHRIST in every crumme.
In broken formes à stable FAITH
Untouch't her pretious TOTALL hath.

XI.

Lo the life-food of ANGELLS then
Bow'd to the lowly mouths of men!
The children's BREAD; the Bridegroom's WINE.
Not to be cast to dogges, or swine.

XII.

Lo, the full, finall, SACRI[F]ICE
On which all figures fix't their eyes.
The ransom'd ISACK, & his ramme;
The MANNA, & the PASCHAL Lamb.

XIII.

JESU MASTER, Just & true!
Our Food, & faithfull SHEPHARD too!
O by thy self vouchsafe to keep,
As with thy selfe thou feed'st thy SHEEP.

XIV.

O let that love which thus makes thee
Mix with our low Mortality,
Lift our lean Soules, & sett us up
Convi&ors of thine own full cup,
Coheirs of SAINTS. That so all may
Drink the same wine; and the same WAY.
Nor chang the PASTURE, but the PLACE;
To feed of THEE in thine own FACE.

AMEN.

CARMEN DEO NOSTRO

THE

HYMN.

OF THE

CHURCH,

IN MEDITATION OF

THE DAY OF

JUDGMENT.

I.

H Ears't thou, my soul, with serious things
Both the Psalm and sybyll sings
Of a sure judge, from whose sharp Ray
The world in flames shall fly away.

II.

O that fire! before whose face
Heavn & earth shall find no place.
O those eyes! whose angry light
Must be the day of that dread Night.

III.

O that trump! whose blast shall r[u]n
An even round with the circling Sun.
And urge the murmuring graves to bring
Pale mankind forth to meet his king.

IV.

Horror of nature, hell & Death!
When a deep Groan from beneath
Shall cry we come, we come & all
The caves of night answer one call

RICHARD CRASHAW

V.

O that Book! whose leaves so bright
Will sett the world in severe light.
O that Judge! whose hand, whose eye
None can indure; yet none can fly

VI.

Ah then, poor soul, what wilt thou say?
And to what Patron chuse to pray?
When starres themselves shall stagger; and
The most firm foot no more then stand.

VII.

But thou giv'st leave (dread Lord) that we
Take shelter from thy self, in thee;
And with the wings of thine own dove
Fly to thy scepter of soft love.

VIII.

Dear, remember in that Day
Who was the cause thou cams't this way.
Thy sheep was stray'd; And thou wouldst be
Even lost thy self in seeking me.

IX.

Shall all that labour, all that cost
Of love, and ev'n that losse, be lost?
And this lov'd soul, judg'd worth no lesse
Then all that way, and wearynesse?

X.

Just mercy then, thy Reckning be
With my price, & not with me:
'Twas pay'd at first with too much pain,
To be pay'd twice; or once, in vain.

XI.

Mercy (my judge) mercy I cry
With blushing Cheek & bleeding ey,
The conscious colors of my sin
Are red without & pale within.

CARMEN DEO NOSTRO

XII.

O let thine own soft bowells pay
Thy self; And so discharge that day.
If sin can sigh, love can forgive.
O say the word my Soul shall live.

XIII.

Those mercyes which thy MARY found
Or who thy crosse confes't & crown'd,
Hope tells my heart, the same loves be
Still alive; and still for me.

XIV.

Though both my Prayres & teares combine,
Both worthlesse are; For they are mine.
But thou thy bounteous self still be;
And show thou art, by saving me.

XV.

O when thy last Frown shall proclaim
The flocks of goates to folds of flame,
And all thy lost sheep found shall be,
Let come ye blessed then call me.

XVI.

When the dread ITE shall divide
Those Limbs of death from thy left side,
Let those life-speaking lipps command
That I inheritt thy right hand.

XVII.

O hear a suppliant heart; all crush't
And crumbled into contrite dust.
My hope, my fear! my Judge, my Freind!
Take charge of me, & of my END.

RICHARD CRASHAW

THE

HIMN

O GLORIOSA DOMINA.

Hail, most high, most humble one!
  Above the world; below thy Son
Whose blush the moon beauteously marres
And staines the timerous light of stares.
He that made all things, had not done
Till he had made Himself thy son
The whole world's host would be thy guest
And board himself at thy rich Brest.
O boundles Hospitality!
The Feast of all thing feeds on the[e].
  The first Eve, mother of our Fall,
E're she bore any one, slew all.
Of Her unkind gift might we have
The inheritance of a hasty Grave;
Quick burye'd in the wanton Tomb
    Of one forbidden bitt;
Had not à Better Fruit forbidden it.
    Had not thy healthfull womb
The world's new eastern window bin
And given us heav'n again, in giving Him.
Thine was the Rosy Dawn that sprung the Day
Which renders all the starres she stole away.
  Let then the Aged world be wise, & all
Prove nobly, here, unnaturall.
'Tis gratitude to forgett that other
And call the maiden Eve their mo[t]her.
  Yee redeem'd Nations farr & near,
Applaud your happy selves in her,
(All you to whom this love belongs)
And keep't alive with lasting songs.

CARMEN DEO NOSTRO

Let hearts & lippes speak lowd; and say
Hail, door of life: & sourse of day!
The door was shutt, the fountain seal'd;
Yet LIGHT was seen & LIFE reveald.
The fountain seald, yet life found way.
    Glory to thee, great virgin's son
In bosom of thy FATHER's blisse.
    The same to thee, sweet SPIRIT be done;
As ever shall be, was, & is.

AMEN.

RICHARD CRASHAW

IN THE
GLORIOUS
ASSUMPTION
OF
OUR BLESSED
LADY.

THE HYMN.

HArk! she is call'd, the parting houre is come
Take thy Farewell, poor world! heavn must goe home.
A peice of heav'nly earth; Purer & brighter
Then the chast starres, whose choise lamps come to light her
While through the crystall orbes, clearer then they
She climbes; and makes a farre more milkey way.
She's calld. Hark, how the dear immortall dove
Sighes to his sylver mate rise up, my love!
Rise up, my fair, my spottlesse one!
The winter's past, the rain is gone.
The spring is come, the flowrs appear
No sweets, but thou, are wanting here.

    Come away, my love!
    Come away, my dove! cast off delay,
     The court of heav'n is come
      To wait upon thee home; Come come away!
    The flowrs appear.

Or quickly would, wert thou once here
The spring is come, or if it stay,
'Tis to keep time with thy delay.
The rain is gone, except so much as we
Detain in needfull teares to weep the want of thee.

    The winter's past.
    or if he make lesse hast,
His answer is, why she does so.
If sommer come not, how can winter goe.

    Come away, come away.
The shrill winds chide, the waters weep thy stay;

256

CARMEN DEO NOSTRO

The fountains murmur; & each loftyest [t]ree,
Bowes low'st his heavy top, to look for thee.
      Come away, my love.
      Come away, my dove &c.
She's call'd again. And will she goe?
When heavn bidds come, who can say no?
Heavn calls her, & she must away.
Heavn will not, & she cannot stay.
Goe then; goe Glorious.
      On the golden wings
Of the bright youth of heavn, that sings
Under so sweet a Burthen. Goe,
Since thy dread son will have it so.
And while thou goest, our song & we
Will, as we may, reach after thee.
Hail, holy Queen of humble hearts!
We in thy prayse will have our parts.
      Thy pretious name shall be
      Thy self to us; & we
      With holy care will keep it by us.
      We to the last
      Will hold it fast
      And no Assumption shall deny us.
      All the sweetest showres
      Of our fairest flowres
      Will we strow upon it.
      Though our sweets cannot make
      It sweeter, they can take
      Themselves new sweetnes from it.
Maria, men & Angels sing
Maria, mother of our King.
  Live, rosy princesse, Live. And may the bright
Crown of a most incomparable light
Embrace thy radiant browes. O may the best
      Of everlasting joyes bath thy white brest.
      Live, our chast love, the holy mirth
      Of heavn; the humble pride of earth.
      Live, c[r]own of woemen; Queen of men.
      Live mistresse of our song. And when
      Our weak desires have done their [b]est,
      Sweet Angels come, and sing the rest.

RICHARD CRASHAW

SANITE

MARY

MAGDALENE

OR

THE WEEPER.

Loe where à WOUNDED HEART with Bleeding EYES conspire.
Is she a FLAMING Fountain, or a Weeping fire!

CARMEN DEO NOSTRO

THE

WEEPER.

I.

H Ail, sister springs!
  Parents of sylver-footed rills!
Ever bubling things!
 Thawing crystall! snowy hills,
Still spending, never spent! I mean
Thy fair eyes, sweet MAGDALENE!

II.

 Heavens thy fair eyes be;
Heavens of ever-falling starres.
 'Tis seed-time still with thee
 And starres thou sow'st, whose harvest dares
Promise the earth to counter shine
Whatever makes heavn's forhead fine.

III.

 But we'are deceived all.
Starres indeed they are too true;
 For they but seem to fall,
 As Heavn's other spangles doe.
It is not for our earth & us
To shine in Things so pretious.

IV.

 Upwards thou dost weep.
Heavn's bosome drinks the gentle stream.
 Where th'milky rivers creep,
 Thine floates above; & is the cream.
Waters above th'Heavns, what they be
We'are taught best by thy TEARES & thee.

RICHARD CRASHAW

V.

Every morn from hence
A brisk Cherub somthing sippes
Whose sacred influence
Addes sweetnes to his sweetest Lippes.
Then to his musick. And his song
Tasts of this Breakfast all day long.

VI.

Not in the evening's eyes
When they Red with weeping are
For the Sun that dyes,
Sitts sorrow with a face so fair,
No where but here did ever meet
Sweetnesse so sad, sadnesse so sweet.

VII.

When sorrow would be seen
In her brightest majesty
(For she is a Queen)
Then is she drest by none but thee.
Then, & only then, she weares
Her proudest pearles; I mean, thy TEARES.

VIII.

The deaw no more will weep
The prim rose's pale cheek to deck,
The deaw no more will sleep
Nuzzel'd in the lilly's neck;
Much reather would it be thy TEAR,
And leave them Both to tremble here.

IX.

There's no need at all
That the balsom-sweating bough
So coyly should let fall
His med'cinable teares; for now
Nature hath learn't to'extract a deaw
More soveraign & sweet from you.

CARMEN · DEO · NOSTRO

X.

Yet let the poore drops weep
(Weeping is the ease of woe)
Softly let them creep,
Sad that they are vanquish't so.
They, though to others no releife,
Balsom maybe, for their own greife.

XI.

Such the maiden gemme
By the purpling vine put on,
Peeps from her parent stemme
And blushes at the bridegroomes sun.
This watry Blossom of thy eyn,
Ripe, will make the richer wine.

XII.

When some new bright Guest
Takes up among the starres a room,
And Heavn will make a feast,
Angels with crystall violls come
And deaw from these full eyes of thine
Their master's Water: their own Wine.

XIII.

Golden though he be,
Golden Tagus murmures tho;
Were his way by thee,
Content & quiet he would goe.
So much more rich would he esteem
Thy sylver, then his golden stream.

XIV.

Well does the May that lyes
Smiling in thy cheeks, confesse
The April in thine eyes.
Mutuall sweetnesse they expresse.
No April ere lent kinder showres,
Nor May return'd more faithfull flowres.

RICHARD CRASHAW

XV.

O c[h]eeks! Bedds of chast loves
By your own showres seasonably dash't
Eyes! nests of milky doves.
In your own wells decently washt.
O wit of love! that thus could place
Fountain & Garden in one face.

[XVI.]

O sweet Contest; of woes
With loves, of teares with smiles disputing!
O fair, & Freindly Foes,
Each other kissing & confuting!
While rain & sunshine, Cheekes & Eyes
Close in kind contrarietyes.

XVII.

But can these fair Flouds be
Freinds with the bosom fires that fill you!
Can so great flames agree
Æternall Teares should thus distill thee!
O flouds, o fires! o suns ô showres!
Mixt & made freinds by love's sweet powres.

XVIII.

Twas his well-pointed dart
That digg'd these wells, & drest this wine;
And taught the wounded HEART
The way into these weeping Eyn.
Vain loves avant! bold hands forbear!
The lamb hath dipp't his white foot here.

XIX.

And now where're he strayes,
Among the Galilean mountaines,
Or more unwellcome wayes,
He's follow'd by two faithfull fountaines;
Two walking baths; two weeping motions;
Portable, & compendious oceans.

262

CARMEN DEO NOSTRO

XX.

O Thou, thy lord's fair store!
In thy so rich & rare expenses,·
Even when he show'd most poor,
He might provoke the wealth of Princes.
What Prince's wanton'st pride e're could
Wash with Sylver, wipe with Gold.

XXI.

Who is that King, but he
Who calls't his Crown to be call'd thine,
That thus can boast to be
Waited on by a wandring mine,
A voluntary mint, that strowes
Warm sylver shoures where're he goes!

XXII.

O pretious Prodigall!
Fair spend-thrift of thy self! thy measure
(Mercilesse love!) is all.
Even to the last Pearle in thy threasure.
All places, Times, & objects be
Thy teare's sweet opportunity.

XXIII.

Does the day-starre rise?
Still thy starres doe fall & fall;
Does day close his eyes?
Still the FOUNTAIN weeps for all.
Let night or day doe what they will,
Thou hast thy task; thou weepest still.

XXIV.

Does thy song lull the air?
Thy falling teares keep faithfull time.
Does thy sweet-breath'd paire
Up in clouds of incense climb?
Still at each sigh, that is, each stop,
A bead, that is, A TEAR, does drop,

RICHARD CRASHAW

XXV.

At these thy weeping gates,
(Watching their watry motion)
Each winged moment waits,
Takes his TEAR, & gets him gone.
By thine Ey's tinct enobled thus
Time layes him up; he's pretious.

XXVI.

Not, so long she lived,
Shall thy tomb report of thee;
But, so long she greived,
Thus must we date thy memory.
Others by moments, months, & yeares
Measure their ages; thou, by TEARES.

XXVII.

So doe perfumes expire.
So sigh tormented sweets, opprest
With proud unpittying fires.
Such Teares the suffring Rose that's vext
With ungentle flames does shed,
Sweating in a too warm bed.

XXVIII.

Say, the bright brothers,
The fugitive sons of those fair Eyes
Your fruitfull mothers!
What make you here? what hopes can tice
You to be born? what cause can borrow
You from Those nests of noble sorrow?

XXIX.

Whither away so fast?
For sure the sordid earth
Your Sweetnes cannot tast
Nor does the dust deserve their birth.
Sweet, whither hast you then? o say
Why you trip so fast away?

CARMEN DEO NOSTRO

XXX.

We goe not to seek,
The darlings of Auroras bed,
The rose's modest Cheek
Nor the violet's humble head.
Though the Feild's eyes too WEEPERS be
Because they want such TEARES as we.

XXXI.

Much lesse mean we to trace
The Fortune of inferior gemmes,
Preferr'd to some proud face
Or pertch't upon fear'd Diadems.
Crown'd Heads are toyes. We goe to meet
A worthy object, our lord's FEET.

A HYMN
TO
THE NAME AND HONOR
OF
THE ADMIRABLE
SANITE
TERESA,
FOUNDRESSE
of the Reformation of the Discalced
CARMELITES, both
men & Women;

A

WOMAN
for Angelicall heig[ht] of speculation, for
Masculine courage of performance,
more then a woman.

WHO
Yet a child, out ran maturity, and
durst plott a Martyrdome;

CARMEN DEO NOSTRO

THE

HYMNE.

LOve, thou art Absolute sole lord
Of Life & Death. To prove the word,
Wee'l now appeal to none of all
Those thy old Souldiers, Great & tall,
Ripe Men of Martyrdom, that could reach down
With strong armes, their triumphant crown;
Such as could with lusty breath
Speak lowd into the face of death
Their Great Lord's glorious name, to none
Of those whose spatious Bosomes spread a throne
For Love at larg to fill, spare blood & sweat;
And see him take a private seat,
Making his mansion in the mild
And milky soul of a soft child.
  Scarse has she learn't to lisp the name
Of Martyr; yet she thinks it shame
Life should so long play with that breath
Which spent can buy so brave a death.
She never undertook to know
What death with love should have to doe;
Nor has she e're yet understood
Why to show love, she should shed blood
Yet though she cannot tell you why,
She can Love, & she can Dy.
  Scarse has she Blood enough to make
A guilty sword blush for her sake;
Yet has she'a Heart dares hope to prove
How much lesse strong is Death then Love.
  Be love but there; let poor six yeares
Be pos'd with the maturest Feares
Man trembles at, you st[r]aight shall find
Love knowes no nonage, nor the Mind.
'Tis Love, not Yeares or Limbs that can
Make the Martyr, or the man.

RICHARD CRASHAW

Love touch't her HEART, & lo it beates
High, & burnes with such brave heates;
Such thirsts to dy, as dares drınk up,
A thousand cold deaths in one cup.
Good reason. For she breathes All fire.
Her [weake] brest heaves with strong desire
Of what she may with fruitles wishes
Seek for amongst her MOTHER's [Kisses].
Since 'tis not to be had at home
She'l travail to à Mar[t]yrdom.
No home for hers confesses she
But where she may à Martyr be.
She'l to the Moores; And trade with them,
For this unvalued Diadem.
She'l offer them her dearest Breath,
With CHRIST's Name in't, in change for death.
She'l bargain with them; & will give
Them GOD; teach them how to live
In him: or, if they this deny,
For him she'l teach them how to DY.
So shall she leave amongst them sown
Her LORD's Blood; or at lest her own.
FAREWEL then, all the world! Adieu.
TERESA is no more for you.
Farewell, all pleasures, sports, & joyes,
(Never till now esteemed toyes)
[Farewell what ever deare may be,]
MOTHER's armes or FATHER's knee.
Farewell house, & farewell home!
SHE's for the Moores, & MARTYRDOM.
SWEET, not so fast! lo thy fair Spouse -
Whom thou seekst with so swift vowes,
Calls thee back, & bidds thee come
T'embrace a milder MARTYRDOM.
Blest powres forbid, Thy tender life
Should bleed upon a barborous knife;
Or some base hand have power to race
Thy Brest's chast cabinet, & uncase
A soul kept there so sweet, ô no;
Wise· heavn will never have it so.

CARMEN DEO' NOSTRO

Thou art love's victime; & must dy
A death more mysticall & high.
Into love's armes thou shalt let fall
A still-surviving funerall.
His is the Dart. must make the Death
Whose stroke shall tast thy hallow'd breath;
A Dart thrice dip't in that rich flame
Which writes thy spouse's radiant Name
Upon the roof of Heav'n; where ay
It shines, & with a soveraign ray
Beates bright upon the burning faces
Of soules which in that name's sweet graces
Find everlasting smiles. So rare,
So spirituall, pure, & fair
Must be th'immortall instrument
Upon whose choice point shall be sent
A life so lov'd; And that there be
Fitt executioners for Thee,
The fair'st & first-born sons of fire
Blest Seraphim, shall leave their quire
And turn love's souldiers, upon Thee
To exercise their archerie.

O how oft shalt thou complain
Of a sweet & subtle Pain.
Of intolerable Joyes;
Of a Death, in which who dyes
Loves his death, and dyes again.
And would for ever so be slain.
And lives, & dyes; and knowes not why
To live, But that he thus may never leave to Dy.

How kindly will thy gentle Heart
Kisse the swee[t]ly-killing Dart!
And close in his embraces keep
Those delicious Wounds, that weep
Balsom to heal themselves with. Thus
When These thy Deaths, so numerous,
Shall all at last dy into one,
And melt thy Soul's sweet mansion;
Like a soft lump of incense, hasted
By too hott a fire, & wasted

RICHARD CRASHAW

Into perfuming clouds, so fast
Shalt thou exhale to Heavn at last
In a resolving SIGH, and then
O what? Ask not the Tongues of men.
Angells cannot tell, suffice,
Thy selfe shall feel thine own full joyes
And hold them fast for ever there
So soon as you first appear,
The MOON of maiden starrs, thy white
MISTRESSE, attended by such bright
Soules as thy shining self, shall come
And in her first rankes make thee room;
Where 'mongst her snowy family
Immortall well comes wait for thee.
    O what delight, when reveal'd LI[FE] shall stand
And teach thy lipps heav'n with his hand;
On which thou now maist to thy wishes
Heap up thy consecrated kisses.
What joyes shall seize thy soul, when she
Bending her blessed eyes on thee
(Those second Smiles of Heav'n) shall dart
Her mild rayes through thy melting heart!
    Angels, thy old freinds, there shall greet thee
Glad at their own home now to meet thee.
    All thy good WORKES which went before
And waited for thee, at the door,
Shall own thee there; and all in one
Weave a constellation
Of CROWNS, with which the KING thy spouse
Shall build up thy triumphant browes.
    All thy old woes shall now smile on thee
And thy paines sitt bright upon thee
All thy SUFFRINGS be divine.
TEARES shall take comfort, & turn gemms
And WRONGS repent to Diademms.
Ev'n thy Death shall live; & new
Dresse the soul that erst they slew.
Thy wounds shall blush to such bright scarres
As keep account of the LAMB's warres.
    Those rare WORKES where thou shalt leave writt.

CARMEN DEO NOSTRO

Love's noble history, with witt
Taught thee by none but him, while here
They feed our soules, shall cloth THINE there.
Each heavnly word by whose hid flame
Our hard Hearts shall strike fire, the same
Shall flourish on thy browes, & be
Both fire to us & flame to thee;
Whose light shall live bright in thy FACE
By glory, in our hearts by grace.
   Thou shalt look round about, & see
Thousands of crown'd Soules throng to be
Themselves thy crown. Sons of thy vowes
The virgin-births with which thy soveraign spouse
Made fruitfull thy fair soul, goe now
And with them all about thee bow
To Him, put on (hee'l say) put on
(My rosy love) That thy rich zone
Sparkling with the sacred flames
Of thousand soules, whose happy names
Heav'n keep upon thy score. (Thy bright
Life brought them first to kisse the light
That kindled them to starrs.) and so
Thou with the LAMB, thy lord, shalt goe;
And whereso'ere he setts his white
Stepps, walk with HIM those wayes of light
Which who in death would live to see,
Must learn in life to dy like thee.

RICHARD CRASHAW

AN

APOLOGIE

FOR

THE FORE-GOING HYM[NE]

as having been writt when the author was yet among the
protestantes.

THus have I back again to thy bright name
(Fair floud of holy fires!) transfus'd the flame
I took from reading thee, tis to thy wrong
I know, that in my weak & worthlesse song
Thou here art sett to shine where thy full day
Scarse dawnes. O pardon if I dare to say
Thine own dear bookes are guilty. For from thence
I learn't to know that love is eloquence.
That hopefull maxime gave me hart to try
If, what to other tongues is tun'd so high,
Thy praise might not speak English too; forbid
(By all thy mysteryes that here ly hidde)
Forbid it, mighty Love! let no fond Hate
Of names & wordes, so farr præjudicate.
Souls are not SPANIARDS too, one freindly floud
Of BAPTISM blends them all into a blood.
CHRIST's faith makes but one body of all soules
A[n]d love's that body's soul, no law controwlls
Our free traffique for heav'n we may maintaine
Peace, sure, with piety, though it come from SPAIN.
What soul so e're, in any language, can
Speak heav'n like her's is my souls country-man.

272

CARMEN DEO NOSTRO

O 'tis not spanish, but 'tis heav'n she speaks !
'Tis heav'n that lyes in ambush there, & breaks
From thence into the wondring reader's brest;
Who feels his warm HEART into a nest
Of little EAGLES & young loves, whose high
Flights scorn the lazy dust, & things that dy.
  There are now, whose draughts (as deep as hell)
Drink up al SPAIN in sack. Let my soul swell
With thee, strong wine of love! let others swimme
In puddles; we will pledge this SERAPHIM
Bowles full of richer blood then blush of grape
Was ever guilty of, Change we too 'our shape
(My soul,) Some drink from men to beasts, o then
Drink we till we prove more, not lesse, then men,
And turn not beasts, but Angels. Let the king
Me ever into these his cellars bring
Where flowes such wine as we can have of none
But HIM who trod the wine-presse all alone.
Wine of youth, life, & the sweet Deaths of love;
Wine of immortall mixture; which can prove
It's Tincture from the rosy nectar; wine
That can exalt weak EARTH; & so refine
Our dust, that at one draught, mortality
May drink it self up, and forget to dy.

RICHARD CRASHAW

THE

FLAMING HEART

UPON THE BOOK AND

Picture of the seraphicall saint

TERESA,

(AS SHE IS USUALLY EX-

pressed with a SERAPHIM

b[e]side her.)

WEll meaning readers! you that come as freinds
And catch the pretious name this peice pretends;
Make not too much hast to' admire
That fair-cheek't fallacy of fire.
That is a SERAPHIM, they say
And this the great TERESIA.
Readers, be rul'd by me; & make
Here a well-plac't & wise mistake
You must transpose the picture quite,
And spell it wrong to read it right;
Read HIM for her, & her for him;
And call the SAINT the SERAPHIM.
    Painter, what didst thou understand
To put her dart into his hand!
See, even the yeares & size of him
Showes this the mother SERAPHIM.
This is the mistresse flame; & duteous he
Her happy fire-works, here, comes down to see.
O most poor-spirited of men!
Had thy cold Pencil kist her PEN

CARMEN DEO NOSTRO

Thou couldst not so unkindly err
To show us This faint shade for HER.
Why man, this speakes pure mortall frame;
And mockes with female FROST love's manly flame.
One would suspect thou meant'st to print
Some weak, inferiour, woman saint.
But had thy pale-fac't purple took
Fire from the burning cheeks of that bright Booke
Thou wouldst on her have heap't up all
That could be found SERAPHICALL;
What e're this youth of fire weares fair,
Rosy fingers, radiant hair,
Glowing cheek, & glistering wings,
All those fair & flagrant things,
But before all, that fiery DART
Had fill'd the Hand of this great HEART.
  Doe then as equall right requires,
Since HIS the blushes be, & her's the fires,
Resume & rectify thy rude design;
Undresse thy Seraphim into MINE.
Redeem this injury of thy art;
Give HIM the vail, give her the dart.
  Give Him the vail; that he may cover
The Red cheeks of a rivall'd lover.
Asham'd that our world, now, can show
Nests of new Seraphims here below.
  Give her the DART for it is she
(Fair youth) shootes both thy shaft & THEE
Say, all ye wise & well-peirc't hearts
That live & dy amidst her darts,
What is't your tastfull spirits doe prove
In that rare life of Her, and love?
Say & bear wittnes. Sends she not
A SERAPHIM at every shott?
What magazins of immortall ARMES there shine!
Heavn's great artillery in each love-spun line.
Give then the dart to her who gives the flame;
Give him the veil, who gives the shame.
  But if it be the frequent fate
Of worst faults to be fortunate;

RICHARD CRASHAW

If all's præscription; & proud wrong
Hearkens not to an humble song;
For all the gallantry of him,
Give me the suff[r]ing SERAPHIM.
His be the bravery of all those Bright things,
The glowing cheekes, the glistering wings;
The Rosy hand, the radiant DART;
Leave HER alone THE FLAMING HEART.
Leave her that; and thou shalt leave her
Not one loose shaft but love's whole quiver.
For in love's feild was never found
A nobler weapon then a WOUND.
Love's passives are his activ'st part,
The wounded is the wounding heart.
O HEART! the æquall poise of love's both parts
Bigge alike with wound & darts.
Live in these conquering leaves; live all the same;
And walk through all tongues one triumphant FLAME.
Live here, great HEART; & love and dy & kill;
And bleed & wound; and yeild & conquer still.
Let this immortall life wherere it comes
Walk in a crowd of loves & MARTYRDOMES.
Let mystick DEATHS wait on't; & wise soules be
The love-slain wittnesses of this life of thee.
O sweet incendiary! shew here thy art,
Upon this carcasse of a hard, cold, hart,
Let all thy scatter'd shafts of light, that play
Among the leaves of thy larg Books of day,
Combin'd against this BREST at once break in
And take away from me my self & sin,
This gratious Robbery shall thy bounty be;
And my best fortunes such fair spoiles of me.
O thou undanted daughter of desires!
By all thy dowr of LIGHTS & FIRES;
By all the eagle in thee, all the dove;
By all thy lives & deaths of love;
By thy larg draughts of intellectuall day,
And by thy th[ir]sts of love more large then they;
By all thy brim-fill'd Bowles of feirce desire
By thy last Morning's draught of liquid fire;

CARMEN DEO NOSTRO

By the full kingdome of that finall kisse
That seiz'd thy parting Soul, & seal'd thee his;
By all the heav'ns thou hast in him
(Fair sister of the SERAPHIM!)
By all of HIM we have in THEE;
Leave nothing of my SELF in me.
Let me so read thy life, that I
Unto all life of mine may dy.

A SONG.

Lord, when the sense of thy sweet g[r]ace
 Sends up my soul to seek thy face.
Thy blessed eyes breed such desire,
I dy in love's delicious Fire.
O love, I am thy SACRIFICE.
Be still triumphant, blessed eyes.
Still shine on me, fair suns! that I
Still may behold, though still I dy.
   Second part.
 Though still I dy, I live again;
Still longing so to be still slain,
So gainfull is such losse of breath.
I dy even in desire of death.
 Still live in me this loving strife
Of living DEATH & dying LIFE.
For while thou sweetly slayest me
Dead to my selfe, I live in Thee.

RICHARD CRASHAW

PRAYER.

AN ODE, WHICH WAS
Præfixed to a little Práyer-book
giv[e]n to a young

GENTLE-WOMAN.

L O here a little volume, but great Book!
    A nest of new-born sweets;
    Whose native fires disdaining
    To ly thus folded, & complaining
    Of these ignoble sheets,
    Affect more comly bands
    (Fair one) from the kind hands
    And confidently look
    To find the rest
Of a rich binding in your BREST.
It is, in one choise handfull, heavenn; & all
Heavn's Royall host; incamp't thus small
To prove that true schooles use to tell,
Ten thousand Angels in one point can dwell.
It is love's great artillery
Which here contracts i[t] self, & comes to ly
Close couch't in their white bosom : & from thence
As from a snowy fortresse of defence,
Against their ghostly foes to take their part,
And fortify the hold of their chast heart.
It is an armory of light
Let constant use but keep it bright,
    You'l find it yeilds
To holy hands & humble hearts
    More swords & sheilds
Then sin hath snares, or Hell hath darts.
    Only be sure
    The hands be pure

CARMEN DEO NOSTRO

That hold these weapons; & the eyes
Those of turtles, chast & true;
  Wakefull & wise;
Here is a freind shall fight for you,
Hold but this book before their heart;
Let prayer alone to play his part,
   But ô the heart
   That studyes this high ART
   Must be a sure house-keeper;
   And yet no sleeper.
   Dear soul, be strong.
   MERCY will come e're long
And bring his besom fraught with blessings,
Flowers of never fading graces
To make immortall dressings
For worthy soules, whose wise embraces
Store up themselves for HIM, who is alone
The SPOUSE of Virgins & the Virgin's son.
But if the noble BRIDEGROOM, when he come,
Shall find the loytering HEART from home;
   Leaving her chast abroad
   To gadde abroad
Among the gay mates of the god of flyes;
To take her pleasure & to play
And keep the devill's holyday;
To dance th'sunshine of some smiling
   But beguiling
Spheares of sweet & sugred Lyes,
   Some slippery Pair
Of false, perhaps as fair,
Flattering but forswearing eyes;
Doubtlesse some other heart
   Will gett the start
Mean while, & stepping in before
Will take possession of that sacred store
Of hidden sweets & holy joyes.
WORDS which are not heard with EARES
(Those tumultuous shops of noise)
Effectuall wispers, whose still voice
The soul it selfe more feeles then heares;

RICHARD CRASHAW

Amorous languishments; luminous trances;
SIGHTS which are not seen with eyes;
Spirituall & soul-peircing glances
Whose pure & subtil lightning flyes
Home to the heart, & setts the house on fire
And melts it down in sweet desire:
      Yet does not stay
To ask the windows leave to passe that way;
Delicious DEATHS; soft exalations
Of soul; dear & divine annihilations;
      A thousand unknown rites
Of joyes & rarefy'd delights;
A hundred thousand goods, glories, & graces,
      And many a mystick thing
      Which the divine embraces
Of the deare spouse of spirits with them will bring
      For which it is no shame
That dull mortality must not know a name.
      Of all this store
Of blessings & ten thousand more
      (If when he come
      He find the Heart from home)
      Doubtlesse he will unload
      Himself some other where,
      And poure abroad
      His pretious sweets
On the fair soul whom first he meets.
O fair, ô fortunate! O riche, ô dear!
O happy & thrice happy she
      Selected dove
      Who ere she be,
      Whose early love
      With winged vowes
Makes hast to meet her morning spouse
And close with his immortall kisses.
Happy indeed, who never misses
To improve that pretious hour,
      And every day
      Seize her sweet prey
All fresh & fragrant as he rises

CARMEN DEO NOSTRO

Dropping with a baulmy Showr
A delicious dew of spices;
O let the blissfull heart hold fast
Her heavnly arm-full, she shall tast
At once ten thousand paradises;
       She shall have power
         To rifle & deflour
The rich & roseall spring of those rare sweets
Which with a swelling bosome there she meets
       Boundles & infinite
       Bottomles treasures
Of pure inebriating pleasures.
Happy proof! she shal discover
       What joy, what blisse,
How many Heav'ns at once it is
To have her GOD become her LOVER.

RICHARD CRASHAW

TO
THE SAME PARTY
COUNCEL
CONCERNING HER.
CHOISE.

Dear, heavn-designed Soul!
  Amongst the rest
Of suters that beseige your Maiden brest,
   Why m[a]y not I
   My fortune try
And venture to speak one good word
Not for my self alas, but for my dearer Lord?
You'ave seen allready, in this lower sphear
Of froth & bubbles, what to look for here.
Say, gentle soul, what can you find
   But painted shapes,
   Peacocks & Apes,
   Illustrious flyes,
Guilded dunghills, glorious Lyes,
   Goodly surmises
   And deep disguises,
Oathes of water, words of wind?
Truth biddes me say, 'tis time you cease to trust
Your soul to any son of dust.
'Tis time you listen to a braver love,
   Which from above
   Calls you up higher
   And biddes you come
   And choose your roome
Among his own fair sonnes of fire,
   Where you among
   The golden throng
That watches at his palace doores
   May passe along

282

CARMEN DEO NOSTRO

And follow those fair starres of yours;
Starrs much too fair & pure to wait upon
The false smiles of a sublunary sun.
Sweet, let me prophesy that at last t'will prove
      Your wary love
Layes up his purer & more pretious vowes,
And meanes them for a farre more worthy SPOUSE
Then this world of Lyes can give ye
Ev'n for Him with whom nor cost,
Nor love, nor labour can be lost;
Him who never will deceive ye.
Let not my lord, the Mighty lover
Of soules, disdain that I discover
      The hidden art
Of his high stratagem to win your heart,
      It was his heavnly art
      Kindly to crosse you
      In your mistaken love,
      That, at the next remove
      Thence he might tosse you
      And strike your troubled heart
Home to himself; to hide it in his brest
      The bright ambrosiall nest,
Of love, of life, & everlasting rest.
      Happy Mystake!
      That thus shall wake
Your wise soul, never to be wonne
Now with a love below the sun.
Your first choyce failes, ô when you choose agen
May it not be amongst the sonnes of Men.

RICHARD CRASHAW

ALEXIAS.

THE

COMPLAINT

OF

THE FORSAKEN WIFE

OF SANITE ALEXIS.

THE FIRST ELEGIE.

I Late the roman youth's lov'd prayse & pride,
  Whom long none could obtain, though thousands try'd,
Lo here am left (alas), For my lost mate
T'embrace my teares, & kisse an unkind FATE.
Sure in my early woes starres were at strife,
And try'd to make a WIDOW ere a WIFE.
Nor can I tell (and this new teares doth breed)
In what strange path my lord's fair footsteppes bleed.
O knew I where he wander'd, I should see
Some solace in my sorrow's certainty
I'd send my woes in words should weep for me.
(Who knowes how powrfull well-writt praires would be?)
Sending's too slow a word, my selfe would fly.
Who knowes my own heart's woes so well as I?
But how shall I steal hence? ALEXIS thou
Ah thou thy self, alas, hast taught me how.
Love too, that leads the, would lend the wings
To bear me harmlesse through the hardest things.
And where love lends the wing, & leads the way,
What dangers can there be dare say me nay?
If I be shipwrack't Love shall teach to swimme.
If drown'd; sweet is the death indur'd for HIM,
The noted sea shall change his name with me;
I, 'mongst the blest STARRES a new name shall be.

284

CARMEN DEO NOSTRO

And sure where lovers make their watry graves
The weeping mariner will augment the waves.
For who so hard, but passing by that way
Will take acquaintance of my woes, & say
Here't was the roman MAID found a hard fate
While through the world she sought her wandring mate.
Here perish't she, poor heart, heavns, be my vowes
As true to me, as she was to her spouse.
O live, so rare a love! live! & in thee
The too frail life of femal constancy.
Farewell; & shine, fair soul, shine there above
Firm in thy crown, as here fast in thy love.
There thy lost fugitive thou'hast found at last.
Be happy; and for ever hold him fast.

RICHARD CRASHAW

THE

SECONDE ELEGIE.

THough All the joyes I had fleed hence with Thee,
Unkind! yet are my TEARES still true to me.
I'am wedded ore again since thou art gone;
Nor couldst thou, cruell, leave me quite alone.
ALEXIS' widdow now is sorrow's wife.
With him shall I weep out my weary life.
Wellcome, my sad sweet Mate! Now have I gott
At last a constant love that leaves me not.
Firm he, as thou art false, Nor need my cryes
Thus vex the earth & teare the skyes.
For him, alas, n'ere shall I need to be
Troublesom to the world, thus, as for thee.
For thee I talk to trees; with silent groves
Expostulate my woes & much-wrong'd loves.
Hills & relentlesse rockes, or if there be
Things that in hardnesse more allude to thee;
To these I talk in teares, & tell my pain;
And answer too for them in teares again.
How oft have I wept out the weary sun!
My watry hour-glasse hath old time outrunne.
O I am learned grown, Poor love & I
Have study'd over all astrology.
I'am perfect in heavn's state, with every starr
My skillfull greife is grown familiar.
Rise, fairest of those fires; whate're thou be
Whose rosy beam shall point my sun to me.
Such as the sacred light that erst did bring
The EASTERN princes to their infant king.
O rise, pure lamp! & lend thy golden ray
That weary love at last may find his way.

286

CARMEN DEO NOSTRO

THE

THIRD ELEGIE.

Rich, churlish Land! that hid'st so long in thee,
  My treasures, rich, alas, by robbing mee.
Needs must my miseryes owe that man a spite
Who e're he be was the first wandring knight.
O had he nere been at that cruell [c]ost
Nature's virginity had nere been lost.
Seas had not bin rebuk't by sawcy oares
But ly'n lock't up safe in their sacred shores.
Men had not spurn'd at mountaines; nor made warrs
With rocks; nor bold hands struck the world's strong barres.
Nor lost in too larg bounds, our little Rome
Full sweetly with it selfe had dwell't at home.
My poor Alexis, then in peacefull life,
Had under some low roofe lov'd his plain wife
But now, ah me, from where he has no foes
He flyes; & into willfull exile goes.
Cruell return. Or tell the reason why
Thy dearest parents have deserv'd to dy.
And I, what is my crime I cannot tell,
Unlesse it be a crime to'have lov'd too well.
If Heates of holyer love & high desire
Make bigge thy fair brest with immortall fire,
What needes my virgin lord fly thus from me,
Who only wish his virgin wife to be?
Wittnesse, chast heavns! no happyer vowes I know
Then to a virgin Grave untouch't to goe.
Love's truest Knott by venus is not ty'd;
Nor doe embraces onely make a bride.
The Queen of angels, (and men chast as You)
Was Maiden Wife & Maiden Mother too.
Cecilia, Glory of her name & blood
With happy gain her maiden vowes made good.
The lusty bridegroom made approach: young man
Take heed (said she) take heed, Valerian!

287

RICHARD CRASHAW

My bosome's guard, a SPIRIT great & strong,
Stands arm'd, to sheild me from all wanton wrong.
My Chastity is sacred; & my sleep
Wakefull, her dear vowes undefil'd to keep.
PALLAS beares armes, forsooth, and should there be
No fortresse built for true VIRGINITY?
No gaping gorgon, this. None, like the rest
Of your learn'd lyes. Here you'l find no such jest.
I'am yours, O were my GOD, my CHRIST. so too,
I'd know no name of love on earth but you.
He yeilds, and straight Baptis'd, obtains the grace
To gaze on the fair souldier's glorious face.
Both mixt at last their blood in one rich bed
Of rosy MARTYRDOME, twice Married.
O burn our hymen bright in such high 'Flame.
Thy torch, terrestriall love, have here no name.
How sweet the mutuall yoke of man & wife,
When holy fires maintain love's Heavnly life!
But I, (so help me heavn my hopes to see)
When thousand sought my love, lov'd none but Thee.
Still, as their vain teares my firm vowes did try,
ALEXIS, he alone is mine (said I)
Half true, alas, half false, proves that poor line.
ALEXIS is alone; But is not mine.

CARMEN DEO NOSTRO

DESCRIPTION

OF

A RELIGIOUS HOUSE

AND CONDITION

OF LIFE

(OUT OF BARCLAY.)

NO roofes of gold o're riotous tables shining
Whole dayes & suns devour'd with endlesse dining;
No sailes of tyrian sylk proud pavements sweeping;
Nor ivory couches costlyer slumbers keeping;
False lights of flairing gemmes; tumultuous joyes;
Halls full of flattering men & fris[k]ing boyes;
Whate're false showes of short & slippery good
Mix the mad sons of men in mutuall blood.
But WALKES & unshorn woods; and soules, just so
Unforc't & genuine; but not shady tho.
Our lodgings hard & homely as our fare.
That chast & cheap, as the few clothes we weare.
Those, course & negligent, As the naturall lockes
Of these loose groves, rough as th'unpolish't rockes.
A hasty Portion of præscribed sleep;
Obedient slumbers; that can wake & weep,
And sing, [&] sigh, & work, and sleep again;
Still rowling à round spear of still-returning pain.
Hands full of harty labours; doe much, that more they may,
And work for work, not wages; let to morrow's
New drops, wash off the sweat of this daye's sorrows.
A long & dayly-d[y]ing life, which breaths
A respiration of reviving deaths.
But neither are there those ignoble stings
That nip the bosome of the world's best things,

RICHARD CRASHAW

And lash Earth-laboring souls.
No cruell guard of diligent cares, that keep
Crown'd woes awake; as things too wise for sleep.
But reverent discipline, & religious fear,
And soft obedience, find sweet biding here;
Silence, & sacred rest; peace, & pure joyes;
Kind loves keep house, ly close, make no noise,
And room enough for Monarchs, while none swells
Beyond the kingdomes of contentfull Cells.
The self-remembring SOUL sweetly recovers
Her kindred with the starrs; not basely hovers
Below; But meditates her immortall way
Home to the originall sourse of LIGHT & intellectuall Day.

CARMEN DEO NOSTRO

AN

EPITAPH

UPON

A YOUNG MARRIED COUPLE

DEAD AND BURYED

TOGETHER.

TO these, whom DEATH again did wed,
This GRAVE's their second Marriage-bed;
For though the hand of fate could force
'Twixt SOUL & BODY à Divorce,
It could not sunder man & WI[F]E,
'Cause They Both lived but one life.
Peace, good Reader. Doe not weep.
Peace, The Lovers are asleep.
They, sweet Turtles, folded ly
In the last knott love could ty.
And though they ly as they were dead,
Their Pillow stone, their sheetes of lead,
(Pillow hard, & sheetes not warm)
Love made the bed; They'l take no harm
Let them sleep: let them sleep on.
Till this stormy night be gone,
Till the 'Æternall morrow dawn;
Then the curtaines will be drawn
'And they wake into a light.
Whose day shall never dy in Night.

RICHARD CRASHAW

DEATH'S LECTURE
AND THE
FUNERAL
OF
A YOUNG GENTLEMAN,

DEar Reliques of a dislodg'd Soul, whose lack
Makes many a mourning paper put on black!
O stay a while, ere thou draw in thy head
And wind thy self up close in thy cold bed.
Stay but à little while, untill I call
A summons worthy of thy funerall.
Come then, Youth, Beauty, & blood!
      All the soft powres.
Whose sylken flatteryes swell a few fond howres
Into a false æternity. Come man;
Hyperbolized Nothing! know thy span;
Take thine own measure here down, down, & bow
Before thy self in thine idæa; thou
Huge emptynes! contraƈt thy self; & shrinke
All thy Wild circle to a Point. O sink
Lower & lower yet; till thy leane size
Call heavn to look on thee with n[a]rrow eyes.
Lesser & lesser yet; till thou begin
To show a face, fitt to confesse thy Kin,
Thy neig[h]bourhood to Nothing.
Proud lookes, & lofty eyliddes, here putt on
Your selves in your unfaign'd reflexion,
Here, gallant ladyes! this unpartiall glasse
(Though you be painted) showes you your true face.
These death-seal'd lippes are they dare give the ly
To the lowd Boasts of poor Mortality.
These curtain'd windows, this retired eye
Outstares the liddes of larg-look't tyranny.
This posture is the brave one this that lyes
Thus low, stands up (me thinkes,) thus & defies
The world. All-daring dust & ashes! only you
Of all interpreters read Nature True.

TEMPERANCE.

OF THE

CHEAP PHYSITIAN

UPON

THE TRANSLATION OF

LESSIUS.

Goe now; and with some daring drugg
Bait thy disease. And whilst they tugge,
Thou to maintain their pretious strife
Spend the dear treasures of thy life.
Goe, take physick Doat upon
Some big-nam'd composition.
Th'Oraculous Doctor's mystick bills;
Certain hard Words made into pills,
And what at last shalt' gain by these?
Only a costlyer disease.
That which makes us have no need
Of physick, that's Physick indeed.
Hark hither, Reader! wilt thou see
Nature her own physitian be?
Wilt' see a man, all his own wealth,
His own musick, his own health;
A man whose sober soul can tell
How to wear her garments well.
Her garments, that upon her sitt
As garments should doe, close & fitt;
A well-cloth'd soul; that's not opp[r]est
Nor choak't with what she should be drest.
A soul sheath'd in a christall shrine;
Through which all her bright features shine;
As when a peice of wanton lawn
A thinne, aeriall veil, is drawn

RICHARD CRASHAW

Or'e beauty's face seeming to hide
More sweetly showes the blushing bride.
A soul, whose intellectuall beames
No mists doe mask, no lazy steames.
A happy soul, that all the way,
To HEAVN rides in a summer's day.
Wouldst' see a man, whose well-warm'd blood
Bathes him in a genuine flood!
A man, whose tuned humors be
A seat of rarest harmony?
Wouldst' see blith lookes, fresh cheekes beguil
Age? wouldst see december smile?
Wouldst' see nests of new roses grow
In a bed [o]f re[v]erend snow?
Warm thoughts, free spirits flattering
Winter's selfe into a S[P]RING.
In summe, wouldst see a man that can
Live to be old, and still a man?
Whose latest & most leaden houres
Fall with soft wings, stuck with soft flowres;
And when life's sweet fable ends,
Soul & body part like freinds;
No quarrells, murmurs, no delay;
A KISSE, a SIGH, and so away.
This rare one, reader, wouldst thou see?
Hark hither; and thy self be HE.

CARMEN DEO NOSTRO

H O P E.

HOpe whose weak beeing ruin'd is
  Alike if it succeed or if it misse!
Whom ill or good does equally confound
And both the hornes of fate's dilemma wound.
     Vain shadow; that dost vanish quite
     Both at full noon & perfect night!
The starres have not a possibility
    Of blessing Thee.
If thinges then from their end we happy call,
'Tis hope is the most hopelesse thing of all.
  Hope, thou bold Taster of delight!
Who in stead of doing so, devourst it quite.
Thou bringst us an estate, yet leav'st us poor
By clogging it with legacyes before.
     The joyes which we intire should wed
     Come deflour'd-virgins to our bed.
Good fortunes without gain imported be
    Such mighty custom's paid to Thee.
For joy like wine kep't close, does better tast;
If it take air before his spirits wast.
  Hope fortun's cheating lottery
Where for one prize, an hundred blankes there be.
Fond archer, hope. Who tak'st thine aime so farr
That still or short or wide thine arrowes are;
     Thinne empty cloud which th-ey deceives
     With shapes that our own fancy gives.
A cloud which gilt & painted now appeares
     But must drop presently in teares
When thy false beames o're reason's light prevail,
By IGNES FATUI for north starres we sail.
  Brother of fear more gayly clad.
The merryer fool oth two, yet quite as mad.
Sire of repen[t]ance, child of fond desire
That blow'st the chymick & the lover's fire.

295

RICHARD CRASHAW

Still leading them insensibly'on
With the strong witchcraft of Anon.
By thee the one does changing nature through
Her endlesse labyrinth's pursue,
And th'other chases woman ; while she goes
More wayes & turnes then hunted nature knowes.

M. COWLEY.

CARMEN DEO NOSTRO

M. CRASHAWS

ANSWER

FOR HOPE.

Ear hope! earth's dowry, & heavn's debt!
The entity of those that are not yet.
Subtlest, but surest beeing! Thou by whom
Our nothing has a definition!
    Substantiall shade! whose sweet allay
    Blends both the noones of night & day.
Fates cannot find out a capacity
    Of hurting thee.
From Thee their lean dilemma, with blunt horn,
Shrinkes, as the sick moon from the wholsome morn.
    Rich hope! love's legacy, under lock
Of faith! still spending, & still growing stock!
Our crown-land lyes above yet each meal brings
A seemly portion for the sonnes of kings.
    Nor will the virgin joyes we wed
    Come lesse unbroken to our bed,
Because that from the bridall c[h]eek of blisse
    Thou steal'st us down a distant kisse.
Hope's chast stealth harmes no more joye's maidenhead
Then spousall rites prejudge the marriage bed.
  Fair hope! our earlyer heav'n by thee
Young time is taster to eternity.
Thy generous wine with age growes strong, not sowre.
Nor does it kill thy fruit, to smell thy flowre.
    Thy golden, growing, head never hangs down
    Till in the lappe of loves full noone
It falls; and dyes! o no, it melts away
    As does the dawn into the day.
As lumpes of sugar loose themselves; and twine
Their supple essence with the soul of wine.

RICHARD CRASHAW

Fortune? alas, above the world's low warres
Hope walks; & kickes the curld heads of conspiring starres.
Her keel cutts not the waves where These winds stirr,
Fortune's whole lottery is one blank to her.
    Sweet hope! kind cheat! fair fallacy by thee
    We are not WHERE nor What we be,
But WHAT & WHERE we would be. Thus art thou
Our absent PRESENCE, and our future Now.
Faith's sister! nurse of fair desire!
Fear's anti[dot]e! a wise & well-stay'd fire!
Temper twixt chill despair, & torrid joy!
Queen Regent in yonge love's minority!
    Though the vext chymick vainly chases
    His fugitive gold through all her faces;
Though love's more feirce, more fruitlesse, fires assay
    One face more fugitive then all they;
True hope's a glorious hunter & her chase,
The GOD of nature in the feilds of grace.

VIVE JESU.

298

Richardi Crashawi

POEMATA

ET

EPIGRAMMATA,

Quæ scripsit Latina & Græca,

Dum *Aulæ Pemb*. Alumnus fuit,

Et

Collegii *Petrensis* Socius.

Editio Secunda, Auctior & emendatior.

Εἴνεκεν εὐμαθίης πινυτόφρονος, ἥν ὁ Μελιχρὸς
Ἤσκησεν, Μουσῶν ἄμμιγα καὶ Χαρίτων.   'Ανθολ.

CANTABRIGIÆ,

Ex Officina *Joan. Hayes*, Celeberrimæ Academiæ
Typographi. 1 6 7 o.

Luc. 18.

Pharisæus & Publicanus.

Ἄνδρες, ἰδοὺ, (ἑτέροισι νόοις) δύω ἱρον ἐσῆλθον·
Τήλοθεν ὀῤῥωδεῖ κεῖνος ὁ φρικαλέος,

Ἀλλ' ὁ μὲν ὡς σοβαρὸς νηοῦ μυχὸν ἐγγὺς ἱκάνει·
Πλεῖον ὁ μὲν νηοῦ, πλεῖον ὁ δ' εἶχε θεοῦ.

Marc. 12. 44.

Obolum viduæ.

Κερματίοιο βραχεῖα ῥάνις, βιότοιο τ' ἀφαυρῆς
Ἕρκος, ἀποστάζει χειρὸς ἀπὸ τρομέρας.

Τοῖς δὲ ἀνασκιρτᾷ πολὺς ἀφρὸς ἀναίδεος ὄλβου·
Οἱ μὲν ἀπόῤῥιπτον· κεῖνα δέδωκε μόνον.

Matth. 28.

Ecce locus ubi jacuit Dominus.

Φαίδιμε, μοὶ αὐτὸν μᾶλλόν μοι δείκνυθι αὐτόν.
Αὐτός μου, δέομαι, αὐτὸς ἔχῃ δάκρυα.

Εἰ δὲ τόπόν μοι δεικνύναι ἅλις ἐστὶ, καὶ εἰπεῖν
Ὧδε τεὸς Μαριὰμ (ἤνιδε) κεῖτο ἄναξ.

Ἀγκοινάς μου δεικνύναι δύναμαι γε, καὶ εἰπεῖν
Ὧδε τεὸς Μαριὰμ (ἤνιδε) κεῖτο ἄναξ.

301

RICHARD CRASHAW

In descensum Spiritûs sanⳓi.

Ὀὐρανοῦ ἐκτύπησε βρόμος· πόλεμον καὶ ἀπειλὰς
Ἦγε τρέχων ἄνεμος σὺν φλογὶ σμιρδαλέῃ.

Αὖεν Ἰουδαῖος. μιαρὰ στυγερῶν τὰ κάρηνα
Ἔφθασε τῆς ὀργῆς τὸ πρέπον οὐρανίης.

Ἀλλὰ γαληναίῳ ὅτε κεῖται ἥσυχον ἄστρῳ
Φλέγμα, καὶ ἀβλήτους λεῖχε φιλὸν πλοκαμούς,

Ἐκθαμβεῖ. ὅτι γὰρ κείνοις οὐκ ἦεν ἀληθής,
Νυνὶ ἐτεὸν διότι τῷδε κεραυνὸς ἔῃ.

In S. Columbam ad Christi caput sedentem.

Πῆ^ ταχυεργὸς ἄγει πτέρυγ' ἀστερόεσσαν ἐρετμός;
Ἦ τινὶ κεῖνα φέρει τὴν πόδα χιονέτην;

Χριστὲ τεῇ κεφαλῇ πάσαις πτερύγεσσιν ἐπείγει·
Πῇ σκιὰ τοι δασιόις παῖζε μάλα πλοκάμοις.

Ποῖά σοι ἀρρήτῳ ψιθυρίσματι κεῖν' ἀγορεύει;
Ἄρρητ', οὐκ ἠχῆς ἴσα μὲν ἀνδρομέης.

Μοῦνα μὲν ἠδ' ὄρνις καλιᾶς ἐσ' ἄξια ταύτης·
Ἄξια δ' ὄρνιθος μοῦνα μὲν ἡ καλιά.

Ad D. Lucam medicum.

Ὀὐδὲν ἐγὼ, Λουκᾶ, παρά σου μοι φάρμακον αἰτῶ,
Κἂν σὺ δ' ἰατρὸς ἔῃς, κἂν μεν ἐγὼ νοσερός.

Ἀλλ' ἐν ὅσῳ παράδειγμα πέλεις μοι πίστιος, αὐτός,
Αὐτὸς ἰατρὸς, ἐμοὶ γ' ἐσσὶ ἀκεστορίη.

302

EPIGRAMMATA SACRA

In stabulum ubi natus est Dominus.

Ἴκος ὅδ' ἐς' αὔλη. οὐ μή. [τ]εὸς οἶκος, Ἰησοῦ,
 Ἐν θ' ᾧ τὺ τίκτῃ αὔλιον οὐ πέλεται.

Οἴκων μὲν πάντων μάλα δὴ κάλλιστος ἐκεῖνος·
 Οὐρανοῦ οὐδὲ τεοῦ μικρότερος πέλεται.

Ἤνιδε κεῖνο νεῷ δῶμ' ἐμπυρίζετο χρύσῳ,
 Ἤνιδε κεῖνο νεοῖς δῶμα ῥόδοισι γελᾷ.

Ἦν ῥόδον οὐχὶ γελᾷ, ἦν οὐδέ τε χρύσον ἐκεῖθεν·
 Ἐκ σου δ' ὀφθαλμῶν ἐστιν ἐλεγχέμεναι.

Μ α τ τ η. 4.

Hic lapis fiat panis.

Ἄρτος ἔην τοι δῆτ' (εἰπεῖν θέμις ἐστὶν) ἐκεῖνος
 Χριστέ τοι ἄρτος ἔην καὶ λίθος· ἀλλὰ τεός.

Ἤ[ν] οὕτως τοῦ πατρὸς ἐῇ μεγάλου τὸ θέλημα
 Ἄρτος ὅτ' οὐκ ἦν τοι, Χριστὲ, τοι ἄρτος ἔην.

In die Ascensionis Dominicæ.

Ντ̓ν ἔτι ἡμέτερον σε, Χριστέ, ἔχομεν τὸν ἔρωτα;
 Οὐρανοῦ οὖν ὅσσον τὸν φθόνον ὡς ἔχομεν·

Ἀλλὰ ἔχωμεν. ἔχει ἐὰ μὲν τὰ δ' ἀγάλματα αἰθήρ·
 Ἄστρατε, καὶ φοῖβον, καὶ καλὰ τῶν νεφέλων.

Ὅσσον ἔην, ἡμῖν ὄφρ' εἴη ἐν τόδε ἄστρον;
 Ἄστρον ἐν ἡμῖν ἤ· εἰσι τοι ἄστρ' ἕκατον.

Πάντα μάτην. ὅτι Χριστὲ συ οὐκ ἀνάβαινες ἐς αὐτὸν,
 Αὐτὸς μὲν κατέβη οὐρανὸς εἰς σε τεός.

RICHARD CRASHAW

Luc. 18.

Cæcus implorat Christum.

IMproba turba tace. Mihi tam mea vota propinquant,
    Et linguam de me vis tacuisse meam?

Tunc ego tunc taceam, mihi cùm meus ille loquetur:
    Si nescis, oculos vox habet ista meos.

O noĉtis miserere meæ, miserere; per illam
    In te quæ primo riserit ore, diem.

O noĉtis miserere meæ, miserere; per illam
    Quæ, nisi te videat, nox velit esse, diem.

O noĉtis miserere meæ, miserere; per illam
    In te quam fidei nox habet ipsa, diem.

Hæc animi tam clara dies rogat illam oculorum:
    Illam, oro, dederis; hanc mihi nè rapias.

ΝΥκτ' ἐλέησον ἐμήν. ἐλέησον. ναί τοι ἐκεῖνο
    Χριστὲ ἐμοῦ ἦμαρ, νὺξ ὅδ' ἐμεῖο ἔχει.

Ὀφθαλμῶν μὲν ἐκεῖνο, Θεὸς, δέεται τόδε γνώμης.
    Μή μοι τοῦτ' αἴρῃς, δός μοι ἐκεῖνο φάος.

304

EPIGRAMMATA SACRA

Luc. 15. 4.

Quis ex vobis si habeat centum oves, & perdiderit
    unam ex illis ----- &c.

O *Ut ego angelicis fiam bona gaudia turmis,*
    Me quoq; sollicito quære per arva gradu.

Mille tibi tutis ludunt in montibus agni,
    Quos potes haud dubiâ dicere voce tuos.

Unus ego erravi quò me meus error agebat,
    Unus ego fuerim gaudia plura tibi.

Gaudia non faciunt, quæ nec fecêre timorem;
    Et plus, quæ donant ipsa peric'la, placent.

Horum, quos retines, fuerit tibi latior usus.
    De me, quem recipis, dulcior usus erit.

Ἐ῀Ις μὲν ἐγὼ, ἦ μου πλάνη περιῆγεν, ἄλημι·
    Ἐις δέ τοι σῶς ἔσομαι γηθοσύναι πλέονες.

Ἀμνὸς ὁ μή ποιῶν φόβον, οὐ ποιεῖ δέ τε χάρμα.
    Μείζων τῶν μὲν, ἐμοῦ χρεία δὲ γλυκυτέρη.

Herodi D. Jacobum obtruncanti.

N *Escis Jacobus quantum hunc tibi debeat iĉtum,*
    Quæq; tua in sacrum sæviit ira caput.

Scilicet ipso illi donâsti hoc ense coronam,
    Quo sacrum abscideras scilicet ense caput.

Abscissum pensare caput quæ possit abundè,
    Sola hæc tam sæva & sacra corona fuit.

Ἐ῀Ν μὲν, Ἰάκωβε, κεφαλὴν τοι ξίφος ἀπῆρεν,
    Ἐν τόδε καὶ στέφανον ξίφος ἔδωκε τεόν.

Μοῦνον ἀμείβεσθαι κεφαλὴν, Ἰάκωβε, δύναιτο
    Κεῖνος ὁδ' ὡς καλὸς μαρτυρίου στέφανος.

RICHARD CRASHAW

MATTH. 20. 34.

Cæci receptis oculis Christum sequuntur.

ECce manu impositâ Christus nova sidera ponit.
    Sectantur patriam sidera fidæ manum.

Hæc manus his, credo, cœlum est. Hæc scilicet astra
    Suspicor esse, olim quæ geret ille *manu.

        * Revel. 1. 16.

ΧΕὶρ ἐπιβαλλομένη Χριστοῦ ἐπίβαλλεν ὀπωπῶν
    Ἄστρα. ὀπηδεύει κεῖνά γε χειρὶ Θεοῦ.

Χεὶρ αὕτη τούτοις πέλεν οὐρανός. ἄστρα γὰρ ὄιμαι,
    Ἐν χερὶ ταῦτ' ὄισει Χριστὸς ἔπειτα ἑῇ.

LUC. 19. 4.

Zachæus in Sycomoro.

QUid te, quid jactas alienis fructibus, arbor?
    Quid tibi cum foliis non (Sycomore) tuis?

Quippe istic ramo qui jam tibi nutat ab alto,
    Mox è divinâ vite racemus erit.

ΤΊπτ' ἐπικομπάζεις κενεόν; ξεινῷ δὲ τε καρπῷ,
    Καὶ φύλλοις σεμνὴ μὴ, συκόμωρε, τεοῖς;

Καί γαρ ὅδ' ἐκκρημνὴς σοῦ νῦν μετέωρος ἀπ' ἔρνους,
    Ἀμπέλου ὁ κλαδὼν ἔσσεται οὐρανίου.

FINIS.

MR CRASHAW'S POËMS

transcrib'd from his own copie, before they were printed; among wch are some not printed.

From ARCHBISHOP SANCROFT'S Copy,
Vol. 465, Tanner MSS,
Bodleian Library, Oxford.

RICHARD CRASHAW

Ps. 1.

O Te te nimis, & nimis beatum!
    Quem non lubricus implicavit error;
Nec risu misero procax tumultus.
Tu cùm grex sacer undiq execrandis
Strident consiliis, nec aure (felix!)
(Felix!) non animo, vel ore mixtus,
Haud intelligis impios susurros.
Sed tu deliciis ferox repôstis
Cultu simplice, sobriâq curâ
Legem numinis usq, & usq volvis.
Læta sic fidas colit arbor undas:
Quem nec immiti violentus aurâ
Seirius frangit, neq contumacis
       Ira, procellæ.
At tu, profane pulvis, & lusus sacer
Cujusvis auræ; fronte quâ tandem feres
Vindex tribunal? quanta tum, & qualis tuæ
Moles procellæ stabit? ô quàm ferreo
Frangêre nutu, præda frontis asperæ,
Sacriq fulminandus ah procul, procul
A luce vultûs, aureis procul à locis,
Ubi longa gremio mulcet æterno pios
Sincera semper pax, & umbrosâ super
Insurgit alâ, vividiq nectaris
Imbres beatos rore perpetuo pluit.
Sic ille sic ô vindice stat vigil,
Et stabit irâ torvus in impios,
    Seseq sub mentes bonorum
    Insinuat facili favore.

Acts 28. 3.

PAule, nihil metuas. non fert hæc vipera virus:
    Virtutem vestræ vult didicisse manûs.
Oscula, non morsus; supplex, non applicat hostis.
    Nec metuenda venit, sed miseranda magis.

FROM SANCROFT MS.

Joh. 6. 14. 26.

JAm credunt. Deus es. (Deus est, qui teste palato,
   Quiĉ, ipso demum est judice dente Deus.)
Scilicet hæc sapiunt miracula : de quibus alvus
   Proficere, & possit pingue latus fluere.
Hæc sua fecisti populo miracula. credunt.
   Gens pia! & in ventrem relligiosa suum!

In lacrymas Christi patientis.

SÆve dolor! potes hoc? oculos quoĉ, perpluis istos?
   O quàm non meritas hæc arat unda genas!
O lacrymas ego flere tuas, ego dignior istud,
   Quod tibi cunĉ, cadit roris, habere meum.
Siccine? me tibi flere tuas? ah, mi bonē Jesu,
   Si possem lacrymas vel mihi flere meas!
Flere meas? immò immò tuas. hoc si modò possem :
   Non possem lacrymas non ego flere meas.
Flere tuas est flere meas. tua lacryma, Christe,
   Est mea. vel lacryma est si tua, causa mea est.

Joh. 19. *In Sepulchrum Domini.*

JAm cedant, veteris cedant miracula saxi,
   Unde novus subitō fluxerat amne latex.
Tu felix rupes, ubi se lux tertia tollet,
   Flammarum sacro fonte superba flues.

Joh. 13. 14. *ubi amorem præcipit.*

SIc magis in numeros, morituraĉ, carmina vivit
   Dulcior extremâ voce caducus olor ;
Ut tu inter strepitus odii, & tua funera, Jesu,
   Totus amor liquido totus amore sonas.

RICHARD CRASHAW

Act. 12. 23.

EUge Deus! (pleno populus fremit undiq; plausu:)
 Certè non hominem vox sonat. euge Deus!
Sed tamen iste Deus qui sit, vos dicite, vermes,
Intima turba illi; vos fovet ille sinu.

Bonum est nobis esse hîc.

CUr cupis hîc adeo, dormitor Petre, manere?
 Somnia non alibi tam bona, Petre, vides.

Mat. 6. 29. *Videte lilia agrorum—nec Solomon &c.*

CAndide rex campi, cui floris eburnea pompa est,
 Deq; nivis fragili vellere longa toga;
Purpureus Solomon impar tibi dicitur. esto.
Nempe (quod est melius) par fuit ille rosis.

Marc. 7. 33. & 36.

VOce, manuq; simul linguæ tu, Christe, ciendæ:
 Sistendæ nudis vocibus usus eras.
Sanè at lingua equus est pronis effusus habenis:
Vox ciet, at sistit non nisi tota manus.

In Beatæ Virginis verecundiam.

NOn est hoc matris, sed (crede) modestia nati,
 Quòd virgo in gremium dejicit ora suum.
Illîc jam Deus est. oculus jam Virginis ergò,
Ut cœlum videat, dejiciendus erit.

Mitto vos, sicut agnos in medio luporum.

HOs quoq;? an hos igitur sævi lacerabitis agnos?
 Hîc saltem, hîc vobis non licet esse lupis.
At sceleris nulla est clementia. at ergò scietis,
Agnus qui nunc est, est aliquando leo.

310

FROM SANCROFT MS.

MAT. 4. *Christus à dæmone vectus.*

ERgò ille, Angelicis ô sarcina dignior alis,
  Præpete sic Stygio sic volet ille vehi?
Pessime! nec lætare tamen. tu scilicet inde
Non minùs es Dæmon, non minùs ille Deus.

JOH. 1. 23.

VOx ego sum, dicis. tu vox es, sancte Johannes?
  Si vox es, sterilis cur tibi mater erat?
Quàm fuit ista tuæ mira infœcundia matris!
In vocem sterilis rarior esse solet.

Vox Joannis; Christus Verbum.

MOnstrat Joannes Christum. haud res mira videtur:
  Vox unus, verbum scilicet alter erat.
Christus Joanne est prior. hæc res mira videtur:
Voce suâ verbum non solet esse prius.

In natales Domini Pastoribus nuntiatos.

AD te sydereis, ad te, Bone Tityre, pennis
  Purpureus juvenis gaudia tanta vehit.
O bene te vigilem, cui gaudia tanta feruntur,
  Ut neq, dum vigilas, te vigilare putes.
Quem sic monstrari voluit pastoribus æther,
  Pastor, an Agnus erat? Pastor, & Agnus erat.
Ipse Deus cùm Pastor erit, quis non erit agnus?
  Quis non pastor erit, cùm Deus Agnus erit?

RICHARD CRASHAW

APOCAL. XII. 7.

ARma, viri! (ætheriam quocunq̃ sub ordine pubem
　　Siderei proceres ducitis) Arma viri!
Quæq̃ suis, (nec queîs solita est) stet dextra sagittis,
　　Stet gladii sævâ luce corusca sui.
Totus adest, totisq̃ movet se major in iris,
　　Fertq̃ Draco, quicquid vel Draco ferre potest.
Quas secum facies (imæ mala pignora noctis)!
　　Quot secum nigros ducit in arma Deos!
Jam pugnas parat (heu sævus!) jam pugnat. & ecce
　　Vix potui, Pugnat, dicere. jam cecidit.
His tamen ah nimium est quòd frontibus addidit iras;
　　Quòd potuit rugas his posuisse genis:
Hoc torvum decus est, tumidiq̃ ferocia fati,
　　Quòd magni sceleris mors quoq̃ magna fuit.
Quòd neq̃, si victus, jaceat victoria vilis:
　　Quòd meruit multi fulminis esse labor.
Quòd queat ille suas hoc inter dicere flammas,
　　Arma tuli frustra: sed tamen arma tuli.

ACT. 17. *In Atheniensem merum.*

IPsos naturæ thalamos sapis, imaq̃ rerum
　　Concilia, & primæ quicquid agunt tenebræ.
Quid dubitet refluum mare. quid vaga sydera volvant.
　　Christus et est studiis res aliena tuis.
Sic scire, est tantùm nescire loquaciùs illa.
　　Qui nempe illa sapit sola, nec illa sapit.

JOH. 14. *Ego vitis vera.*

CRedo quidem. sed & hoc hostis te credidit ipse
　　Caiaphas, & Judas credidit ipse, reor.
Unde illis, Jesu, vitis nisi vera fuisses,
　　Tanta tui potuit sanguinis esse sitis?

Abscessum Christi queruntur discipuli.

ILle abiit. jamq̃ ô quæ nos mala cunq̃ manetis,
　　Sistite jam in nostras tela parata neces.
Sistite. nam quibus hæc vos olim tela paratis,
　　Abscessu Domini jam periêre sui.

FROM SANCROFT MS.

In descensum Spiritûs Sancti.

QUæ vehit auratos nubes dulcissima nimbos?
  Quis mitem pluviam lucidus imber agit?
Agnosco. nostros hæc nubes abstulit ignes:
  Hæc nubes in nos jam redit igne pari.
O nubem gratam, & memorem! quæ noluit ultrà
  Tam sævè de se nos potuisse queri!
O bene! namq̃ alio non posset rore rependi,
  Cælo exhalatum quod modò terra dedit.

Act. x. 39.

QUis malus appendit de mortis stipite vitam?
  O malus Agricola! hoc inseruisse fuit?
Immò quis appendit vitæ hac ex arbore mortem?
  O bonus Agricola! hoc inseruisse fuit.

Joh. 10. *Ego sum ostium.*

JAmq̃ pates. cordisq̃ seram gravis hasta reclusit,
  Et clavi claves undiq̃ te reserant.
Ah, vereor, sibi ne manus impia clauserit illas,
  Quæ cæli has ausa est sic aperire fores.

In spinas demtas è Christi capite cruentatas.

ACcipe (an ignoscis?) de te sata germina, miles.
  Quàm segeti est messis discolor illa suæ!
O quæ tam duro gleba est tam grata colono?
  Inserit hic spinas: reddit & illa rosas.

313

RICHARD CRASHAW

Joh. iii.

NOx erat, & Christum (Doctor malè docte) petebas,
    In Christo tenebras deposituræ tuas.
Ille autem multo dum te bonus irrigat ore,
    Atq, per arcanas ducit in alta vias,
Sol venit, & primo pandit se flore diei,
    Ludit et in dubiis aureus horror aquis.
Sol oritur. sed adhuc, & adhuc tamen (ô bone) nescis.
    Sol oritur. tecum nox tamen est & adhuc.
Non cæli illa fuit; nox fuit illa tua.

In Baptistam Vocem.

TAntum habuit Baptista loqui, tot flumina rerum,
    Ut bene Vox fuerit, prætereaq, nihil.
Ecce autem Verbum est unum tantùm ille loquutus:
    Uno sed Verbo cuncta loquutus erat.

Act. [3. xii.] 6, 7. In D. Petrum ab Angelo solutum.

MOrs tibi, & Herodes instant: cùm nuncius ales
    Gaudia fert, quæ tu somnia ferre putas.
Quid tantum dedit ille (rogo) tibi? Vincula solvit.
    Mors tibi, & Herodes nonne dedisset idem?

Luc. 5. Relictis omnibus sequuti sunt eum.

AD nutum Domini abjecisti retia, Petre.
    Tam bene non unquam jacta fuere priùs.
Scilicet hoc rectè jacere est tua retia, Petre,
    Nimirum, Christus cùm jubet, abjicere.

Joh. i. Agnus Dei, qui tollit peccata mundi.

ERgò tot heu (torvas facies) tot in ora leonum,
    In tot castra lupûm qui meat, Agnus erit?
Hic tot in horribiles, quot sunt mea crimina, pardos?
    Hic tot in audaces ungue, vel ore feras?
Ah melius! pugiles quis enim commiserit istos?
    Quos sua non faciunt arma, vel ira pares.

FROM SANCROFT MS.

MARC. 8. *Pisces multiplicati.*

QUæ secretâ meant taciti tibi retia verbi,
  Queîs non tam pisces, quàm capis Oceanum?

JOH. 13. *Domine, non solum pedes, sed & caput. &c.*

EN caput! atq̃ suis quæ plus satis ora laborant
  Sordibus! huc fluvios [*blurred*] (ais) adde tuos.
Nil opus est. namq̃ hæc (modò tertius occinat ales)
  E fluviis fuerint, Petre, lavanda suis.

JOH. 12. 19. *Cùm tot signa edidisset, non credebant.*

QUantâ amor ille tuus se cunq̃ levaverit alâ,
  Quo tua cunq̃ opere effloruit alta manus;
Mundus adest, contráq̃ tonat. signisq̃ reponit
  Signa. (adeo sua sunt numina vel sceleri.)
Imò (ô nec nimii vis sit temeraria verbi)
  Ille uno sensu vel tua cuncta premit.
Tot, tantisq̃ tuis mirâclum hoc objicit unum,
  Tot tantisq̃ tuis non adhibere fidem.

ACT. 1. *In nubem, quæ Dominum abstulit.*

O Nigra hæc! Quid enim mihi candida pectora monstrat?
  Pectora Cygneîs candidiora genis.
Sit verò magis alba, suo magis aurea Phœbo,
  Quantumcunq̃ sibi candida; nigra mihi est.
Nigra mihi nubes! et quâ neq̃ nigrior Austros,
  Vel tulit irati nuncia tela Dei.
Nigra! licèt nimbos, noctem neq̃ detulit ullam.
  Si noctem non fert, at rapit, ecce, diem.

LUC. 19. *Vidit urbem, & flevit super eam.*

E Rgò meas spernis lacrymas, urbs perfida? Sperne.
  Sperne meas. quas ô sic facis esse tuas.
Tempus erit, lacrymas poterit cùm lacryma demum
  Nostra (nec immeritò) spernere spreta tuas.

315

RICHARD CRASHAW

Luc. 18. *Nec sicut iste Publicanus.*

TU quoq̖ dùm istius miseri peccata fateris,
    Quæ nec is irato mitiùs ungue notat;
Hic satis est gemino bonus in sua crimina telo.
    Interea quid erit, mi Pharisæe, tuis?

Mat. 8.—*& accedentes discipuli excitavérunt eum.*

AH, quis erat furor hos (tam raros) solvere somnos?
    O vos, queîs Christi vel sopor invigilat!
Illum si somnus tenuit, vos somnia terrent,
    Somnia tam vanos ingeminata metus.
Nil Christi nocuit somnus (mihi credite.) Somnus,
    Qui nocuit, vestræ somnus erat fidei.

Mat. 15. *In mulierem Canaanæam cum Dnᵒ decertantem.*

CEdit io. jam, jamq̖ cadet. modò fortiter urge.
    Jam, tua nî desit dextera, jamq̖ cadet.
Nimirum hoc velit ipse. tuo favet ipse triumpho:
    Ipse tuas tacitus res tuus hostis agit.
Quas patitur, facit ille manus. ictu ille sub omni est;
    Atq̖ in te vires sentit, amatq̖ suas,
Usq̖ adeò haud tuus hic ferus est, neq̖ ferreus hostis!
    Usq̖ adeò est miles non truculentus Amor!
Illo quàm facilis victoria surgit ab hoste,
    Qui, tantùm ut vinci possit, in arma venit!

Mat. 9. *Quare comedit Magister vester cum peccatoribus &c.*

SIccine fraternos fastidis, improbe, morbos,
    Cùm tuus, (& gravior) te quoq̖ morbus habet?
Tantum ausus medicum morbus sibi quærere, magnus;
    Tantum ausus medicum spernere, major erat.

FROM SANCROFT MS.

Marc. 1. & Luc. 14. *In* $\begin{Bmatrix} \textit{febricitantem} \\ \textit{&} \\ \textit{hydropicum} \end{Bmatrix}$ *sanatos.*

NUper lecta gravem extinxit pia pagina febrem:
    Hydropi siccos dat modò lecta sinus.
Hæc vice fraternâ quàm se miracula tangunt,
    Atq, per alternum fida juvamen amant!
Quippe ignes istos his quàm bene mersit in undis!
    Ignibus his illas quàm bene vicit aquas!

In S. Lucam Medicum.

HAnc, mihi quam miseram faciunt mea crimina vitam,
    Hanc, medici, longam vestra medela facit.
Hocné diu est vixisse? diu (mihi credite) non est
    Hoc vixisse; diu sed timuisse mori.
Tu foliis, Medice alme, tuis medicamina præbes,
    Et medicaminibus (quæ mala summa) malis.
Hoc mortem bene vitare est; vitare ferendo.
    Et vixisse diu est hoc; citò posse mori.

Tollat crucem suam—&c.

ERgò tuam pone; ut nobis sit sumere nostram:
    Si nostram vis nos sumere, pone tuam.
Illa illa, ingenti quæ te trabe duplicat, illa
    Vel nostra est, nostras vel tulit illa cruces.

In (Joh. 17.) *Cygnæam D^i Jesû cantionem.*

QUæ mella, ô quot, Christe, favos in carmina fundis!
    Dulcis, & (ah furias!) ah moribundus olor!
Parce tamen; minus hæ si sunt mea gaudia voces:
    Voce quidem dulci, sed moriente canis.

Et conspuebant illum.

QUid non tam fœdè sævi maris audeat ira!
    Conspuit ecce oculos (sydera nostra) tuos.
Forsan & hîc aliquis sputo te excæcat, Jesu,
    Qui debet sputo, quòd videt ipse, tuo.

RICHARD CRASHAW

Joh. 4. Rogavit eum, ut descenderet, & sanaret filium suum.

ILle vt eat tecum, in natiq̃, tuiq̃ salutem?
   Qui petis; ah nescis (credo) quòd Ales Amor.
Ille ut eat tecum? quàm se tua vota morantur!
   Ille ut eat? tantò seriùs esset ibi.
Ne tardus veniat, Christus tecum ire recusat:
   Christi nempe ipsum hoc ire moratur iter.
Christi nempe viis perit hoc quodcunq̃ meatur:
   Christi nempe viis vel properare mora est.
Hîc est, cui tu vota facis tua, Christus: at idem
   (Crede mihi) dabit hæc qui rata, Christus ibi est.

Luc. 5. 9. Pavor enim occupaverat eum super
capturam piscium.

DUm nimiùm in captis per te, Petre, piscibus hæres,
   Piscibus (ut video) captus es ipse tuis.
Rem scio. te prædam Christus sibi cepit: & illi
   Una in te ex istis omnibus esca fuit.

Joh. vidérunt, & odérunt me.

VIdit? & odit adhuc? Ah, te non vidit, Jesu.
   Non vidit te, qui vidit, & odit adhuc.
Non vidit, te non vidit (dulcissime rerum)
   In te qui vidit quid, quod amare neget.

Luc. 18. 39.

TU mala turba tace, mihi tam mea vota propinquant,
   Tuq̃ in me linguam vis tacuisse meam?
Tunc ego, tunc taceam, mihi cùm meus Ille loquetur.
   Si nescis, oculos vox habet ista meos.
O noctis miserere meæ. miserere, per illam,
   Quæ tam læta tuo ridet in ore diem.
O noctis miserere meæ. miserere, per illam
   Quæ, nisi te videat, nox velit esse, diem.
O noctis miserere meæ. miserere, per illam,
   Hæc mea quam (fidei) nox habet ipsa, diem.
Illa dies animi (Jesu) rogat hanc oculorum.
   Illam (oro) dederis; hanc mihi ne rapias.

FROM SANCROFT MS.

Mat. 22. *In Pharisæos Christi verbis insidiantes.*

O Quam te miseri ludunt vaga tædia voti,
    Ex ore hoc speras qui, Pharisæe, malum!
Sic quis ab Auroræ noctem speraverit ulnis,
    Unde solet primis Sol tener ire rosis?
Sic Acheronta petas illinc, unde amne corusco
    Lactea sydereos Cynthia lavit equos.
Sic violas aconita roges: sic toxica nympham,
    Garrula quæ vitreo gurgite vexat humum.
Deniq, (ut exemplo res hæc propiore patescat)
    A te sic speret quis (Pharisæe) bonum.

Mat. 9.

F Alleris. & nudum malè ponis (Pictor) Amorem:
    Non nudum facis hunc, cùm sine veste facis.
Nonne hic est (dum sic digito patet ille fideli)
    Tunc, cùm vestitus, tunc quoq, nudus amor?

Tolle oculos, tolle ô tecum (tua sydera) nostros.
    Ah quid enim, quid agant hîc sine sole suo?
Id, quod agant sine sole suo tua sydera, cœlum:
    Id terræ hæc agerent hîc sine sole suo.
Illa suo sine sole suis cæca imbribus essent:
    Cæca suis lacrymis hæc sine sole suo.

Act. 21. *Nam ego non solum vinciri—&c.*

Q Uid mortem objicitis nostro, quid vincla timori?
    Non timor est illinc, non timor inde meus.
Vincula, quæ timeam, sunt vincula sola timoris:
    Sola timenda mihi est mors, timuisse mori.

RICHARD CRASHAW

MAT. 11. *Legatio Baptistæ ad Christum.*

ORo, quis es? legat ista suo Baptista Magistro.
   Illi quæ referant, talia Christus habet.
Cui cæcus cernit, mutus se in verba resolvit,
   It claudus, vivit mortuus; Oro, quis est?

ERgò veni; quicunq ferant tua signa timores:
   Quæ nos cunq vocant tristia, Christe, veni.
Christe, veni. suus avulsum rapiat labor axem,
   Nec sinat implicitas ire redire vias.
Mutuus attonito titubet sub fœdere mundus,
   Nec Natura vagum dissona volvat opus.
Christe, veni. roseos ultrà remeare per ortus
   Nolit, & ambiguos Sol trahat æger equos.
Christe, veni. ipsa suas patiatur Cynthia noctes,
   Plus quàm Thessalico tincta tremore genas.
Astrorum mala cæsaries per inane dolendum
   Gaudeat, horribili flore repexa caput.
Sole sub invito subitæ vis improba noctis
   Corripiat solitam, non sua jura, diem.
Importuna dies, nec Eöi conscia pacti,
   Per desolatæ murmura noctis eat.
Christe, veni. tonet Oceanus pater; & sua nolit
   Claustra. vagi montes sub nova sceptra meent.
Christe, veni. quodcunq audet metus, audeat ultrà.
   Fata id agant, quod agent. tu modò, Christe, veni.
Christe, veni. quàcunq venis mercede malorum.
   Quanti hoc constiterit cunq venire, veni.
Teq, tuosq oculos tanti est potuisse videre!
   Oh tanti est te vel sic potuisse frui!
Quicquid id est, Pater, omne tuo pensabitur ore;
   Quicquid id est, veniat: Tu modò, Christe, veni.

FROM SANCROFT MS.

FElices! properâstis io, properâstis. & altam.
    Vicistis gyro sub breviore viam.
Vos per non magnum vestri mare sanguinis illuc
    Cymba tulit nimiis non operosa notis.;
Quò nos tam lento sub remigio luctantes
    Ducit inexhausti vis malè fida freti.
Nos mora, nos longi consumit inertia lethi.
    In ludum mortis, luxuriemq̃ sumus.
Nos ævo, & senio, & latis permittimur undis.
    Spargimur in casus,—porrigimur furiis.
Nos miseri sumus ex amplo; spatioq̃ perimus.
    In nos inquirunt fata; probantq̃ manus.
Ingenium fati sumus, ambitioq̃ malorum;
    Conatus mortis, consiliumq̃ sumus.
In vitæ multo multæ patet area mortis.

Non vitam nobis numerant, quot viximus, anni:
    Vita brevis nostra est; sit licèt acta diu.
Vivere non longum est, quod longam ducere vitam:
    Res longa vitâ sæpe peracta brevi est.
Nec vos tam vitæ Deus in compendia misit,
    Quàm vetuit vestræ plus licuisse neci.
Accedit vitæ quicquid decerpitur ævo.
    Atq̃ illó breviùs, quò citiùs morimur.

Domitiano. De S. Johanne ad portam Lat.

ERgò ut inultus eas? Sed nec tamen ibis inultus,
    Sic violare ausus meq̃, meosq̃ Deos.
Ure oleo, Lictor. Oleo parat urere Lictor:
    Sed quem uri Lictor credidit, unctus erat.
Te quoq̃ sic olei virtus malefida fefellit?
    Sic tua te Pallas, Domitiane, juvat?

Εἰς τὸν τοῦ Στεφάνου ϛέφανον.

ECce tuos lapides! nihil est pretiosius illis;
    Seu pretium capiti dent, capiantve tuo.
Scilicet hæc ratio vestri diadematis: hoc est,
    Unde coronatis nos decet ire comis.
Quisq̃ lapis quantò magis in se vilis habetur,
    Ditior hôc capiti est gemma futura tuo.

RICHARD CRASHAW

AH ferus, ah culter! qui tam bona lilia primus
    In tam crudeles jussit abire rosas.
Virgineûm hoc qui primus ebur violavit ab ostro;
    Inq̃ sui instituit muricis ingenium.
Scilicet hinc olim quicunq̃ cucurrerit amnis,
    Ex hoc purpurei germine fontis erit.
Scilicet hunc mortis primum puer accipit unguem:
    Inijciunt hodie fata, furorq̃ manus.
Ecce illi sanguis fundi jam cæpit; & ecce,
    Qui fundi possit, vix bene sanguis erat.
Excitat è dolio vix dum bene musta recenti,
    Atq̃ rudes furias in nova membra vocat.
Improbus! ut nimias jam nunc accingitur iras!
    Armaq̃ non molli sollicitanda manu!
Improbus! ut teneras audet jam ludere mortes!
    Et vitæ ad modulum, quid puerile mori!
Improbus! ut tragici impatiens præludia fati
    Ornat, & in socco jam negat ire suo!
Scilicet his pedibus manus hæc meditata cothurnos!
    Hæc cum blanditiis mens meditata minas?
Hæc tam dura brevem decuêre crepundia dextram?
    Dextra Gigantæis hæc satis apta genis?
Sic cunis miscere cruces? cumq̃ ubere matris
    Commisisse neces, & scelus, & furias?
Quo ridet patri, hoc tacite quoq̃ respicit hastam;
    Quoq̃ oculo matrem mulcet, in arma redit.
Dii Superi! furit his oculis! hoc asper in ore est!
    Dat Marti vultus, quos sibi mallet Amor.
Deliciæ irarum! torvi, tenera agmina, risus!
    Blande furor! terror dulcis! amande metus!
Præcocis in pœnas pueri lascivia tristis!
    Cruda rudimenta! & torva tyrocinia!
Jam parcum, breviusq̃ brevi pro corpore vulnus,
    Proq̃ brevi brevior vulnere sanguis eat:
Olim, cùm nervi, vitæq̃ ferocior haustus
    Materiam morti, luxuriemq̃ dabunt;
Olim maturos ultrò conabitur imbres;
    Robustum audebit tunc, solidumq̃ mori.
Ergò illi, nisi qui in sævos concreverit usus,
    Nec nisi quem possit fundere, sanguis erit?

FROM SANCROFT MS.

Euge puer trux! Euge tamen mitissime rerum!
   Quiq́ tibi tantùm trux potes esse, puer!
Euge tibi trux! Euge mihi mitissime rerum!
   Euge Leo mitis! trux sed & Agne tamen!
Macte puer! macte hoc tam duræ laudis honore!
   Macte ô pœnarum hac indole, & ingenio!
At ferus ah culter! sub quo, tam docte dolorum,
   In tristem properas sic, puer, ire virum.
Ah ferus, ah culter! sub quo, puer auree, crescis
   Mortis proficiens hac quasi sub ferulâ.

NE, pia, ne nimium, Virgo, permitte querelis:
   Haud volet, haud poterit natus abesse diu.
Nam quid eum teneat? vel quæ magis oscula vellet?
   Vestri illum indigenam quid vetet esse sinûs?
Quippe illis quæ labra genis magis apta putentur?
   Quæve per id collum dignior ire manus?
His sibi quid speret puer ambitiosiùs ulnis?
   Quóve sub amplexu dulciús esse queat?
O quæ tam teneram sibi vitis amicior ulmum
   Implicet, alternis nexibus immoriens?
Cui circum subitis eat impatientior ulnis?
   Aut quæ tam nimiis vultibus ora notet?
Quæ tam prompta puer toties super oscula surgat?
   Quâ signet gemmâ nobiliore genam?
Illa ubi tam vernis adolescat mitiùs auris,
   Tamve sub apricis pendeat uva jugis?
Illi quâ veniat languor tam gratus in umbrâ?
   Commodiùs sub quo murmure somnus agat?
O ubi tam charo, tam casto in carcere regnat,
   Maternoq́ simul, virgineoq́ sinu?
Ille ut ab his fugiat? nec tam bona gaudia vellet?
   Ille ut in hos possit non properare sinus?
Ille sui tam blanda sinûs patrimonia spernet?
   Hæres tot factus tam bene deliciis?
Ne tantum, ne, Diva, tuis permitte querelis:
   Quid dubites? Non est hic fugitivus Amor.

RICHARD CRASHAW

ACcipe dona, Puer; parvæ libamina laudis.
    Accipe, non meritis accipienda suis.
Accipe dona, Puer dulcis. dumq̇ accipis illa,
    Digna quoq̇ efficies, quæ, puer, accipies.
Sive oculo, sive illa tuâ dignabere dextrâ;
    Dextram, oculumq̇ dabis posse decere tuum.
Non modò es in dantes, sed & ipsa in dona benignus;
    Nec tantùm donans das, sed & accipiens.

In partum B. Virg'. non difficilem.

NEc facta est tamen illa Parens impune; quòd almi
    Tam parcens uteri venerit ille Puer.
Una hæc nascentis quodcunq̇ pepercerit hora,
    Toto illum vitæ tempore parturiit.
Gaudia parturientis erat semel ille parenti;
    Quotidie gemitus parturientis erat.

CIrculus hic similem quàm par sibi pergit in orbem!
    Principiumq̇ suum quàm bene finis amat!
Virgineo thalamo quàm pulchrè convenit ille
    (Quo nemo jacuit) virgineus tumulus!
Undiq̇ ut hæc æquo passu res iret; & ille
    Josepho desponsatus, & ille fuit.

In Sanctum igneis linguis descendentem Spiritum.

ABsint, qui ficto simulant pia pectora vultu,
    Ignea quos luteo pectore lingua beat.
Hoc potius mea vota rogant, mea thura petessunt,
    Ut mihi sit mea mens ignea, lingua luti.

FROM SANCROFT MS.

Cùm horum aliqua dedicâram
Præceptori meo colendissimo,
Amico amicissimo, R. Brooke.

EN tibi Musam, (Præceptor colendissime) quas ex tuis modò scholis, quasi ex Apollinis officinâ, accepit, alas timidè adhuc, nec aliter quàm sub oculis tuis jactitantem.

Qualiter è nido multâ jam floridus alâ
Astra sibi meditatur avis, pulchrosq, meatus
Aërios inter proceres; licèt æthera nunquam
Expertus, rudibusq, illi sit in ardua pennis
Prima fides; micat ire tamen, quatiensq, decorâ
Veste leves humeros, querulumq, per aëra ludens
Nil dubitat vel in astra vagos suspendere risus.
At verò simul immensum per inane profundis
Exhaustus spatiis, vacuoq, sub æthere pendens,
Arva procul, sylvasq, suas, procul omnia cernit,
Cernere quæ solitus; tum verò victa cadit mens,
Spesq, suas, & tanta timens conamina, totus
Respicit ad matrem, pronisq, revertitur auris.

Quòd tibi enim hæc feram (Vir ornatissime) non ambitio dantis est, sed justitia reddentis: neq, te libelli mei tam elegi patronum, quàm dominum agnosco. Tua sanè sunt hæc, et mea. neq, tamen ita mea sunt, quin si quid in illis boni est, tuum hoc sit totum: neq, interim in tantum tua, ut quantumcunq, est in illis mali illud non sit ex integro meum. ita medio quodam, & misto jure utriusq, sunt. ne vel mihi, dum me in societatem tuarum laudum elevarem, invidiam facerem; vel injuriam tibi, ut qui te in tenuitatis mea consortium deducere conarer. Ego enim de meo nihil ausim boni mecum agnoscere, nedum profiteri palàm, præter hoc unum (quo tamen nihil melius) animum nempe non ingratum tuorumq, beneficiorum historiam religiosissimâ fide in se reponentem. hoc quibuscunq, testibus coram, hoc palàm in os cœli, meæq, conscientiæ meum jacto. effero me in hoc ultra æmuli patientiam. Enim vero elegantiore obsequio venerentur te (& venerantur, scio) tuorum alii: nemo me sincero magis, vel ingenuo poterit. Horum deniq, rivulorum, tenuium utcunq, nulliusq, nominis, hæc saltem laus erit propria, quòd suum nempe nôrint Oceanum.

RICHARD CRASHAW

Hymnus Veneri.
dum in illius tutelam transĕunt virgines.

TU tuis adsis, Venus alma, sacris:
    Rideas blandùm, Venus, & benignùm,
Quale cùm Martem premis, aureoq̃
      Frangis ocello.

Rideas. ô tum neq̃ flamma Phœbum,
Nec juvent Phœben sua tela. gestat
Te satis contra tuus ille tantùm
      - Tela Cupido.

Sæpe in ipsius pharetrâ Dianæ
Hîc suas ridens posuit sagittas.
Ausus et flammæ Dominum magistris
      Urere flammis.

Virginum te orat chorus (esse longùm
Virgines nollent) modò servientûm
Tot columbarum tibi, passerumq̃ au-
      gere catervam.

Dedicant quicquid labra vel rosarum,
Colla vel servant tibi liliorum:
Dedicant totum tibi ver genarum,
      Ver oculorum.

Hinc tuo sumas licet arma nato,
Seu novas his ex oculis sagittas;
Seu faces flamma velit acriori
      Flave comatas.

Sume. et ô discant, quid amica; quid nox,
Quid bene, & blandè vigilata nox sit;
Quid sibi dulcis furor, & protervus
      Poscat amator.

Sume. per quæ tot tibi corda flagrant.
Per quod arcanum tua cestus halat.
Per tuus quicquid tibi dixit olim, aut
      Fecit Adonis.

FROM SANCROFT MS.

SPes Diva salve. Diva avidam tuo
⠀⠀Necessitatem numine prorogans;
⠀Vindicta fortunæ furentis;
⠀⠀Una salus mediis ruinis.

Regina quamvis, tu solium facis
Depressa parvi tecta tugurii
⠀Surgunt jacentes inter; illic
⠀⠀Firma magis tua regna constant.

Cantus catenis, carmina carcere,
Dolore ab ipso gaudiaq̃ exprimis.
⠀Scintilla tu vivis sub imo
⠀⠀. Pectoris, haud metuens procellas.

Tu regna servis; copia pauperi:
Victis triumphus: littora naufrago:
⠀Ipsisq̃ damnatis patrona:
⠀⠀Anchora sub medio profundo.

Quin ipse alumnus sum tuus. ubere
Pendemus isto; & hinc animam traho.
⠀O, Diva nutrix, ô foventes
⠀⠀Pande sinus. sitiens laboro.

RICHARD CRASHAW

Non accipimus brevem vitam, sed facimus.

ERgò tu luges nimiùm citatam
    Circulo vitam properante volvi?
Tu Deos parcos gemis, ipse cùm sis
    Prodigus ævi?

Ipse quod perdis, quereris perire?
Ipse tu pellis, sed et ire ploras?
Vita num servit tibi? servus ipse
    Cedet abactus.

Est fugax vitæ (fateor) fluentum:
Prona sed clivum modò det voluptas,
Amne proclivi magis, & fugace
    Labitur undâ.

Fur Sopor magnam hinc (oculos recludens)
Surripit partem. ruit inde partem
Temporis magnam spolium reportans
    Latro voluptas.

Tu creas mortes tibi mille. & æva
Plura quò perdas, tibi plura poscis.

FROM SANCROFT MS.

Pulchra non diuturna.

EHeu ver breve, & invidum!
  Eheu floriduli dies!
Ergò curritis. improbâ
Et quæ nunc face fulgurat,
Dulcis forma tenacibus
Immiscebitur infimæ
Heu! noctis nebulis; amor
Fallax, umbraq̇ somnii.
Quin incumbitis. (invida
Sic dictat colus, & rota
Cani temporis incito
Currens orbe volubilis)
O deprendite lubricos
Annos; et liquidum jubar
Verni syderis, ac novi
Floris fulgura, mollibus
Quæ debetis amoribus,
Non impendite luridos
In manes, avidum & chaos.
 Quanquam sydereis genis,
Quæ semper nive sobriâ
Synceris spatiis vigent
Floris germine simplicis,
Flagrant ingenuæ rosæ:
 Quanquam perpetuâ fide
Illic mille Cupidines,
Centum mille Cupidines,
Pastos nectareâ dape
Blandis sumptibus educas;
Istis qui spatiis vagi,
Plenis lusibus ebrii,
Udo rore beatuli,
Uno plus decies die
Istis ex oculis tuis
Istis ex oculis suas
Sopitas animant faces,
Et languentia recreant
Succo spicula melleo;

RICHARD CRASHAW

Tum flammis agiles novis
Lascivâ volitant face,
Tum plenis tumidi minis,
Tum vel sydera territant,
Et cælum, & fragilem Jovem:
 Quanquam fronte sub arduâ
Majestas gravis excubans,
Dulces fortiter improbis
Leges dictat amoribus:
 Quanquam tota, per omnia,
Cælum machina præferat;
Tanquam pagina multiplex
Vivo scripta volumine
Terris indigitans polos,
Et compendia syderum:
 Istis heu tamen heu genis,
Istis purpureis genis,
Oris sydere florido,
Regno frontis amabili,
Mors heu crastina forsitan
Crudeles faciet notas,
Naturǽq superbiam
Damnabit tumuli specu.

FROM SANCROFT MS.

Veris descriptio.

TEmpus adest, placidis quo Sol novus auctior horis
Purpureos mulcere dies, & sydere verno
Floridus, augusto solet ire per æthera vultu,
Naturæ communis amor; spes aurea mundi;
Virgineum decus; & dulcis lascivia rerum,
Ver tenerum, ver molle subit; jam pulchrior annus
Pube novâ, roseæq, recens in flore juventæ
Felici fragrat gremio, & laxatur odorâ
Prole parens; per aquas, perq, arva, per omnia latè
Ipse suas miratur opes, miratur honores.
Jam Zephyro resoluta suo tumet ebria tellus,
Et crebro bibit imbre Jovem.   Sub frondibus altis
Flora sedens, audit (fælix!) quo murmure lapsis
Fons patrius minitetur aquis, quæ vertice crispo
Respiciunt tantùm, & strepero procul agmine pergunt.
Audit & arboreis siquid gemebunda recurrens
Garriat aura comis.   audit quibus ipsa susurris
Annuit, & facili cervice remurmurat arbor.
Quin audit querulas audit quodcunq, per umbras
Flebilibus Philomela modis miserabile narrat.
Tum quoq, præcipuè blandis Cytheræa per orbem
Spargitur imperiis; molles tum major habenas
Incutit increpitans, cestus magis ignea rores
Ingeminat, tumidosq, sinus flagrantior ambit;
Nympharum incedit latè, charitumq, coronâ
Amplior, & plures curru jam nectit olores:
Quin ipsos quoq, tum campis emittit apricis
Læta parens, gremioq, omnes effundit Amores.
Mille ruunt equites blandi, peditumq, protervæ
Mille ruunt acies: levium pars terga ferarum
Insiliunt, gaudentq, suis stimulare sagittis;
Pars optans gemino multum properare volatu
Aërios conscendit equos; hic passere blando
Subsiliens lene ludit iter; micat huc, micat illuc
Hospitio levis incerto, & vagus omnibus umbris:
Verùm alter gravidis insurgens major habenis
Maternas molitur aves: ille improbus acrem
Versat apem similis, seseq, agnoscit in illo.

RICHARD CRASHAW

Et brevibus miscere vias, ac frangere gyris:
Pars leviter per prata vagi sua lilia dignis
Contendunt sociare rosis; tum floreus ordo
Consilio fragrante venit: lascivit in omni
Germine læta manus: nitidis nova gloria pennis
Additur; illustri gremio sedet aurea messis;
Gaudet odoratas coma blandior ire sub umbras.
Excutiunt solitas (immitia tela) sagittas,
Ridentesq̃ aliis pharetræ spectantur in armis.
Flore manus, & flore sinus, flore omnia lucent.
Undiq̃ jam flos est. vitreas hic pronus ad undas
Ingenium illudentis aquæ, fluitantiaq̃ ora,
Et vaga miratur tremulæ mendacia formæ.
Inde suos probat explorans, & judice nymphâ
Informat radios, ne non satis igne protervo
Ora tremant, agilesq̃ docet nova fulgura vultus,
Atq̃ suo vibrare jubet petulantiùs astro.

Hæc est, quæ sacrâ didicit florere figurâ,
    Non nisi per lachrymas charta videnda tuas.
Scilicet ah dices, hæc cùm spectaveris ora,
    Ora sacer sic, ô sic tulit ille pater.
Sperabis solitas illinc, pia fulmina, voces;
    Sanctaq̃ tam dulci mella venire viâ.
Sic erat illa, suas Famæ cùm traderet alas,
    Ad calamum (dices) sic erat illa manus.
Tale erat & pectus, celsæ domus ardua mentis,
    Tale suo plenum sydere pectus erat.
O bene fallacis mendacia pulchra tabellæ!
    Et, qui tam simili vivit in ære, labor!
Cùm tu tot chartis vitam, Pater alme, dedisti;
    Hæc meritò vitam charta dat una tibi.

FROM SANCROFT MS.

Meliùs purgatur stomachus per vomitum, quàm per secessum.

DUm vires refero vomitûs, & nobile munus,
  Da mihi de vomitu, grandis Homere, tuo.
Nempe olim, multi cùm carminis anxia moles
  Vexabat stomachum, magne Poëta, tuum;
Ægraq; jejuno tenuabat pectora morsu,
  Jussit & in crudam semper hiare famem:
Phœbus (ut est medicus) vomitoria pocula præbens
  Morbum omnem longos expulit in vomitus.
Protinus & centum incumbunt toto ore Poëtæ,
  Certantes sacras lambere relliquias.
Quod vix fecissent, (scio) si medicamen ineptum
  Venisset miserè posteriore viâ.
Quippe per amfractus, cæciq; volumina ventris
  Sacra (putas) hostem vult medicina sequi?
Tam turpes tenebras hæc non dignatur. at ipsum
  Sedibus ex imis imperiosa trahit.
          Ergò
Per vomitum stomachus meliùs purgabitur. alvus
  Quàm quà secretis exit opaca viis.

RICHARD CRASHAW

In Natales Mariæ Principis.

PArce tuo jam, bruma ferox, ô parce furori.
Pone animos. ô pacatæ da spiritus auræ
Afflatu leniore gravem demulceat annum.
Res certè, & tempus meruit. Licèt improbus Auster.
Sæviat, & rabido multùm se murmure volvat;
Imbriferis licèt impatiens Notus ardeat alis;
Hîc tamen, hîc certè, modò tu non (sæva)·negares,
Nec Notus impatiens jam, nec foret improbus Auster.
Scilicet hoc decuit? dum nos tam lucida rerum
Attollit series, adeò commune serenum
Lætitiæ, vernisq; animis micat alta voluptas;
Jam torvas acies, jam squallida bella per auras
Volvere? & hybernis annum corrumpere nimbis?
Ah melius! quin luce novæ reparata juventæ
Ipsa hodie vernaret hyems; pulchroq; tumultu
Purpureas properaret opes; effunderet omnes
Læta sinus, nitidumq; diem fragrantibus horis
Æternùm migrare velit; florumq; beatâ
Luxurie tanta ô circum cunabula surgat,
Excipiatq; novos, & molliter ambiat artus.
  Quippe venit. sacris iterum vagitibus ingens
Aula sonat. venit en roseo decus addita fratri
Blanda soror. tibi se brevibus, tibi porrigit ulnis,
Magne puer! facili tibi torquet hiantia risu
Ora; tibi molles, lacrymas, & nobile murmur
Temperat, inq; tuo ponit se pendula collo.
Tale decus; juncto veluti sub stemmate cùm quis
Dat sociis lucere rosis sua lilia. talis
Fulget honos; medio cùm se duo sydera mundo
Dulcibus intexunt radiis. nec dignior olim
Flagrabat nitidæ felix consortio formæ,
Tunc cùm sydereos inter pulcherrima fratres
Erubuit primùm, & Ledæo cortice rupto
Tyndarida explicuit teneræ nova gaudia frontis.
  Sic socium ô miscete jubar, tu, candide frater,
Tuq; serena soror. sic ô date gaudia patri,
Sic matri. cùmq; ille olim, subeüntibus annis,

FROM SANCROFT MS.

Ire inter proprios magnâ cervice triumphos
Egregius volet, atq̓ suâ se discere dextrâ;
Te quoq̓ tum pleno mulcebit sydere & alto
Flore tui, dulcesq̓ oculos maturior ignis
Indole divinâ, & radiis intinget honoris.
Tunc ô te quoties (nisi quòd tu pulchrior illâ)
Esse suam Phœben falsus jurabit Apollo!
Tunc ô te quoties (nisi quòd tu castior illâ)
Esse suam Venerem Mavors jurabit inanis!
Felix ah! et cui se non Mars, non aureus ipse
Credet Apollo parem! tantâ cui conjuge celsus
In pulchros properare sinus, & carpere sacras
Delicias, oculosq̓ tuos, tua basia solus
Tum poterit dixisse sua; & se nectare tanto
Dum probat esse Deum, superas contemnere mensas.

RICHARD CRASHAW

IGnitum latus, & sacrum tibi gratulor ostrum,
   O amor; atq̃ tuæ gloria magna togæ!
Nam video. Themis ecce humeris, Themis ardet in istis,
   Inq̃ tuos gaudet tota venire sinus.
O ibi purpureo quàm se bene porrigit astro!
   Et docet hîc radios luxuriare suos!
Imò eat æternâ sic ô Themis aurea pompâ!
   Hîc velit ô sydus semper habere suum!
Sic flagret, & nunquam tua purpura palleat intus.
   O nunquam in vultus digna sit ire tuos.
Sanguine ab innocuo nullos bibat illa rubores.
   Nec tam crudeli murice proficiat.
Quæq̃ tibi est (nam quæ non est tibi?) candida virtus
   Fortunam placidè ducat in alta tuam.
Nullius viduæ lacrymas tua marmora sudent.
   Nec sit, quæ inclamet te, tibi facta domus.
Non gemat ulla suam pinus tibi scissa ruinam,
   Ceu cadat in domini murmure mæsta sui.
Fama suas subter pennas tibi sternat eünti;
   Illa tubæ faciat te melioris opus.
Thura tuo (quacunq̃ meat) cum nomine migrent;
   Quæq̃ vehit fęlix te, vehat aura rosas.
Vive tuis (nec enim non sunt æquissima) votis
   Æqualis, quæ te sydera cunq̃ vocant.
Hæc donec niveæ cedat tua purpura pallæ,
   Lilium ubi fuerit, quæ rosa vestis erat.

Serenissimæ Reginæ librum suum commendat Academia.

HUnc quoq̃ maternâ (nimium nisi magna rogamus)
   Aut aviæ saltem sume, Maria, manu.
Est Musâ de matre recens rubicundulus infans,
   Cui pater est partus (quis putet?) ille tuus.
Usq̃ adeo impatiens amor est in virgine Musâ:
   Jam nunc ex illo non negat esse parens.
De nato quot habes olim sperare nepotes,
   Qui simul & pater est, & facit esse patrem!

FROM SANCROFT MS.

Priscianus verberans, & vapulans.

QUid facis? ah! tam perversâ quid volvitur irâ?
  Quid parat iste tuus, posterus iste furor?
Ah, truculente puer! tam fœdo parce furori.
  Nec rapiat tragicas tam gravis ira nates.
Ecce fremit, fremit ecce indignabundus Apollo.
  Castalides fugiunt, & procul ora tegunt.
Sic igitur sacrum, sic insedisse caballum
  Quæris? & (ah) fieri tam malè notus eques?
Ille igitur phaleris nitidus lucebit in istis?
  Hæc erit ad solidum turpis habena latus?
His ille (haud nimium rigidis) dabit ora lupatis?
  Hæc fluet in miseris sordida vitta jubis?
Sic erit ista tui, sic aurea pompa triumphi?
  Ille sub imperiis ibit olentis heri?
Ille tamen neq, terribili stat spumëus irâ;
  Ungula nec celso fervida calce tonat.
O meritò spectatur equi patientia nostri!
  Dicite Iŏ. tantum quis toleravit equus?
Pegasus iste ferox, mortales spretus habenas,
  Bellerophontæâ non tulit ire manu.
Noster equus tamen exemplo non turget in isto:
  Stat bonus, & solito se pede certus habet.
Imò licèt tantos de te tulit ille pudores,
  Te tulit ille iterum. sed meliore modo.
Tunc rubor in scapulas ô quàm bene transiit iste,
  Qui satis in vultus noluit ire tuos!
At mater centum in furias abit, & vomit iram
  Mille modis rabidam: jura, forumq; fremit.
Quin fera tu, taceas; aut jura, forumq; tacebunt:
  Tu legi vocem non sinis esse suam.
O malè vibratæ rixosa volumina linguæ!
  Et satls in nullo verba tonanda foro!
Causidicos (vesana!) tuos tua fulmina terrent.
  Ecce stupent miseri: ah! nec meminêre loqui.
Hinc tua, (fœde puer) fœdati hinc terga caballi
  Exercent querulo jurgia lenta foro.
Obscænas lites, & olentia jurgia ridet
  Turpiter in causam sollicitata Themis.

RICHARD CRASHAW

Juridicus lites quisquis tractaverit istas,
　　Oh satis emunctâ nare sit ille, precor.
At tu de misero quid vis, truculente, caballo?
　　Cur premis insultans, sæve! tyranne puer!
Tené igitur fugiet? fugiet sacer iste caballus?
　　Non fugiet. sed (si vis) tibi terga dabit.

Ad librum super hac re ab ipso
ludi magistro editum, qui dr̈ } Priscianus { *verberans,*
　　　　　　　　　　　　　　　　　　　　　&
　　　　　　　　　　　　　　　　　　　　　vapulans.

SOrdes ô tibi gratulamur istas,
　　O Musa aurea, blanda, delicata!
Sordes ô tibi candidas, suoq̂
Jam nec nomine, jam nec ore notas!
Sacro carmine quippe delinitæ
Se nunc ô bene nesciunt, novâq̂
Mirantur facie novum nitorem.
Ipsas tu facis ô nitere sordes.
Sordes ô tibi gratulamur ipsas!
Si non hic natibus procax malignis
Fœdo fulmine turpis intonâsset:
Unde insurgeret hæc querela vindex,
Docto & murmure carminis severi
Dulces fortiter aggregaret iras?
Ipsæ ô te faciunt nitere sordes.
Sordes ô tibi gratulamur ipsas.
　　Quàm pulchrè tua migrat Hippocrene!
Turpi quam bene degener parenti!
Fœdi filia tam serena fontis.
Has de stercore quis putaret undas?
　　Sic ô lactea surge, Musa, surge.
Surge inter medias serena sordes.
Spumis qualiter in suis Dione,
Cùm prompsit latus aurĕum, atq̂ primas
Ortu purpureo movebat undas.
Sic ô lactea surge, Musa, surge.
Enni stercus erit Maronis aurum.

338

FROM SANCROFT MS.

Horatii Ode.

Ille & nefasto te posuit die &c.

Ἑλληνιϛί.

Ὥρα σε κεῖνος θῆκεν ἀποφράδι
Ὁ πρῶτος ὅϛις, χειρί τε βώμακι
   Ἔθρεψε, δένδρον, τῆς τε κώμης
     Αἴτιον, ἐσσομένων τ' ἔλεγχος.

Κεῖνος τοκῆος θρύψε καὶ αὐχένα,
Κεῖνός γε (φαίην) αἵματι ξεινίῳ
   Μυχώτατον κοιτῶνα ῥαῖνε
     Νύκτιος, ἀμφαφάασε κεῖνος

Τὰ δῆτα κόλχων φάρμακα, καὶ κακοῦ
Πᾶν χρῆμα, δώσας μοι ἐπιχώριον
   Σὲ ϛυγνὸν ἔρνος, δεσπότου σε
     Ἔμπεσον ἐς κεφαλὴν ἀεικῶς.

Πάσης μὲν ὥρης πᾶν ἐπικίνδυνον.
Τίς οἶδε φεύγειν; δείδιε βοσφόρον
   Λιβὺς ὁ πλωτὴρ, οὐδ' ἀνά[γ]κην
     Τὴν κρυφίην ἑτέρωθεν ὀκνεῖ.

Πάρθων μάχημον Ῥωμάικος φυγήν,
Καὶ τόξα· Πάρθος Ῥωμαίκην βίαν,
   Καὶ δεσμὰ· λάους ἀλλὰ μοίρας
     Βάλλε, βαλεῖ τ' ἀδόκητος ὁρμή.

Σχέδον σχέδον πῶς Περσεφόνης ἴδον
Αὔλην μελαίνην, καὶ κρίσιν Αἰακοῦ,
   Καλήν τ' ἀπόϛασιν μακαίρων,
     Αἰολίαις κινύρην τε χορδαῖς.

Σαπφὼ πατρίδος μεμφομένην κόραις,
Ἡχοῦντα καί σε πλεῖον ἐπιχρύσῳ,
   Ἀλκαῖε, πλήκτρῳ σκληρὰ νῆος,
     Σκληρὰ φυγῆς, πολέμου τε σκληρά.

RICHARD CRASHAW

Εὐφημέουσαι δ' ἀμφοτέρων σκιαὶ
Κλύουσι θάμβει, τὰς δὲ μαχὰς πλεόν,
Ἀναςάτους τε μὲν τυράννους
Ὠμιὰς ἔκπιεν ὧσι λᾶος.

Τί θαῦμ'; ἐκείναιρ θὴς ὅτε τρίκρανος
Ἄκην ἀοιδαῖς, οὔατα κάββαλε,
Ἐρινύων τ' ἡδυπαθοῦσι
Βόςρυχες, ἡσυχίων ἐχιδνῶν.

Καὶ δὴ Προμηθεύς, καὶ Πέλοπος πατὴρ
Εὔδουσιν ἠχεῖ τῷ λαθικήδεῖ
Ἄγειν λέοντας Ὠρίων δὲ
Οὐ φιλέει, φοβεράς τε λύγκας.

In Rev^d. Dre. Brooke Epitaphium.

POsuit sub istâ (non gravi) caput terrâ
    Ille, ipsa quem mors arrogare vix ausa
Didicit vereri, plurimumque suspenso
Dubitavit ictu, lucidos procul vultus,
Et sydus oris acre procul prospectans.
Cui literarum fama cùm dedit lumen,
Accepit, atque est ditior suis donis.
Cujus serena gravitas faciles mores
Muliere novit; cujus in senectute
Famaeque riguit, & juventa fortunæ.
Ita brevis ævi, ut nec videri festinus;
Ita longus, ut nec fessus. Et hunc mori credis?

FROM SANCROFT MS.

In obitum Rev. V. D^{ris} Mansell,
Coll. Regin: M^{ri} qui ven. D^s Brooke,
interitum proximè secutus est.

ERgo iterum in lacrymas, & sævi murmura planctûs
  Ire jubet tragicâ mors iterata manu?
Scilicet illa novas quæ jam fert dextra sagittas,
  Dextra priore recens sanguine stillat adhuc.
Vos ô, quos sociâ Lachesis propè miscuit urnâ,
  Et vicina colus vix sinit esse duos;
Ite ô, quos nostri jungunt consortia damni;
  Per nostras lacrymas ô nimis ite pares!
Ite per Elysias felici tramite valles.
  Et sociis animos conciliate viis.
Illic ingentes ultrò confundite manes,
  Noscat & æternam mutua dextra fidem.
Communes eadem spargantur in otia curæ,
  Atque idem felix poscat utrumque labor.
Nectaræ simul ite vagis sermonibus horæ:
  Nox trahat alternas continuata vices.
Una cibos ferat, una suas vocet arbor in umbras.
  Ambobus faciles herba det una toros.
Certum erit interea quanto sit major habenda,
  Quàm quæ per vitam est, mortis amicitia.

RICHARD CRASHAW

LUKE 2. *Quærit Jesum suum Maria, &c.*

ANd is he gone, whom these armes held but now?
   Their hope, their vow?
Did ever greife, & joy in one poore heart
   Soe soone change part?
Hee's gone. the fair'st flower, that e're bosome drest,
   My soules sweet rest.
My wombes chast pride is gone, my heaven-borne boy;
   And where is joy?
Hee's gone. & his lov'd steppes to wait upon,
   My joy is gone.
My joyes, & hee are gone; my greife, & I
   Alone must ly.
Hee's gone. not leaving with me, till he come,
   One smile at home.
Oh come then. bring Thy mother her lost joy:
   Oh come, sweet boy.
Make hast, & come, or e're my greife, & I
   Make hast, & dy.
Peace, heart! the heavens are angry. all their spheres
   Rivall thy teares.
I was mistaken. some faire sphære, or other
   Was thy blest mother.
What, but the fairest heaven, could owne the birth
   Of soe faire earth?
Yet sure thou did'st lodge heere. this wombe of mine
   Was once call'd thine.
Oft have these armes thy cradle envied,
   Beguil'd thy bed.
Oft to thy easy eares hath this shrill tongue
   Trembled, & sung.
Oft have I wrapt thy slumbers in soft aires,
   And stroak't thy cares.
Oft hath this hand those silken casements kept,
   While their sunnes slept.
Oft have my hungry kisses made thine eyes
   Too early rise.

FROM SANCROFT MS.

Oft have I spoild my kisses daintiest diet,
        To spare thy quiet.
Oft from this breast to thine my love-tost heart
        Hath leapt, to part.
Oft my lost soule have I bin glad to seeke
        On thy soft cheeke.
Oft have these armes alas ! show'd to these eyes
        Their now lost joyes.
Dawne then to me, thou morne of mine owne day,
        And lett heaven stay.
Oh, would'st thou heere still fixe thy faire abode,
        My bosome God :
What hinders, but my bosome still might be
        Thy heaven to Thee?

Whosoever shall loose his life &c. MATH. 16. 25.

SOe I may gaine thy death, my life I'le give.
    (My life's thy death, & in thy death I live.)
Or else, my life, I'le hide thee in his grave,
By three daies losse æternally to save.

343

RICHARD CRASHAW

In cicatrices Domini Jesu.

COme, brave soldjers, come, & see
    Mighty love's Artillery.
This was the conquering dart; & loe
There shines his quiver, there his bow.
These the passive weapons are,
That made great Love, a man of warre.
The quiver, that he bore, did bide
Soe neare, it prov'd his very side.
In it there sate but one sole dart;
A peircing one. his peirced heart.
His weapons were nor steele, nor brasse:
The weapon, that he wore, he was.
For bow his unbent hand did serve,
Well strung with many a broken nerve.
Strange the quiver, bow, & dart!
A bloody side, & hand, & heart!
But now the feild is wonne: & they
(The dust of Warre cleane wip'd away)
The weapons now of triumph be,
That were before of Victorie.

In amorem divinum (Hermannus Hugo).

AEternall love! what 'tis to love thee well,
    None, but himselfe, who feeles it, none can tell.
But oh, what to be lov'd of thee as well,
None, not himselfe, who feeles it, none can tell.

FROM SANCROFT MS.

Upon a Gnatt burnt in a candle.

Little—buzzing—wanton elfe,
    Perish there, & thanke thy selfe.
Thou deserv'st thy life to loose,
For distracting such a Muse.
Was it thy ambitious aime
By thy death to purchase fame?
Didst thou hope he would in pitty
Have bestow'd a funerall ditty
On thy ghoast? & thou in that
To have outlived Virgills gnatt?
No. the treason, thou hast wrought,
Might forbid the[e] such a thought.
If that night's worke doe miscarry,
Or a syllable but vary,
A greater foe thou shalt me find,
The destruction of thy kind.
Phœbus, to revenge thy fault,
In a fiery trapp thee caught;
That thy winged mates might know it,
And not dare disturbe a Poet.
Deare, & wretched was thy sport,
Since thyselfe was crushed for't.
Scarcely had that life a breath,
Yet it found a double death;
Playing in the golden flames,
Thou fell'st into an inky Thames;
Scorch'd, & drown'd. That petty sunne
A pretty Icarus hath undone.

RICHARD CRASHAW.

Petronius.

Ales Phasiacis petita Colchis &c.

THe bird, that's fetch't from Phasis floud,
    Or choicest hennes of Africk-brood;
These please our palates. & why these?
'Cause they can but seldome please.
Whil'st the goose soe goodly white,
And the drake yeeld noe delight,
Though his wings conceited hewe
Paint each feather, as if new.
These for vulgar stomacks be,
And rellish not of rarity.
But the dainty Scarus, sought
In farthest clime; what e're is bought
With shipwracks toile, oh, that is sweet,
'Cause the quicksands hanselld it.
The pretious Barbill, now groune rife,
Is cloying meat. How stale is Wife?
Deare wife hath ne're a handsome letter,
Sweet mistris sounds a great deale better.
Rose quakes at name of Cinnamon.
Unlesse't be rare, what's thought upon?

FROM SANCROFT MS.

Horatius.

Ille & ne fasto te posuit die &c.

SHame of thy mother soyle! ill-nurtur'd tree!
Sett to the mischeife, of posteritie!
That hand, (what e're it wer) that was thy nurse,
Was sacrilegious, (sure) or somewhat worse.
Black, as the day was dismall, in whose sight
Thy rising topp first staind the bashfull light.
That man (I thinke) wrested the feeble life
From his old father. that mans barbarous knife
Conspird with darknes 'gainst the strangers throate;
(Whereof the blushing walles tooke bloody note)
Huge high-floune poysons, ev'n of Colchos breed,
And whatsoe're wild sinnes black thoughts doe feed,
His hands have padled in; his hands, that found
Thy traiterous root a dwelling in my ground.
Perfidious totterer! longing for the staines
Of thy kind Master's well-deserving braines.
Mans daintiest care, & caution cannot spy
The subtile point of his coy destiny,
W^{ch} way it threats. with feare the merchant's mind
Is plough'd as deepe, as is the sea with wind,
(Rowz'd in an angry tempest), Oh the sea!
Oh! that's his feare; there flotes his destiny:
While from another (unseene) corner blowes
The storme of fate, to wch his life he owes.
By Parthians bow the soldier lookes to die,
(Whose hands are fighting, while their feet doe flie.)
The Parthian starts at Rome's imperiall name,
Fledg'd with her eagles wing; the very chaine
Of his captivity rings in his eares.
Thus, ò thus fondly doe wee pitch our feares
Farre distant from our fates. our fates, that mocke
Our giddy feares with an unlook't for shocke.
   A little more, & I had surely seene
Thy greisly Majesty, Hell's blackest Queene;
And Œacus on his Tribunall too,

347

RICHARD CRASHAW

Sifting the soules of guilt; & you, (oh you!)
You ever-blushing meads, where doe the Blest
Farre from darke horrors home appeale to rest.
There amorous Sappho plaines upon her Lute
Her loves crosse fortune, that the sad dispute
Runnes murmuring on the strings. Alcæus there
In high-built numbers wakes his golden lyre,
To tell the world, how hard the matter went,
How hard by sea, by warre, by banishment.
There these brave soules deale to each wondring eare,
Such words, soe precious, as they may not weare
Without religious silence; above all
Warres ratling tumults, or some tyrants fall.
The thronging clotted multitude doth feast.
What wonder? when the hundred-headed beast
Hangs his black lugges, stroakt with those heavenly
            lines;
The Furies curl'd snakes meet in gentle twines,
And stretch their cold limbes in a pleasing fire.
Prometheus selfe, & Pelops sterved sire
Are cheated of their paines; Orion thinkes
Of Lions now noe more, or spotted Linx.

348

FROM SANCROFT MS.

On ye Gunpowder-Treason.

I Sing Impiety beyond a name:
Who stiles it any thinge, knowes not the same.
Dull, sluggish Ile! what more than lethargy
Gripes thy cold limbes soe fast, thou canst not fly,
And start from of[f] thy center? hath heaven's love
Stuft thee soe full with blisse, thou can'st not move?
If soe, oh Neptune, may she farre be throwne
By thy kind armes to a kind world unknowne:
Lett her survive this day, once mock her fate,
And shee's an Island truely fortunate.
Lett not my suppliant breath raise a rude storme
To wrack my suite. oh keepe pitty warme
In thy cold breast, & yearely on this day
Mine eyes a tributary streame shall pay.
Do'st thou not see an exhalation
Belch'd from the sulph'ry lungs of Phlegeton?
A living Comet, whose pestiferous breath
Adulterates the Virgin aire? with death
It labours. stif'led nature's in a swound,
Ready to dropp into a chaos, round
About horror's displai'd; It doth portend,
That earth a shoure of stones to heaven shall send,
And crack the Christall globe; the milky streame
Shall in a silver rain runne out, whose creame
Shall choake the gaping earth, wch then shall fry
In flames, & of a burning fever dy.
That wonders may in fashion be, not rare,
A winter's thunder with a groane shall scare,
And rouze the sleepy ashes of the dead,
Making them skip out of their dusty bed.
Those twinckling eyes of heaven, wch ev'n now shin'd,
Shall with one flash of lightning be struck blind.
The sea shall change his youthfull greene, & slide
Along the shore in a grave purple tide.
It does præsage, that a great Prince shall climbe,
And gett a starry throne before his time.

RICHARD CRASHAW

To usher in this shoale of Prodigies,
Thy infants, Æolus, will not suffice.
Noe, noe, a giant wind, that will not spare
To tosse poore men like dust into the aire;
Justle downe mountaines: Kings courts shall be sent,
Like bandied balles, into the firmament.
Atlas shall be tript upp, Jove's gate shall feele
The weighty rudenes of his boysterous heele.
All this it threats, & more: Horror, that flies
To th' Empyræum of all miseries.
Most tall Hyperbole's cannot descry it;
Mischeife, that scornes expression should come nigh it.
All this it only threats. the Meteor ly'd;
It was exhal'd, a while it hung, & dy'd.
Heaven kickt the Monster downe. downe it was throwne,
The fall of all things it præsag'd, its owne
It quite forgott. the fearfull earth gave way,
And durst not touch it, heere it made noe stay.
At last it stopt at Pluto's gloomy porch;
He streightway lighted upp his pitchy torch.
Now to those toiling soules it gives its light,
Wch had the happines to worke i'th' night.
They banne the blaze, & curse its curtesy,
For lighting them unto their misery.
Till now hell was imperfect; it did need
Some rare choice torture; now 'tis hell indeed.
Then glutt thy dire lampe with the warmest blood,
That runnes in violett pipes: none other food
It can digest. then watch the wildfire well,
Least it breake forth, & burne thy sooty cell.

FROM SANCROFT MS.

Upon the Gunpowder-Treason.

REach me a quill, pluckt from the flaming wing
   Of Pluto's Mercury, that I may sing
Death to the life. My inke shall be the blood
Of Cerberus, or Alecto's viperous brood.
Unmated malice! Oh unpeer'd despight!
Such as the sable pinions of the night
Never durst hatch before: extracted see
The very Quintessence of villanie.
I feare to name it; least that he, wch heares,
Should have his soule frighted beyond the spheres.
Heaven was asham'd, to see our mother Earth
Engender with the Night, & teeme a birth
Soe foule, one minutes light had it but seene,
The fresh face of the morne had blasted beene.
Her rosy cheekes you should have seene noe more
Dy'd in vermilion blushes, as before:
But in a vaile of clouds mufling her head
A solitary life she would have led.
Affrighted Phœbus would have lost his way,
Giving his wanton palfreys leave to play
Olympick games in the' Olympian plaines,
His trembling hands loosing the golden raines.
The Queene of night gott the greene sicknes then,
Sitting soe long at ease in her darke denne,
Not daring to peepe forth, least that a stone
Should beate her headlong from her jetty throne.
Jove's twinckling tapers, that doe light the world,
Had beene puft out, & from their stations hurl'd.
Æol kept in his wrangling sonnes, least they
With this grand blast should have bin bloune away.
Amazed Triton with his shrill alarmes
Bad sporting Neptune to pluck in his armes,
And leave embracing of the Isles, least hee
Might be an actor in this Tragœdy.
Nor should wee need thy crisped waves, for wee
An Ocean could have made t' have drowned thee.
Torrents of salt teares from our eyes should runne,

RICHARD CRASHAW

And raise a deluge, where the flaming sunne
Should coole his fiery wheeles, & never sinke
Soe low to give his thirsty stallions drinke.
Each soule in sighes had spent its dearest breath,
As glad to waite upon their King in death.
Each winged Chorister would swan-like sing
A mournfull Dirge to their deceased King.
The painted meddowes would have laught no more
For joye of their neate coates; but would have tore
Their shaggy locks, their flowry mantles turn'd
Into dire sable weeds, & sate, & mourn'd.
Each stone had streight a Niobe become,
And wept amaine; then rear'd a costly tombe,
T' entombe the lab'ring earth.   for surely shee
Had died just in her delivery.
But when Jove's winged Heralds this espied,
Upp to th' Almighty thunderer they hied,
Relating this sad story.   streight way hee
The monster crusht, maugre their midwiferie.
And may such Pythons never live to see
The Light's faire face, but still abortive bee.

FROM SANCROFT MS.

Upon the Gunpowder-Treason.

GRow plumpe, leane Death; his Holinesse a feast
   Hath now præpar'd, & you must be his guest.
Come grimme destruction, & in purple gore
Dye sev'n times deeper than they were before
Thy scarlet robes. for heere you must not share
A common banquett. noe, heere's princely fare.
And least thy bloodshott eyes should lead aside
This masse of cruelty, to be thy guide
Three coleblack sisters, (whose long sutty haire,
And greisly visages doe fright the aire;
When Night beheld them, shame did almost turne
Her sable cheekes into a blushing morne,
To see some fowler than herselfe) these stand,
Each holding forth to light the aery brand,
Whose purer flames tremble to be soe nigh,
And in fell hatred burning, angry dy,
Sly, lurking treason is his bosome freind,
Whom faint, & palefac't feare doth still attend.
These need noe invitation. onely thou
Black dismall horror, come; make perfect now
Th' Epitome of hell: oh lett thy pinions
Be a gloomy Canopy to Pluto's minions.
In this infernall Majesty close shrowd
Your selves, your Stygian states; a pitchy clowd
Shall hang the roome, & for your tapers bright,
Sulphureous flames, snatch'd from æternall night.
But rest, affrighted Muse; thy silver wings
May not row neerer to these dusky Kings.
Cast back some amorous glances on the cates,
That heere are dressing by the hasty fates,
Nay. stopp thy clowdy eyes. it is not good,
To droune thy selfe in this pure pearly flood.
But since they are for fire-workes, rather prove
A Phenix, & in chastest flames of love
Offer thy selfe a Virgin sacrifice
To quench the rage of hellish deities.

RICHARD CRASHAW

But dares destruction eate these candid breasts,
The Muses, & the Graces sugred neasts?
Dares hungry death snatch of one cherry lipp?
Or thirsty treason offer once to sippe
One dropp of this pure Nectar, wch doth flow
In azure channells warme through mounts of snow?
The roses fresh, conserved from the rage,
And cruell ravishing of frosty age,
Feare is afraid to tast of: only this,
He humbly crav'd to banquett on a kisse.
Poore meagre horro^{r} streightwaies was amaz'd,
And in the stead of feeding stood, & gaz'd.
Their appetites were gone at th' very sight;
But yet their eyes surfett with sweet delight.
Only the Pope a stomack still could find;
But yett they were not powder'd to his mind.
Forthwith each God stept from his starry throne,
And snatch'd away the banquett. every one
Convey'd his sweet delicious treasury
To the close closet of æternity:
Where they will safely keepe it, from the rude,
And rugged touch of Pluto's multitude.

354

FROM SANCROFT MS.

Upon the King's Coronation.

SOund forth, cœlestiall Organs, lett heavens quire
Ravish the dancing orbes, make them mount higher
With nimble capers, & force Atlas tread
Upon his tiptoes, e're his silver head
Shall kisse his golden burthen. Thou, glad Isle,
That swim'st as deepe in joy, as Seas, now smile;
Lett not thy weighty glories, this full tide
Of blisse, debase thee; but with a just pride
Swell: swell to such an height, that thou maist vye
With heaven itselfe for stately Majesty.
Doe not deceive mee, eyes: doe I not see
In this blest earth heaven's bright Epitome,
Circled with pure refined glory? heere
I veiw a rising sunne in this our sphere,
Whose blazing beames, maugre the blackest night,
And mists of greife, dare force a joyfull light.
The gold, in wch he flames, does well præsage
A precious season, & a golden age.
Doe I not see joy keepe his revels now,
And sitt triumphing in each cheerfull brow?
Unmixt felicity with silver wings
Broodeth this sacred place. hither peace brings
The choicest of her olive-crownes, & praies
To have them guilded with his courteous raies.
Doe I not see a Cynthia, who may
Abash the purest beauties of the day?
To whom heavens lampes often in silent night
Steale from their stations to repaire their light.
Doe I not see a constellation,
Each little beame of wch would make a sunne?
I meane those three great starres, who well may scorn
Acquaintance with the Usher of the morne.
To gaze upon such starres each humble eye
Would be ambitious of Astronomie.
Who would not be a Phœnix, & aspire
To sacrifice himselfe in such sweet fire?
Shine forth, ye flaming sparkes of Deity,
Yee perfect emblemes of divinity.
Fixt in your spheres of glory, shed from thence,
The treasures of our lives, your influence.
For if you sett, who may not justly feare,
The world will be one Ocean, one great teare.

RICHARD CRASHAW

Upon the King's Coronation.

STrange metamorphosis! It was but now
The sullen heaven had vail'd its mournfull brow
With a black maske: the clouds with child by greife
Traveld th' Olympian plaines to find releife.
But at the last (having not soe much power
As to refraine) brought forth a costly shower
Of pearly drops, & sent her numerous birth
(As tokens of her greife) unto the earth.
Alas, the earth, quick drunke with teares, had reel'd
From of[f] her center, had not Jove upheld
The staggering lumpe: each eye spent all its store,
As if heereafter they would weepe noe more.
Streight from this sea of teares there does appeare
Full glory flaming in her owne free sphere.
Amazed Sol throwes of[f] his mournfull weeds,
Speedily harnessing his fiery steeds,
Up to Olympus stately topp he hies,
From whence his glorious rivall hee espies.
Then wondring starts, & had the curteous night
With held her vaile, h' had forfeited his sight.
The joyfull sphæres with a delicious sound
Afright th' amazed aire, & dance a round
To their owne Musick, nor (untill they see
This glorious Phœbus sett) will quiet bee.
Each aery Siren now hath gott her song,
To whom the merry lambes doe tripp along
The laughing meades, as joyfull to behold
Their winter coates cover'd with flaming gold.
Such was the brightnesse of this Northerne starre,
It made the Virgin Phœnix come from farre
To be repaird: hither she did resort,
Thinking her father had remov'd his court.
The lustre of his face did shine soe bright,
That Rome's bold Eagles now were blinded quite,
The radiant darts, shott from his sparkling eyes,
Made every mortall gladly sacrifice
A heart burning in love; all did adore
This rising sunne, their faces nothing wore,
But smiles, & ruddy joyes, & at this day
All melancholy clowds vanisht away.

356

FROM SANCROFT MS.

Upon the birth of the Princesse Elizabeth.

BRight starre of Majesty, oh shedd on mee,
A precious influence, as sweet as thee.
That with each word, my loaden pen letts fall,
The fragrant spring may be perfum'd withall.
That Sol from them may suck an honied shower,
To glutt the stomack of his darling flower.
With such a sugred livery made fine,
They shall proclaime to all, that they are thine.
Lett none dare speake of thee, but such as thence
Extracted have a balmy eloquence.
But then, alas, my heart! oh how shall I
Cure thee of thy delightfull tympanie?
I cannot hold, such a springtide of joy
Must have a passage, or 'twill force a way.
Yet shall my loyall tongue keepe this command:
But give me leave to ease it with my hand.
And though these humble lines soare not soe high,
As is thy birth; yet from thy flaming eye
Drop downe one sparke of glory, & they'l prove
A præsent worthy of Apollo's love.
My quill to thee may not præsume to sing:
Lett th' hallowed plume of a seraphick wing
Bee consecrated to this worke, while I
Chant to my selfe with rustick melodie.
    Rich, liberall heaven, what, hath yor treasure store
Of such bright Angells, that you give us more?
Had you, like our great Sunne, stamped but one
For earth, t' had beene an ample portion.
Had you but drawne one lively coppy forth,
That might interpret our faire Cynthia's worth,
Y' had done enough to make the lazy ground
Dance, like the nimble spheres, a joyfull round.
But such is the cœlestiall Excellence,
That in the princely patterne shines, from whence
The rest pourtraicted are, that 'tis noe paine
To ravish heaven to limbe them o're againe.
Wittnesse this mapp of beauty; every part
Of wch doth show the Quintessence of art.

357

See! nothing's vulgar, every atome heere
Speakes the great wisdome of th' artificer.
Poore Earth hath not enough perfection,
To shaddow forth th' admired paragon.
Those sparkling twinnes of light should I now stile
Rich diamonds, sett in a pure silver foyle;
Or call her cheeke a bed of new-blowne roses;
And say that Ivory her front composes;
Or should I say, that with a scarlet wave
Those plumpe soft rubies had bin drest soe brave;
.Or that the dying lilly did bestow
Upon her neck the whitest of his snow;
Or that the purple violets did lace
That hand of milky downe: all these are base;
Her glories I should dimme with things soe grosse,
And foule the cleare text with a muddy glosse.
Goe on then, Heaven, & limbe forth such another,
Draw to this sister miracle a brother;
Compile a first glorious Epitome
Of heaven, & earth, & of all raritie;
And sett it forth in the same happy place,
And I'le not blurre it with my Paraphrase.

FROM SANCROFT MS.

EX EUPHORMIONE.

O Dea syderei seu tu stirps alma Tonantis &c.

BRight Goddesse, (whether Jove thy father be;
 Or Jove a father will be made by thee)
Oh crowne these praie'rs (mov'd in a happy hower)
But with one cordiall smile for Cloe. that power
Of Loue's all-daring hand, that makes me burne,
Makes me confess't. Oh, doe not thou with scorne,
Great Nymph, o'relooke my lownesse. heav'n you know
And all their fellow Deities will bow
Even to the naked'st vowes. thou art my fate;
To thee the Parcæ have given up of late
My threds of life. if then I shall not live
By thee; by thee yet lett me die. this give,
High beauties soveraigne, that my funerall flames
May draw their first breath from thy starry beames.
The Phœnix selfe shall not more proudly burne,
That fetcheth fresh life from her fruitfull urne.

RICHARD CRASHAW

An Elegy upon the Death of Mr. Stanninow,

Fellow of Queenes Colledge.

HAth aged winter, fledg'd with feathered raine,
   To frozen Caucasus his flight now tane?
Doth hee in downy snow there closely shrowd
His bedrid limmes, wrapt in a fleecy clowd?
Is th' earth disrobed of her apron white,
Kind winter's guift, & in a greene one dight?
Doth she beginne to dandle in her lappe
Her painted infants, fedd with pleasant pappe,
W^ch their bright father in a pretious showre
From heavens sweet milky streame doth gently powre?
Doth blith Apollo cloath the heavens with joye,
And with a golden wave wash cleane away
Those durty smutches, wch their faire fronts wore,
And make them laugh, wch frown'd, & wept before?
If heaven hath now forgot to weepe; ô then
W^t meane these showres of teares amongst us men?
These Cataracts of griefe, that dare ev'n vie
With th' richest clowds their pearly treasurie?
If winters gone, whence this untimely cold,
That on these snowy limmes hath laid such hold?
What more than winter hath that dire art found,
These purple currents hedg'd with violets round.
To corrallize, wch softly wont to slide
In crimson waveletts, & in scarlet tide?
If Flora's darlings now awake from sleepe,
And out of their greene mantletts dare to peepe:
O tell me then, what rude outragious blast
Forc't this prime flowre of youth to make such hast
To hide his blooming glories, & bequeath
His balmy treasure to the bedd of death?
'Twas not the frozen zone; One sparke of fire,
Shott from his flaming eye, had thaw'd it's ire,
And made it burne in love: 'Twas not the rage,
And too ungentle nippe of frosty age:
'Twas not the chast, & purer snow, whose nest
Was in the modest Nunnery of his brest:

360

FROM SANCROFT MS.

Noe. none of these ravish't those virgin roses,
The Muses, & the Graces fragrant posies.
W^{ch}, while they smiling sate upon his face,
They often kist, & in the sugred place
Left many a starry teare, to thinke how soone
The golden harvest of our joyes, the noone
Of all our glorious hopes should fade,
And be eclipsed with an envious shade.
Noe. 'twas old doting Death, who stealing by,
Dragging his crooked burthen, look't awry,
And streight his amorous syth (greedy of blisse)
Murdred the earth's just pride with a rude kisse.
A winged Herald, gladd of soe sweet a prey,
Snatch't upp the falling starre, soe richly gay,
And plants it in a precious perfum'd bedd,
Amongst those Lillies, wch his bosome bredd.
Where round about hovers with silver wing
A golden summer, an æternall spring.
Now that his root such fruit againe may beare,
Let each eye water't with a courteous teare.

RICHARD CRASHAW

An Elegie on the death of Dr. Porter.

STay, silver-footed Came, strive not to wed
  Thy maiden streames soe soone to Neptunes bed:
Fixe heere thy wat'ry eyes upon these towers,
Unto whose feet in reverence of the powers,
That there inhabite, thou on every day
With trembling lippes an humble kisse do'st pay.
See all in mourning now; the walles are jett,
With pearly papers carelesly besett.
Whose snowy cheekes, least joy should be exprest,
The weeping pen with sable teares hath drest.
Their wronged beauties speake a Tragœdy,
Somewhat more horrid than an Elegy.
Pure, & unmixed cruelty they tell,
Wᶜʰ poseth mischeife's selfe to Parallel.
Justice hath lost her hand, the law her head;
Peace is an Orphan now; her father's dead.
Honesties nurse, Vertues blest Guardian,
That heavenly mortall, that Seraphick man.
Enough is said, now, if thou canst crowd on
Thy lazy crawling streames, pri'thee be gone,
And murmur forth thy woes to every flower,
That on thy bankes sitts in a verdant bower,
And is instructed by thy glassy wave
To paint its perfum'd face wᵗʰ colours brave.
In vailes of dust their silken heads they'le hide,
As if the oft departing sunne had dy'd.
Goe learne that fatall Quire, soe sprucely dight
In downy surplisses, & vestments white,
To sing their saddest Dirges, such as may
Make their scar'd soules take wing, & fly away.
Lett thy swolne breast discharge thy strugling groanes
To th' churlish rocks; & teach the stubborne stones
To melt in gentle drops, lett them be heard
Of all proud Neptunes silver-sheilded guard;
That greife may crack that string, & now untie
Their shackled tongues to chant an Elegie.
Whisper thy plaints to th' Oceans curteous eares,
Then weepe thyselfe into a sea of teares.

362

FROM SANCROFT MS.

A thousand Helicons the Muses send
In a bright Christall tide, to thee they tend,
Leaving .those mines of Nectar, their sweet fountaines,
They force a lilly path through rosy mountaines.
Feare not to dy with greife; all bubling eyes
Are teeming now with store of fresh supplies.

RICHARD CRASHAW

FROM BRITISH MUSEUM
ADDITIONAL MS. 33,219.

AT th' Ivory Tribunall of your hand
(Faire one) these tender leaves doe trembling stand.
Knowing 'tis in the doome of your sweet Eye
Whether the Muse they cloth shall live or die.
Live shee, or dye to Fame; each Leafe you meet
Is her Lifes wing, or her death's winding-sheet.

THough now 'tis neither May nor June
And Nightingales are out of tune,
Yet in these leaves (Faire one) there lyes
(Sworne servant to your sweetest Eyes)
A Nightingale, who may shee spread
In your white bosome her chast bed,
Spite of all the Maiden snow
Those pure untroden pathes can show,
You streight shall see her wake and rise
Taking fresh Life from your fayre Eyes.
And with clasp't winges proclayme a Spring
Where Love and shee shall sit and sing:
For lodg'd so ne're your sweetest throte
What Nightingale can loose her noate?
Nor lett her kinred birds complayne
Because shee breakes the yeares old raigne:
For lett them know shee's none of those
Hedge-Quiristers whose Musicke owes
Onely such straynes as serve to keepe
Sad shades and sing dull Night asleepe.
No shee's a Priestesse of that Grove
The holy chappell of chast Love
Your Virgin bosome. Then what e're
Poore Lawes divide the publicke yeare,
Whose revolutions wait upon
The wild turnes of the wanton Sun;
Bee you the Lady of Loves Yeere:
Where your Eyes shine his Suns appeare:
There all the yeare is Loves long Spring.
There all the year Loves Nightingales
    shall sitt and sing.

FROM BRITISH MUSEUM MS.

Out of Grotius his Tragedy of Christes sufferinges.

O Thou the Span of whose Omnipotence
   Doth graspe the fate of thinges, and share th' events
Of future. chance! the world's grand Sire; and mine
Before the world. Obedient lo! I joyne
An æquall pace thus farre; thy word my deedes
Have flow'd together. if ought further needes
I shrinke not but thus ready stand to beare
(ffor else why came I?) ev'n what e're I feare.
Yett o what end? where does the period dwell
Of my sad labours? no day yett could tell
My soule shee was secure. Still have I borne
A still increasing burden; worse hath torne
His way through bad, to my successive hurt.
I left my glorious Fathers star-pav'd Court
E're borne was banish't; borne was glad t' embrace
A poore (yea scarce a) roofe. whose narrow place
Was not so much as cleane; a stable kind;
The best my cradle and my birth could find.
Then was I knowne; and knowne unluckily
A weake a wretched child; ev'n then was I
For Juryes king an enemy, even worth
His feare; the circle of a yeares round growth
Was not yett full, (a time that to my age
Made litle, not a litle to his rage)
When a wild sword ev'n from their brests, did lop
The Mothers Joyes in an untimely crop.
The search of one child (cruell industry!)
Was losse of multitudes; and missing mee
A bloud drunke errour spilt the costly ayme
Of their mad sin; (how great! and yett how vayne!)
I cal'd a hundred miracles to tell
The world my father, then does envy swell
And breake upon mee: my owne virtues height
Hurtes mee far worse then Herods highest spite;
A riddle! (father) still acknowledg'd thine
Am still refus'd; before the Infant Shrine
Of my weake feet the Persian Magi lay
And left their Mithra for my star: this they.

365

RICHARD CRASHAW

But Isaacks issue the peculiar heyres,
Of thy old goodnesse, know thee not for theires,
Basely degenerous. Against mee flocke
The stiffe neck'd Pharisees that use to mocke
Sound goodnesse with her shadow which they weare,
And 'gainst religion her owne colours beare.
The bloud hound brood of Priests against mee draw
Those Lawlesse tyrant masters of the Law.
Profane Sadocus too does fiercely lead
His court-fed impes against this hated head.
What would they more? th' ave seene when at my nod
Great Natures selfe hath shrunke and spoke mee god.
Drinke fayling there where I a guest did shine
The water blush'd, and started into wine.
Full of high sparkeling vigour: taught by mee
A sweet inebriated extasy.
And streight of all this approbation gate
Good wine in all poynts. but the easy rate;
Other mens hunger with strange feasts I quell'd:
Mine owne with stranger fastings, when I held
Twice twenty dayes pure abstinence, To feed
My minds devotion in my bodyes need.
A subtle inundation of quicke food
Sprang in the spending fingers, and o'reflow'd
The peoples hunger, and when all were full
The broken meate was much more then the whole.
The Wind in all his roaring brags stood still
And listned to the whisper of my will;
The wild waves couch'd; the sea forgott to sweat
Under my feet, the waters to bee wett.
In death-full desperate ills where art and all
Was nothing, there my voyce was med'cinall.
Old clouds of thickest blindnesse fled my sight
And to my touch darke Eyes did owe the light.
Hee that ne're heard now speakes, and finds a tongue
To chaunt my prayses in a new-strung song.
Even hee that belches out a foaming flood
Of hot defiance 'gainst what e're is good
Father and Heyre of darkenesse, when I chide
Sinkes into Horrours bosome, glad to hide

366

FROM BRITISH MUSEUM MS.

Himselfe in his owne hell; and now lets loose
Mans brest (his tenement) and breakes up house.
Yett here's not all: nor was't enough for mee
To freind the living world even death did see
Mee ranging in his quarters; and the land
Of deepest silence answered my command.
Heav'n, Earth, and Sea, my triumphs. what remain'd
Now but the Grave? the Grave it selfe I tam'd.

&c:

THE END.

APPENDIX

In the following references the lines are numbered from the top of the page, including titles.

A=1646, B=1648, C=1652, D=British Museum Addit. MS. 33,219, E=Sancroft MS., F=B. M. Addit. MS. 34,692, G=Harl. MS. 6,917 and 18.

EPIGRAMMATA SACRA. p. 25, l. 5. Printed *est* but altered to *sit* in ink in copies seen. The original editions have been followed in printing the second letter of each initial word as a capital, and, for the sake of uniformity, the same style has been adopted in printing from MSS.

STEPS TO THE TEMPLE and DELIGHTS OF THE MUSES. p. 65, l. 6. A] With other Delights. ll. 11, 12. A] Printed and Published according to Order. l. 14. A] Printed by T. W. for

p. 67, l. 20. A] fancied their dearest.

p. 70. Behind the page containing *The Authors Motto* A prints] Reader, there was a sudden mistake ('tis too late to recover it) thou wilt quickly find it out, and I hope as soone passe it over, some of the humane Poems are misplaced amongst the Divine.

p. 71, l. 4. E] eye expends. l. 27. E] that's vext.

p. 72, l. 5. D and E] manly sun. l. 29. D and E] in a too warm bed.

p. 73, l. 2. Title in E] Upon the Water wch baptiz'd Christ. l. 8. Title in E] Upon the Æthiopian. l. 15. E gives the ref.] John 6. l. 17. A, D and E] be sound. l. 20. Title in E] On our Saviour's Sepulcher. This epigram and one or two others were selected by Crawshaw to form part of *Carmen Deo Nostro*. As the Divine Epigrams form a series by themselves I thought it better to print twice the very few so chosen, instead of omitting them here and giving only the later forms, as in the longer and separate poems (see pp. 230, 79 and 233, 83 and 243, 85 and 244). l. 23. E] widows two mites. Last line. E] other threw.

p. 74, l. 1. Title in E] Upon the rich young man, Luke 15, 13. A also gives the ref.] Luke 15. l. 7. Title in E] The sick crave the shadow of Peter. l. 12. Title in E] Upon the print of Christ's wounds Joh. 20. 20. l. 24. Title in E] Upon the tongue. E also adds as lines 5 and 6 of the epigram]
> Oh wild fire! oh rude tongue! if nought will shame thee,
> Hell hath a wilder fire, and that shall tame thee.

p. 75, l. 2. Title in E] Mary to the Angell, shewing her the place, where Jesus lay. l. 9. Title in E] Pilate washes his hands. l. 13. D and E] his fountaine in thy. l. 17. E] milkie founts. l. 21. Title in E] On Christ's Miracle at the Supper,

APPENDIX

p. **76**, l. 19. Title in E] Upon the Virgins looking on our Saviour. l. 29. E] those teares.

p. **78**, l. 3. E] (Lord) hath. l. 10. B] wor'ds A] word's. l. 17. Title in E] Christ accused answered nothing. l. 20. D and E] spake when first he. l. 24. Title in E] Christ turnes water into wine. l. 26. D and E] sweet acts.

p. **79**, l. 18. D] Had not. l. 29. D] never was man. Title in E] In Sepulchrum Domini Luke 23 where was never man laid; see also p. 233. Last line] A full stop has been supplied here, and elsewhere at the end of a poem, where it is left out in the original by a printer's error.

p. **80**, l. 1. Title in E] It is better to enter into the Kingdome of God with one eye, &c. l. 5. E] Or if. l. 7. E] of thee. ll. 9, 10. Title in E] Christ casteth out two divells at once. l. 12. A] on B] one. l. 14. A] is B] his. ll. 16, 17. Title in E] To them yt passed by at o^r Savio^{rs} passion. l. 24. Title in E] Blessed is—& the papps, wch thou hast suckt &c.

p. **81**, l. 1. Title in E] On Pilate washing his hands B] blood-stanied. l. 12. E] its own l. 15. E] sad murmur...that staines. l. 16. E] Oh leave, for shame. l. 23. E] of him that. Last line. E] Roses heere.

p. **82**, l. 7. D and E] Oh thou alone. l. 8. E] thou giv'st us none.

p. **83**, l. 1. D and E *add*] Joh. l. 6. A *reads*]

> *Upon the Thornes taken downe from our Lords head bloody.*
>
> Know'st thou this Souldier? 'tis a much chang'd plant, which yet
> Thy selfe did'st set,
> 'Tis chang'd indeed, did Autumn e're such beauties bring
> To shame his Spring?
> O! who so hard an husbandman could ever find
> A soyle so kind?
> Is not the soile a kind one (think ye) that returnes
> *Roses* for *Thornes*?

See also p. 243. ll. 16, 17. Title in E] Upon Mary Magdalene. l. 17. D] hayre. l. 28. Title in E] Joh 3 19 Light is come into the world. l. 30. D and E] his darknesse. l. 31. B] Worl'ds A] World's. B] Hell. A] Hell, l. 32. D and E] Hee will not love his.

p. **84**, l. 2. Title in E] Pauls resolution. l. 3. E] Come bonds, come death. l. 4. E] hard names. l. 5. E] other bonds. l. 6. A] Nor other death E] than that. l. 7. Title in E] On Peter's casting the nett. l. 12. A, D and E] Our Lord. In E the poem is arranged in couplets. l. 14. B] life? A] life?) l. 18. E] floodgates. l. 19. E] Then shall hee drinke: and drinke shall doe his worst. l. 21. E] My paines are in their Nonage: my young feares. l. 22. D] yet but. l. 23. D, E] darke woes. l. 24. E] are tender. l. 25. B] unfleg'd A] unfledg'd. l. 26. E] a towardnesse. l. 30. E] The knife.

p. **85**, l. 22. See also p. 244. l. 27. A] O never could bee found Garments too [B to] good. l. 28. A] but these.

p. **86**, l. 5. E] these paths. l. 6. A] One whose. l. 17. E] Makes high noon. l. 22. D] And when simple. l. 28. E] weary wonder. l. 29. E] giddy steps. l. 30. A and E] Spreads a Path cleare as the Day. l. 34. E] learne new. l. 35. B] Sepheards A] Shepheards.

APPENDIX

p. 87, l. 1. D] and covers. l. 4. E] that shade. l. 19. E] his brims. l. 23. E] about my. l. 29. A] eternity, B] eternity.

p. 88, l. 1. E adds after title] Paraphrasi Poëticâ. l. 5. E] On the willowes nodding. l. 28. E] that cryd'st. l. 29. D] and never, never rise.

p. 89, l. 1. Title in A] Easter Day E] Upon Christ's Resurrection. l. 13. A and E] annalls live.

p. 90, l. 1. E indexes this poem, but the leaves are missing in the MS.

p. 91, l. 27. A full stop replaces a comma at the end of the line.

p. 97, l. 4. The full stop in B has been changed to a comma at the end of the line. l. 16. A full stop has been added at the end of the line.

p. 98, l. 8. A semicolon has been added at the end of the line.

p. 101, l. 6. A colon has been added at the end of the line.

p. 103, l. 27. A parenthesis has been taken away before *said*.

p. 105, l. 2. A *omits*] snake. l. 24. B] murmurs. A] murmurs,

p. 106, l. 36. B] Breasts, A] Beasts

p. 107, l. 21. E] ut tenerae. l. 30. B misprints] *tanqnam*.

p. 108, l. 9. E] volvit opes l. 19. E] Divitiisque.

p. 109, l. 6. B misprints] *qnæ*.

p. 110, l. 1. A] G. Herberts. Title in E] Upon Herbert's Temple, sent to a Gentlewoman. l. 5. E] fire from your faire eyes. l. 7. E] hand unties; l. 8. A] you have an Angell by th' wings. l. 9. E] gladly would. l. 10. E] waite on your chast morning. l. 14. E] That every.

p. 111, l. 1. The poem originally appeared in Robert Shelford's 'Five Pious and Learned Discourses,' Cambridge, 1635, 4to., where it is entitled 'Upon the ensuing Treatises,' and signed 'Rich. Crashaw, Aul. Penb. A.B.' l. 13. A and Shelford *read*] this booke. l. 18. Shelford] thy altars wake. l. 31. Shelford] Pure sluttishnesse.

p. 112, l. 22. In Shelford the poem ends with the following additional ten lines]

> Nor shall our zealous ones still have a fling
> At that most horrible and horned thing,
> Forsooth the Pope: by which black name they call
> The Turk, the Devil, Furies, Hell and all,
> And something more. O he is Antichrist:
> Doubt this, and doubt (say they) that Christ is Christ.
> Why, 'tis a point of Faith. What e're it be,
> I'm sure it is no point of Charitie.
> In summe, no longer shall our people hope,
> To be a true Protestant's, but to hate the Pope.

p. 113, l. 12. Grosart prints] 'In tu quas.'

p. 119, l. 1. E] Fidicinis & Philomelæ Bellum Musicum. l. 20. D, E] the warres.

p. 120, l. 2. E] slick passage. l. 6. D] evenly shear'd. l. 32. D] floods of. l. 33. A] when in E] whence in.

p. 121, l. 7. A] There might you. l. 23. A] grave Noat.

APPENDIX

p. 122, l. 9. E] Those pathes. l. 16. E] thus does he D] some grace. Thus doth he. l. 25. E] murmure melting in mild. l. 28. A] he dare. l. 35. E] so long & loud. l. 40. E] full mouth'd.

p. 123, l. 7. E] chatting strings.

p. 124, l. 17. A] decet tantus.

p. 125, l. 1. D adds] Upon Ælia. l. 7. D] businesse there.

p. 126, ll. 1, 2. Title in E] E. Virg. Georg. particula In laudem veris. l. 4. A and E] Their gentlest. l. 19. E] his most loved blossome to. l. 36. E] but that Heav'ns.

p. 127, l. 7. D] Send no. l. 8. D, E] I shall. l. 10. Title in E] The Faire Æthiopian. l. 12. A, D] in a tender. l. 16. E] that great. l. 24. D, E] her third. l. 30. E] their glimmering.

p. 129, l. 10. A superfluous parenthesis has been taken out after *Jove*. l. 14. D] mens feare. l. 22. B] Cease. l. 23. D] Pitty him not. l. 28. A full stop has been added at the end of the line.

p. 130, l. 1. D] Out of the Greeke. No title in A. l. 3. A full stop has been added at the end of the line. l. 8. D adds] Out of Ausonius. l. 9. D and E] sweet Cytherea. l. 15. E] thus, let us thus be.

p. 131, l. 1. B] In Senerissimæ Reginæ patrum [partum A] hyemalem. l. 35. A capital has been supplied here at the beginning of the line and elsewhere in similar cases.

p. 132, l. 13. A] huc nempe.

p. 133, l. 10. A] Sub praeside. l. 22. B] sacilitate, feveritas A] facilitate, severitas. l. 28. A] mortem. l. 32. A] nimirum. l. 35. A] Anglicana ad. l. 36. A] ne malitia.

p. 134, l. 3. A] ipsa nec dum...quem monstrat. l. 4. A] totam solus. l. 13. E] mox sacrum. l. 14. E] ad ætheriis. l. 15. E] Porrexit astris. l. 16. E] chartâ. cæteris audies quoq̨. l. 17. Published unsigned under a portrait of Bishop Andrewes facing the second edition (folio) of his sermons, 1631. The copy in the University Library, Cambridge, possesses the portrait apparently lacking in the volume Grosart examined (see his edition, Vol. I. p. 217), and gives the following variations: l. 18. See heer a shadow from that. l. 19. through this. l. 20. of our. l. 22. Whose rare industrious. l. 28. a flaming. l. 29. Where still she reads. l. 20. B] duil A] dull. l. 22. E] Whose rare.

p. 135, l. 1. Title in D] Upon the Death of Mr Chambers Fellow of Queens Colledge in Cambridge. Title in E] In obitum desideratissimi Mrl Chambers, Coll: Reginal. Socii. l. 5. E] leest joyes. l. 6. G omits] a. l. 11. E adds]

For soe many hoped yeares
Of fruit, soe many fruitles teares.

l. 16. A] snacht. l. 19. E adds]

Leaving his death ungarnished
Therefore, because hee is dead,

l. 20 E] If yet at least. l. 21. G] Thee the. l. 29. E] there are. l. 35. A] rest. B] rest,

p. 136, l. 1. Title in D] Upon the Death of Mr Herris Fellow of Pembrooke Hall in Cambridge. Title in E] In ejusdem præmatur. obitu. Allegoricum. l. 10. E] gratious tree. l. 25. E] Peept out of their. l. 26. E] on each. l. 32. D] in th' shade. l. 34. E] blooming joyes. l. 35. D] Lavish't the.

APPENDIX

p. 137, l. 13.   E] Fecêre tantae terra impar.

p. 138, l. 1.   Title in D] Upon the same.   Title in E] An Elegie on Mr Herris.   l. 17. D and E] thy Easterne.   l. 19. E] his can.   l. 20. D omits] it.   l. 22. D] thou Death.   l. 27. E] to lend.   l. 30. E] given to day.   Last line. E] shower new.

p. 139, l. 15.   E] rugged storme.   l. 23. D] Spare then Death.   l. 25. E] And let not.   l. 34. E adds]

    Keepe him close, close in thine armes,
    Seal'd upp with a thousand charmes.

p. 140, l. 31.   E] its spleen.   l. 35. D, E] That quotes.

p. 141, l. 1.   Title in D] Another upon the same.   l. 6. E] each lease   D] every lease.   l. 13. E] Could bin found.   l. 26. E] here is dead.

p. 142, l. 1.   Title in E] Epitaphium in eundem.   l. 5. D] Ere thou.

p. 143, l. 8.   E] with downy.   l. 9. E] untimely wave.   ll. 15, 16. Title in D] An Epitaph upon the reverend Dr Brooke.   Title in E] In obitum D^ris Brooke.   l. 23. E] loved banck.

p. 144, l. 1.   Title in E] An Invitation to faire weather.   In itinere ad urgeretur matutinum cœlum tali carmine invitabatur serenitas.   l. 4. G] thy hight's.   l. 6. G] on yond faire flockes.   l. 8. G] thy front, and then there.   l. 13. E] command smooth.   l. 15. E] Those tender drops that   D and G] thy cheeke.   l. 17. G] these delicious.   l. 18. E] Will rise.   G] and disclose.   l. 19. D] To every blushing bed of new-blowne Roses.   E] Two ever-blushing beds of new-blowne roses.   G] To every blushing bedd the new-borne Rose.   l. 24. E] soft and dainty.   l. 27. G] in golden.   l. 29. D] golden Mother.   G] to meete.   l. 30. D] how shee.   G] holy flight.   l. 31. E] in liquid.   D] in liquid Night.   l. 37. E] joy is.

p. 145, l. 4.   D] Sea by Land.   l. 5. D] at her.

p. 146, ll. 1, 2.   Title in E] Ad Auroram Somnolentiæ expiatio.   l. 4. G] my Muses.   l. 9. E] call back   D and G] thy eyes.   l. 15. D] which still hides.   l. 18. D, E] Mine owne.   l. 21. E] no winge.   G] Since this my humble.   l. 22. E] raptures [so A] start   E] and bringe.   l. 27. D] His starry.   l. 28. D] lift up.   l. 29. D]

    To rayse mee from my lazy urne, and clime
    Upon the stooping [A stooped].
Last line. D] where Pitty.

p. 147, l. 3.   E] Bee gentle then.   D] and next time hee doth rise.   l. 5. E] radiant face.   l. 8. E] tell how true.   l. 10. G] and duty.   l. 13. G] And that.   l. 17. D and G] thy altar.   l. 22. D] Why shakest thou thy leaden.   l. 28. An exclamation mark has been supplied.

p. 148, l. 15.   E] man's fate.   l. 20. D omits] the.   l. 31. D] warme.

p. 150, l. 17.   A] tenet ille.

p. 151, l. 27.   D] those treasures.   l. 31. D] So made men, Both ..friends for ever.

p. 153, l. 1.   Title in D] Italian.   l. 4. D] have reft.   l. 16. D] Italian.

p. 155, l. 1.   Printed in both A and B as Crashaw's but it is now generally attributed to Dr Edward Rainbow, Bishop of Carlisle (see 'Notes and Queries,' 2nd Ser. iv. 286).   Only the second of the two poems is given in E.   Both (see next page) face the title-page of Henry Isaacson's 'Saturni Ephemerides,' 1633, where they are entitled ' The Frontispiece explained.'

APPENDIX

p. 156, l. 4. E and Isaacson] die, if (Phoenix-like). l. 5. E and Isaacson] Nature take. l. 6. A comma takes the place of a full stop at the end of the line.

p. 157, ll. 1, 2. Title in D] An Epitaph upon the Death of Mr Ashton Citizen of London. l. 14. D *adds*]
For every day his deeds put on
His Sundayes repetition.

l. 21. A full stop has been taken away after *zeale*. D] yett in zeale. l. 25. D] in Life hee lov'd. l. 26. D] to lead him.

p. 158, l. 24. B] trinmphi.

p. 159, l. 1. Title in E] Catull. Vivamus, mea Lesbia &c. l. 5. D and E] Blithest Sol. l. 10. D and E] numerous kisses. l. 11. D] upon our. l..15. A and B] of another. l. 18. D and E] our reckoning. l. 31. A] infans B] infuns.

p. 160, l. 11. G] steps tread our. l. 15. G] Meete her my wishes. l. 20. D] gawdy fair. l. 26. G] a bowe, blush. l. 29. G] commend the.

p. 161, l. 6. G] what their. l. 15. G] Themselves in simple naked-nesse. ll. 16—18. G] displace...outface.. grace. l. 26. G] that dares.

p. 162, l. 10. G] Teares fond and sleight. l. 14. D] And fond. ll. 19, 21. G has this verse after the next one.

p. 163, l. 6. D] Art and all ornament th Shame. l. 26. D] dares apply. Last line. G] but she my story.

p. 164, l. 1. Published in 'Voces Votivæ ab Academicis Cantabrigiensibus pro novissimo Carolo et Mariæ principe filio emissæ, Cantabrigiæ: apud Rogerum Daniel. MDCXL.' l. 2. B] paturientem.

p. 165, l. 1. Published in 'Voces Votivæ.' l. 9. V.V.] to our. l. 14. B] to short...to long.

p. 166, ll. 1—3. Title in E] A Panegyrick Upon the birth of the Duke of Yorke. A and D] Upon the Duke of Yorke his Birth A Panegyricke. The section-titles are not in A, D or E. l. 10. A and D] full glorys. l. 18. A, D and E] O if. l. 19. E] hadst need. l. 20. D] make thee. l. 32. These last four lines are not in A, D or E.

p. 167, l. 2. A] Great Charles. l. 11. B] owne A] one. l. 16. A, D read] in these [E those]. l. 18. E] alablaster. l. 19. A and D] These hands ...these cherries. l. 20. A and D] art of all. l. 21. D] The well-wrought. l. 23. A] mayest thou. l. 24. A and D] th'ast drawn this. l. 31. D] so that. l. 33. The first six lines of this section are not in A, D or E.

p. 168, l. 8. A and E] were the pearls. D] that wept. l. 10. This section is not in A, D or E.

p. 169, l. 38. A and D] may the Light.

p. 170, l. 5. A and D] that's done. l. 24. A, D and E] their offrings.

p. 171, last line. E] Castris quippe.

p. 173, ll. 7, 8. E] Ut sunt.

p. 174, l. 1. E] malorum mala fœmina. l. 10. E] agnoscite vestros. l. 21. B] Mortales. Last line. E] Nempe fuit.

p. 175, l. 1. Title in E] In Phœbum amantem.

p. 177, l. 13. E] ni Dominæ.

374

APPENDIX

p. 178, l. 2. E] ignis habet.   l. 16. E] Troja libentius.   These two words end the previous line in E.

p. 179, l. 1.   Title in E] Pigmalion.

p. 180, l. 20. E] alter vetat ut sit.   l. 21. E] muta it.   ll. 24, 26. E] Genethliacon vel Epicedium.   30. E] Haud parere.

p. 182, l. 16.   Title in E] Turbæ rerum humanarum per errorum insidias.

p. 183, l. 7. E] perfido paratu.

CARMEN DEO NOSTRO. Crashaw's designs will be found at the end of these notes. The lines under one of them do not occur elsewhere in his works and, as they may not be easily read as engraved, I give them here :—

Expostulatio Jesu Christi
cum mundo ingrato.

Sum pulcher : at nemo tamen me diligit.
Sum nobilis : nemo est mihi qui serviat.
Sum dives : a me nemo quicquam postulat.
Et cuncta possum : nemo me tamen timet.
Aeternus exsto : quaeror a paucissimis.
Prudensque sum : sed me quis est qui consulit?
Et sum via : at per me quotusquisque ambulat?
Sum veritas : quare mihi non creditur?
Sum vita : verum rarus est qui me petit.
Sum vera lux : videre me nemo cupit.
Sum misericors : nullus fidem in me collocat.
Tu, si peris, non id mihi imputes, Homo :
Salus tibi est a me parata : hac utere.

p. 185, l. 16. C] heaty.   l. 20. C] ef Paris.

p. 190, ll. 6—8. In the British Museum there is a copy of this letter separately printed in 4to, undated in type but bearing the written date 1653, entitled ' A Letter from Mr. Crashaw to the Countess of Denbigh. Against Irresolution and Delay in matters of Religion. London.' The differences are so many that it seems simpler to print the 1653 version here in full.

WHAT Heav'n-besieged Heart is this
Stands Trembling at the Gate of Blisse :
Holds fast the Door, yet dares not venture
Fairly to open and to enter?
Whose Definition is, A Doubt
'Twixt Life and Death, 'twixt In and Out.
Ah ! linger not, lov'd Soul : A slow
And late Consent was a long No.
Who grants at last, a great while try'de,
And did his best to have Deny'de.
    What Magick-Bolts, what mystick Barrs
Maintain the Will in these strange Warrs?
What Fatall, yet fantastick, Bands
Keep the free Heart from his own Hands?
Say, lingring Fair, why comes the Birth
Of your brave Soul so slowly forth?
Plead your Pretences, O you strong
In weaknesse why you chuse so long
In Labour of your self to ly,
Not daring quite to Live nor Die.

375

APPENDIX

So when the Year takes cold we see
Poor Waters their own Prisoners be:
Fetter'd and lock'd up fast they lie
In a cold self-captivity.
Th' astonish'd Nymphs their Floud's strange Fate deplore,
To find themselves their own severer Shoar.
    Love, that lends haste to heaviest things,
In you alone hath lost his wings.
Look round and reade the World's wide face,
The field of Nature or of Grace;
Where can you fix, to find Excuse
Or Pattern for the Pace you use?
Mark with what Faith Fruits answer Flowers,
And know the Call of Heav'n's kind showers:
Each mindfull Plant hasts to make good
The hope and promise of his Bud.
Seed-time's not all; there should be Harvest too.
Alas! and has the Year no Spring for you?
    Both Winds and Waters urge their way,
And murmure if they meet a stay.
Mark how the curl'd Waves work and wind,
All hating to be left behind.
Each bigge with businesse thrusts the other,
And seems to say, Make haste, my Brother.
The aiery nation of neat Doves.
That draw the Chariot of chast Loves,
Chide your delay: yea those dull things,
Whose wayes have least to doe with wings,
Make wings at least of their own Weight,
And by their Love controll their Fate.
So lumpish Steel, untaught to move,
Learn'd first his Lightnesse by his Love.
    What e're Love's matter be, he moves
By th' even wings of his own Doves,
Lives by his own Laws, and does hold
In grossest Metalls his own Gold.
    All things swear friends to Fair and Good,
Yea Suitours; Man alone is wo'ed,
Tediously wo'ed, and hardly wone:
Only not slow to be undone.
As if the Bargain had been driven
So hardly betwixt Earth and Heaven;
Our God would thrive too fast, and be
Too much a gainer by't, should we
Our purchas'd selves too soon bestow
On him, who has not lov'd us so.
When love of Us call'd Him to see
If wee'd vouchsafe his company,
He left his Father's Court, and came
Lightly as a Lambent Flame,
Leaping upon the Hills, to be
The Humble King of You and Me.
Nor can the cares of his whole Crown

APPENDIX

(When one poor Sigh sends for him down)
Detain him, but he leaves behind
The late wings of the lazy Wind,
Spurns the tame Laws of Time and Place,
And breaks through all ten Heav'ns to our embrace.
Yield to his Siege, wise Soul, and see
Your Triumph in his Victory.
Disband dull Feares, give Faith the day :
To save your Life, kill your Delay.
'Tis Cowardise that keeps this Field ;
And want of Courage not to Yield.
Yield then, O yield, that Love may win
The Fort at last, and let Life in.
Yield quickly, lest perhaps you prove
Death's Prey, before the Prize of Love.
This Fort of your Fair Self if't be not wone,
He is repuls'd indeed, but You'r undone.

l. 22.   A parenthesis has been supplied after *weaknes!*

p. 191, l. 22.   C] rebell-wotd.

p. 193, ll. 1—7.   Title in B] On the name of Jesus.   l. 14.   B *reads*] the bright *instead of* you bright.   l. 24.   A full stop has been taken away after *see*.   l. 31. B] little word.

p. 194, l. 18.   B] This   C] Thas.   l. 20.   A full stop has been added after *sing*.   l. 25.   B] a habit fit of self-tun'd.   l. 29.   A semicolon has been added after *you*.

p. 195, l. 8.   B] Your powers.   l. 9.   C] yours Lutes.   l. 28.   B] aloud.   Last line.   B] yeild.

p. 196, l. 1.   B] Seraphins.   l. 2.   B] Loyall breast.   l. 10.   B] forth from.   l. 11.   A comma has been added after *Light*.   l. 15.   A full stop has been taken away after *Guest*.   l. 28.   B] All heavens.

p. 198, l. 2.   A comma has been supplied after *Paradises*.   l. 3.   B] soules tastes.   l. 18.   B] bare thee.   l. 20.   B] ware thee.   l. 25.   B] served therein thy.   A full stop has been added after *ends*.

p. 200.   Title in B] An [A *in* A *and* E] Hymne of the Nativity, sung as by [A *and* E sung by] the Shepheards.

p. 201, ll. 4—7.   A and E *read*]
Come wee Shepheards who have seene
Dayes King deposed by Nights Queene.
Come lift we up our lofty song,
To wake the Sun that sleeps [E lies] too long.

ll. 8—10.   A and E *read*]
'Hee in this our generall joy,
Slept, and dreampt of no such thing,
While we found out the fair-ey'd Boy,'
l. 19.   C] Thysis.   l. 25.   A and E] thy eyes.   l. 26.   The Chorus lines between the stanzas are not in A or E.   l. 27.   A and E] chid the world.
l. 31.   C] eye's.   l. 32.   A] frosts.

p. 202, l. 2.   A, B and E] Bright dawn.   The second and third stanzas on this page are not in A or E.   l. 3.   E] thy eyes.   A and E] the East   B] their East   C] their Eate.   l. 5.   A comma has been supplied after *sight*.   l. 11.   B] ye powers.   l. 13.   B] ye Powers.   l. 14.   B] Thyrs   C] Thyt.

APPENDIX

l. 17. B] is all one.   l. 18. C] morn. B] morne,   l. 20. B] Babe, &c.
l. 21. B] Tit C] Tir.   l. 23. E] white sheets.   l. 24. A colon has been
supplied after *bed*.   l. 28. In A and E the stanza is as follows]

> I saw th' officious Angels bring,
>   The downe that their soft brests did strow,
> For well they now can spare their wings,
>   When Heaven it selfe lyes here below.
> Faire Youth (said I) be not too rough,
> Thy Downe though soft's not soft enough.

In line 3 of this stanza B prints *wings*, otherwise as in C.   Last line.
B] said we.

    p. 203.   The first stanza on this page reads as follows in A and E]

> The Babe no sooner 'gan to seeke,
>   Where to lay his lovely head,
> But streight his eyes advis'd his Cheeke,
>   'Twixt Mothers Brests to goe to bed.
> Sweet choise (said I) no way but so,
> Not to lye cold, yet sleepe in snow.

l. 1. C] No no. B] No, no,   l. 5. B] said I.   l. 7. B] choice, &c.   l. 16.
A and E] Welcome to our wondring sight.   l. 20. A and E] glorious Birth.
l. 22. A, B and E] not to.   C] silk. A, B] silke,   l. 24. A and E] virgins.
l. 26. A] breathes B] breath's C] brearhes.   l. 27. A, B and E add the
following stanza after this one]

> Shee sings thy Teares asleepe, and dips
>   Her Kisses in thy weeping Eye,
> Shee spreads the red leaves of thy Lips,
>   That in their Buds yet blushing lye,
> Shee 'gainst those Mother-Diamonds tryes
> The points of her young Eagles Eyes.

l. 28.   A full stop has been taken away after *flyes*.   Last three lines.
A and E *read*]

> But to poore Shepheards, simple things,
> That use no varnish, no oyl'd Arts,
> But lift clean hands full of cleare hearts.

    p. 204.   A and B print as two stanzas, as throughout the poem.   l. 6.
B] their sheep A and E] The Shepheards, while they feed their [E the]
sheepe.   l. 11. A and E *omit*] Till burnt.   l. 12. A and E] Wee'l burne,
our owne best sacrifice.

    p. 205, ll. 1, 2.   Title in A] An Himne [B A Hymne] for the Circum-
cision day of our Lord.   l. 3. A] thou first.   l. 7. A] of Laces.   l. 9. A]
Guild thee.   l. 12. B] bosome showes.   l. 16. A] his glorious beames.
l. 18. A] his eyes.   ll. 20, 21. A]

> Rob the rich store her Cabinets keep,
> The pure birth of each sparkling nest.

l. 23. A and B] embrace.   l. 25. A] in them.

    p. 206, l. 1.   A] the sweet.   l. 3. A and B] The Moone.   l. 4. A]
And leave the long adored Sunne.   l. 5. A] Thy nobler beauty.   l. 8. A
and B *add*]

> Nor while they leave him shall they loose the Sunne,
> But in thy fairest eyes find two for one.

378

APPENDIX

p. 207. Title in B] A Hymne for the Epiphanie. Sung as by the three Kings. l. 1. Not in B. l. 4. (2) not in B. l. 6. (3) not in B. l. 15. A full stop has been supplied after *Eyes*. l. 25. C] east. B] East,

p. 208, l. 4. B] halfe spheare C] half-spear. l. 11. B] (1) C] (2). B] world's C] wold's.

p. 210, l. 6. B] thy chast. l. 17. A full stop has been taken away after *worn*. ll. 21—3. B] gives 'But lean and tame' as the beginning of 3's lines and gives the 'Mithra' line only to Chorus.

p. 211, l. 13. A semicolon has been supplied after *song* and a full stop after *us* in line 15. l. 16. B] 1 C] (2). l. 19. B] love-sick world C] love-sick, world. l. 26. B] deere doome. l. 28. C] ludgment. l. 38. B] domesticks. l. 40. C] hour's.

p. 212, l. 6. B] 1 C] (2). l. 10. A full stop has been added after *Light*. l. 24. B] the best. l. 26. B] 1. C] (2). l. 30. B] Use to. l. 31. C] in [it B] self their rorch [torch B], l. 33. B] the conscious. l. 37. C] Ground. l. 38. C] dscant, B] descant. l. 39. B] with what. l. 40. B] his strong.

p. 213, l. 2. B] seize. l. 3. C] ohsequious. l. 7. A full stop has been added after *you*. l. 12. C] negatine.

p. 214, l. 10. B] glorious Tire. l. 13. B] 1 His Gold C] (3) His Gold.

p. 215, l. 3. B adds] upon his dedicating to her the foregoing Hymne. l. 5. B] crownes C] cownes. C] race. B] race, l. 9. C] face. B] face, l. 10. B] Rosie down. l. 14. B] We wade in you (deare Queen). l. 17. B] Royall harvest. l. 21. B] whole groves. l. 23. B] Lamb's great Sire.

p. 216. In B only the hymns for each hour are given, numbered 1 to 7, under the general title 'Upon our B. Saviour's Passion,' followed by 'The Antiphona' for Compline (see p. 229), 'The recommendation of the precedent Poems' (see p. 230) 'A Prayer' 'O Lord Jesus Christ, Son of the Living God, interpose,' etc. and 'Christ's victory,' divided later into 'The Antiphona' for the third, sixth and ninth hours (see pp. 221, 223 and 225).

p. 217, l. 19. B] wakefull dawning. l. 21. C] Father' word. l. 26. B] betrayd and taken.

p. 218, l. 19. B omits here and elsewhere the words 'unto all quick and dead' and reads 'the Church.'

p. 219, l. 14. B] early Morne. l. 15. B] It could. l. 19. B] blotts those. l. 23. C] Antiphona.

p. 220, l. 13. C] O Lrod...living Ood.

p. 221, l. 18. B] then C] them. l. 24. C] rhe. l. 25. A full stop has been taken away after *side*. l. 28. C] Jalyor. Last line. C] word's losse.

p. 222, last line. C] vorld.

p. 223, l. 15. B] For the faint. l. 18. B] The fruit. l. 31. B] the first.

p. 224, l. 5. A full stop has been taken away after Crosse.

p. 225, l. 14. B] rocks C] roeks. l. 18. B] our great sin's sacrifice. l. 29. C] Deard. Last line. C] word's losse.

p. 227, l. 13. B] could not.

p. 229, l. 13. B] The nightening hour. l. 15. A] heartlesse. l. 23. C] Heart. B] Heart, l. 30. B] such rate.

p. 230, ll. 11—13. See p. 73.

APPENDIX

p. 231, ll. 2—5. Not in B. l. 7. B] languishing. Last line. C] warth.

p. 232, l. 6. B. make a throne C] Trhone. l. 13. B] costly crueltie. l. 16. B] heav'n wag'd. ll. 17, 18. B *reads*]

Both with one price were weighed,
Both with one price were paid.

The 7th stanza is not in B. l. 31. B] live for to. l. 32. B] which thy blessed death did.

p. 233. See p. 78.

p. 234, l. 12. A comma replaces a full stop after *merchandise.*

p. 235, l. 1. C] Ler. l. 5. B] Thou.

p. 237, l. 7. C] Nother. l. 13. B] Are more ..Owne heart. l. 33. A semicolon has been supplied after *smart.* l. 34. C] growingt.

p. 238, l. 18. C] nobest. l. 26. B] love. l. 30. B] something to thy. l. 32. B] Oh give me too.

p. 239. B omits stanzas VII and VIII. l. 5. C] etertall. l. 24. B] Shall I in sins sets there. l. 29. C] Is B] If not more just.

p. 240, l. 2. B] Lend, O lend. l. 10. B] studie thee. l. 15. B] thy deare. ll. 19, 20. B]

Let my life end in love, and lye beneath
Thy deare lost vitall death,

l. 22. B] in thy Lords death.

p. 241. E gives 5 stanzas only, 1, 3, 4, 5, 2. ll. 1—6. Title in A and D] On the bleeding wounds [B body] of our crucified Lord. l. 9. A, D and E] thy hands. l. 10. A, D and E] thy head. l. 11. A, D and E] thy purple. l. 12. This verse is 5th in A and D, the order being 1, 3, 4, 5, 2, Water'd (see below) 6, 7, 8, 9. l. 14. A and D] In Teares? l. 16. B] That streames. l. 18. A, D and E] they cannot. l. 20. A] they are wont. D *omits*] ever. l. 21. D and B] own blood. l. 23. A and E] Thy hand. l. 26. E] It dropps.

p. 242, l. 5. A prints stanza 2 here and follows with]

Water'd by the showres they bring,
The thornes that thy blest browes encloses
(A cruell and a costly spring)
Conceive proud hopes of proving Roses.

l. 7. A and D] Not a haire but. l. 18. A and D] Threatning all to overflow.

p. 243. See p. 83. l. 7. A full stop has been taken away after *yet.* l. 12. C] Thrones.

p. 244. See p. 85. ll. 1—6. Title in A] On our crucified Lord Naked, and bloody. l. 11. A] could be found Garments. l. 12. A] but these.

pp. 245 and 246, ll. 1, 2. Title in B] A Hymne to Our Saviour by the Faithfull Receiver of the Sacrament. l. 3. the Power. l. 6. A full stop has been added after *me.*

p. 247, l. 1. B] Help, Lord, my Faith, my Hope increase. ll. 5, 6. B omits these lines.

p. 248, ll. 1—5. Title in B] A Hymne on the B. Sacrament. l. 9. The last two words are omitted in the 1652 copy used. I have supplied them from B. l. 10. B] Heav'n, and Hands. l. 12. B] Ambitions. l. 14. C] Liee. l. 28. B] Law of a new Law.

380

APPENDIX

p. 249, l. 18. B] Names not things.　l. 21. B] on Christ.　l. 24. B]
Nor wound.

p. 250, l. 14. C] Sacrieice.　l. 26. B] meane soules.

p. 251, ll. 1—7. Title in B] A Hymne in meditation of the day of judgement.　l. 10. C] rnn.

p. 252, l. 4. B] the Judge.　l. 28. A colon has been supplied after *me*.

p. 254, ll. 1—3. Title in B] The Virgin Mother.　l. 5. B] below the.
l. 13. C] on the.　l. 24. B] spring.　l. 29. C] their morher　B] your
mother.

p. 255, l. 4. B *adds*] The door was shut, yet let in day.

p. 256, ll. 1—7. Title in B] On the assumption.　E *adds*] of the Virgin
Marie.　l. 10. A and F] heavenly Light.　l. 14. A, E and F] Shee's call'd
againe, harke how th' immortall Dove.　l. 16. E] fair, and.　l. 19. A and
F] No sweets since thou [E save you] art wanting here.　l. 23. A and F
on a fresh line] Come away, come away.　The 16 lines that follow are not in A,
E or F.　l. 28. B] Except as.

p. 257, l. 1.　B] Tree, C] three.　l. 2. B] leavy.　l. 12. B] so great.
l. 13. A, E and F] thy great.　l. 17. A, B, E and F *add*]
　　　And though thy dearest looks must now be [E give] light
　　　　[F now take its flight]
　　　To none but the blest heavens, whose bright
　　　Beholders lost in sweet delight ;
　　　Feed for ever their faire sight
　　　With those divinest eyes, which wee
　　　And our darke world no more shall see.
　　　Though, our poore joyes [E and F eyes] are parted so,
　　　Yet shall our lips never let goe
　　　Thy gracious name, but to [F for] the last,
　　　Our Loving song shall hold it fast.
l. 18. A, E and F] sacred Name.　A full stop has been taken away after *be*.
l. 20. A and F] holy cares.　l. 27. A and F] our sweetness.　l. 28. A and
F] they may.　l. 31. E] mother to.　l. 32. A and F] Live rarest Prıncesse,
and.　l. 33. A and F] of an incomparable.　l. 37. E] humble bragg.　l. 38.
C] ctown.　E] Praise of women, Pride of men.　l. 40. C] brest.

pp. 258—9.　Title in A, B and D] The Weeper.　A omits, B gives, the
couplet on p. 258 under the title.

p. 259.　The order of verses in A is 1, 2, 3, 4, 5, 12, 8, Not the soft Gold
(see below), 7, 6, Sadnesse all the while (see below), 9, 10, 13, 14, Thus dost
thou melt the year (see note to p. 264, ll. 2—4), Time as by thee (see below),
24, 23, 26, 28, 29, 30.　The order in D is as in A save that ' Not the soft
Gold, and 7 are transposed.　The order in E is thus :—1, 2, 3, 4, 5, 12, 8,
Not the soft Gold, 7, 6, Sadnesse all the while, 9, 10, 13, 14, 26, Thus dost
thou melt (see note to p. 264, ll. 2—4), Time as by thee, 24, 23, Say watry
brothers (see note to p. 264), 29, 30.
　The following are the three verses referred to above ; they do not form part
of the later text.
　　　　Not the soft Gold which
　　　Steales from the Amber-weeping Tree,
　　　　Makes sorrow halfe so Rich,
　　　As the drops distil'd from thee.

APPENDIX

Sorrowes best Jewels lye in these
Caskets, of which Heaven keeps the Keyes.

Sadnesse all the while
Shee sits in such a Throne as this,
Can doe nought but smile,
Nor beleeves shee sadnesse is .
Gladnesse it selfe would bee more glad
To bee made so sweetly sad.

Time as by thee he passes,
Makes thy ever-watry eyes
His Hower-Glasses.
By them his steps he rectifies.
The sands he us'd no longer please,
For his owne sands hee'l use thy seas [E thy teares].

l. 5. A, B and D] silver-forded. l. 19. A, D and E] they are indeed. l. 27.
A] rivers meet. l. 28. A, D and E] Thine Crawles. ll. 29, 30. A, D
and E]

Heaven, of such faire floods as this [E these],
Heaven the Christall Ocean is.

p. 260, l. 4. A, D and E] soft influence. l. 21. A, D and E] Her richest
l. 24. E] pale cheeks. l. 27. A, D and E] it tremble heere. A comma as
in B has taken the place of the full stop in C. l. 28. A, D and E] to be
thy Teare.` l. 35. E] and more sweet.

p. 261, l. 3. A] the case. l. 5. B] they are; C] they, are. l. 7. A,
D and E] May Balsame. l. 19. A, D and E] with their bottles. l. 20.
B and E] And draw D] from those. l. 25. A, D and E] Might hee flow
from thee. l. 26. A and D] would he. l. 27. A, D and E] Richer farre
does he esteem. l. 32. E] thy eyes. l. 34. A, D and E] softer showres.
l. 35. A, D and E] returned fairer flowers.

p. 262, l. 2. C] ckeeks. l. 4. A full stop has been taken away after
doves. l. 5. B] washt. C] washt, l. 8. Not numbered in C. l. 9. A
full stop has been taken away after *woes*. l. 10. B] and tears, and smiles.
l. 17. B] balsome fires...fill thee? l. 18. B] Cause great. l. 24. B] this
vine. l. 25. B] that wounded. l. 26. B] those wounded.

p. 263, l. 3. B] large expences. l. 5. B] the wrath. l. 22. A, D and
E] the Night arise? l. 23. A, D and E] thy teares doe. l. 24. A, D and
E] Does night loose her eyes? l. 31. A, D and E] Thy teares just cadence
still keeps time. l. 32. A] Prayer B and E] praier C] paire.

p. 264, ll. 2—4. A, D and E]
Thus dost thou melt the yeare
Into a weeping motion,
Each minute waiteth heere;
l. 4. C] waits. B] waits, l. 10. A and E] Will thy. l. 13. A, D and E]
by Dayes, by Monthes, by Yeares. A full stop has been taken away after
yeares. l. 18. B] fire. l. 23. B] ye bright. The version in A, D and E
is thus]

Say watry Brothers
Yee simpering sons of those faire eyes,
Your fertile [D and E fruitfull] Mothers.
What hath our world that can entice

382

APPENDIX

You to be borne? what is't can borrow
You from her eyes swolne wombes of sorrow.
l. 31. A, D and E] O whither? for the sluttish Earth. l. 33. A, B, D and E] your Birth. l. 34. A, D and E *omit*] Sweet.

p. 265, l. 3. E] The darling. l. 6. A, D and E *read*]
No such thing; we goe to meet
A worthier [D and E worthy] object, Our Lord's [E Lord Jesus] feet.

pp. 266 and 267, ll. 1, 2. Title in A and B]. In memory of the Vertuous and Learned Lady Madre de Teresa that sought an Early Martyrdome.

p. 267, l. 4. C] word. B] word, l. 5. A] Wee need to goe to. l. 6. A] stout and tall. l. 7. A] Ripe and full, growne, that. l. 10. A] unto the. l. 12. A] whose large breasts built a. l. 13. A] For love their Lord, glorious and great. l. 14. A] Weell see. l. 15. A] And make his. l. 16. A full stop has been added after *child*. l. 17. A] had B] hath C] has A] a name. l. 27. A] had B] hath C] has. l. 33. A] wee straight C] you staight.

p. 268, l. 3. A] thirst...dare. l. 6. A and B] Her weake C] Her what. l. 8. A] kisses C] hisles. l. 10. C] Maryrdom B] for a. l. 11. A] for her. l. 13. B] and try. l. 14. A] Shee offers. l. 26. A and B *add*] Farewell what ever deare may bee. l. 27. A full stop has been added after *knee* and after *martyrdom* 6 lines below. l. 37. B] soft cabinet. l. 39. A full stop has been added after *so*.

p. 269, l. 2. A] Loves hand. l. 15. A] be spent B] be sent. l. 17. A comma replaces a full stop after *Thee*. l. 18. A] and the first borne. l. 29. A] he still may dy. l. 32. B] thine embraces. l. 34. Printed thus in A]

Balsome, to heale themselves with——
——————————————thus

When these etc.
In B and C 'thus' follows 'with' in the same line, without any break in C, after a full stop and with a capital T in B.

p. 270, l. 7. A and B] as thou shalt first. l. 13. A] on thee. l. 14. A] when she shall C] Lief. l. 15. A] her hand. l. 18. A] joy. l. 31. A and B add] All thy sorrows here shall shine. l. 32. A and B] And thy. l. 35. A] deaths B] Deat'hs. l. 36. A] soule, which late they.

p. 271, l. 12. A] thy spowse. l. 19. A and B] keeps.

p. 272, ll. 2 and 4. A full stop has been taken away after *Apologie*. C prints *Hymen*. ll. 1—7. Title in A is 'An Apologie for the precedent Hymne.' The title in B is the same, but in B the 'precedent hymne' is 'The Flaming Heart' (see p. 274). l. 9. A] Faire sea. l. 16. A] heavenly maxim. l. 19. A] there lye. l. 23. A] one blood. l. 25. C] aud. l. 27. A] it dwell in Spaine.

p. 273, l. 3. B] a wondring. l. 4. A] Who finds A and B add 'hatch'd' after 'Heart.' l. 7. A and B] are enow. l. 12. A *omits*] too B *prints*] to. l. 18. A full stop has been added after *alone*. l. 19. A] youths Life. l. 23. A and B] in one.

p. 274, l. 4. B *omits*] the seraphicall saint. l. 8. C] biside. l. 11. B] so much. l. 19. B] And Him for Her. l. 26. B] happier. A full stop has been added after *see*.

p. 275, l. 2. A full stop has been added after *Her*. l. 5. B] to paint.

APPENDIX

l. 10. B] form'd Seraphicall.   l. 11. B] But e're...wore faire.   l. 13. B] cheekes.   l. 28. B] shafts.   l. 38. B] who kindly takes the shame.

p. 276, l. 4. C] suffting.   l. 13. C] part. B] part,   l. 14. A full stop has been supplied after *heart* and after *Flame* 4 lines below.,   l. 15. C] lov'es. ll. 25 to end are not in B.   l. 33. C] undanted.   l. 38. C] thrists.

p. 277, l. 4. A parenthesis has been added at the end of the line.   l. 9. Title in B] A Song of divine Love. The second part is more distinctly divided from the first, than in C.   l. 10. C] geace.   l. 23. B] longing strife.

p. 278, ll. 1—5. Title in A] On a prayer-booke sent to Mrs M. R.   Title in B as in C but omits *Prayer* l. 1 and *little* l. 3.   l. 6. A and F] but large. ll. 7—15. For these lines A and F *read*]
(Feare it not, sweet,
It is no hipocrit)
Much larger in it selfe then in its looke.
l. 16. A and F] rich handfull.   l. 17. A and F] royall Hoasts.   l. 19. A and F] A thousand.   l. 21. C] il self.   l. 22. A, B and F] your white. l. 24. A and B] the ghostly...your part   F] your ghostly...your part.   l. 25. A, B and F] your chast.   l. 26. A and F] the Armory.   l. 29. A] hand. l. 31. B] The sinne.

p. 279, l. 1. F] That holds.   l. 5. A, B and F] your heart.   l. 6. B] its part.   l. 13. A] And bring her [B its, F his] bosome full of blessings.   l. 19. A and F] comes.   l. 20. A and F] wandring heart.   l. 24. A] pleasures. l. 26. A and F] dance in the   B] ith'.   l. 28. A and B] Spheare.   l. 34. A, B and F] And stepping.   l. 35. A and B] the sacred.   l. 38. A] These tumultuous.

p. 280, l. 6 A colon has been added after *desire*.   l. 13. A] An hundred thousand loves and graces. F] A hundred loves and graces.   l. 18. F] That dull mortallists.   l. 19. A and F] this hidden store.   l. 30. A and F] Deare silver breasted dove.   l. 33. F] With mingled vows.   l. 35. F] With her immortal.   l. 36. A and F] Happy soule who.

p. 281, l. 3. A and F] O let that [F the] happy soule hold fast.   l. 13. A and F] Happy soule.   l. 16. A and F] a God.

p. 282, l. 9. B] may   C] my.

p. 283, l. 6. B] most pretious.

p. 284, ll. 1—3. A full stop after 'complaint' has been removed to after 'Alexias.'   l. 6. B *omits*] sanite.   l. 8. B] loud Praise.   l. 16. B] Would see.   l. 24. B] leads the way.   l. 30. B] change its.

p. 285, l. 1. B] when lovers. A full stop has been taken away after *graves*.

p. 286, l. 4. A full stop has been added after *me*.   l. 12. B] the beauteous Skies.   l. 22. B] old Times.

p. 287, l. 7. C] eost.   l. 9. B] with sawcy.   l. 15. C] Aleyis.   l. 19. B] O tell.   l. 21. C] tell.   B] tell,   l. 31. B] The Blessed Virgin.   l. 35. A colon has been inserted after *approach*.

p. 288, l. 7. B] No facing Gorgon.   l. 17. B] How sweet's.   l. 20. B] thousands.

p. 289, l. 1. A full stop has been taken away after *Description*. B omits ll. 4—6 of Title.   l. 9. B] pavements weeping.   l. 10. B] costly,   l. 12.

384

C] frishing B] frisking. l. 22. B] slumbers; C] slumbers? l. 23. C] And sing, &, & sigh. l. 24. B] round Spheare. l. 25. B]
> Hands full of hearty labours; Paines that pay
> And prize themselves; doe much, that more they may;

l. 28. C] dayly-ding.

p. 290, l. 7. B] ly close, and keep.

p. 291, ll. 4—6. Title in A and D continues thus] 'Husband and Wife, which died, and were buried together. Title in E] Epitaphium conjugum unâ mortuor. et sepultor. Title in G] A man and his wife who dyed together, and were so buried. l. 8. A] the second. l. 11. A] not sever man and Wife [C Wiee]. l. 12. A, D and G] Because...Liv'd. l. 16. A, D, E and G] knot that love. ll. 17—20. A, D, E and G omit] And though...no harm. l. 23. A, B, D, E and G] And the. G] morning dawn. l. 25. A, E and G] And they waken with that Light [B wake into that]. l. 26. A, D, E and G] never sleepe in.

p. 292, ll. 1—5. Title in A] Upon Mr Staninough's Death. Title in B] At the Funerall of a young Gentleman. Title in D] Upon the Death of Mr Stanninough, Fellow of Queens Colledge in Cambridge. l. 13. A, B and D] ye soft. l. 18. A] thy Idæa. l. 19. A and D] thy bulke. l. 21. A and D] thy small. l. 22. C] norrow. l. 25. C] neigbourhood. In A and D the line ends thus :—'nothing! here put on' and the next line is :—'Thy selfe in this unfeigned reflection'; omitting 'Proud...eyeliddes.' l. 29. A and D] (Through all your painting) showes you your own face. l. 31. A and D] To the proud hopes. A full stop has been added after Mortality. l. 32. A and D] this selfe-prison'd eye.

p. 293. The poem appeared in the English translation of Leonard Lessius's Hygiasticon, see 3rd edn., published at Cambridge in 1636. The first 12 lines of the poem are not there given. ll. 1—6. Title in A and B] In praise of Lessius his rule of health. D] Upon Lessius. E] Upon Lessius, his Hygeiasticon. l. 7. A, B, D and E omit] and. l. 9. A, D and E] cruell strife. l. 15. A, D and E] at length. l. 16. A, D and E add]

> Goe poore man thinke what shall bee
> Remedie against [E 'gainst] thy remedie.

l. 19. A, D and Lessius] wouldst thou. E ends at 'Reader.' l. 21. A, D and Lessius] Wouldst see. l. 22. A and B] His own Physick. l. 27. C] oppest. l. 29. Lessius] Whose soul's.

p. 294, l. 5. C] way. B] way, l. 6. A and D] Heavn hath a. l. 7. A] Would'st thou see. l. 10. A, B, D and Lessius] A set. l. 13. A and Lessius] All a nest of roses D] see a bed of roses grow. l. 14. D] In a nest of. C] nf renerend. l. 16. C] Sring. l. 22. Lessius] His soul. l. 24. D] A sigh, a kisse. The last 8 lines of the poem are not in A.

p. 295, l. 1. Title in A and B] On Hope, By way of Question and Answer, betweene A. Cowley, and R. Crashaw. In both editions this and the answer on pp. 297 and 8 form one poem, ten lines of Cowley being followed by ten of Crashaw, till both are ended, beginning with ten of Cowley and ending with twenty of Crashaw. l. 3. A and B] succeed, and. l. 4. A and B] ill, and. l. 8. A] The Fates have B] The Fates of. l. 10. A and B] ends. l. 11. B] at all. l. 17. Full stops have been added after bed and Thee two lines below. l. 19. A and B] So mighty. l. 21. A and B] its spirits. l. 25. A semicolon has been added after are. l. 26. A and B] Thine empty cloud the eye,

APPENDIX

it selfe deceives. l. 31. A and B] not North. l. 34. C] repenrance. A and B] shield of fond. Last line. A and B] Chymicks.

p. 296, l. 2. A and B] strange witchcraft.

p. 297, l. 1. A full stop has been taken away after *Crashaws*. l. 5. A and B] of things. ll. 8, 9. A, B and G read thus]
> Faire cloud of fire, both shade, and light,
> Our life in death, our day in night.

l. 12. A, B and G] thinne dilemma. l. 13. A, B and G] like the sick Moone at the. A full stop has been added at the end of this line and the twelfth below. l. 14. A, B and G] Thou art Loves. l. 15. A, B and G] Of Faith : the steward of our growing stocke. l. 16. A, B and G] Crown-lands lye above. l. 20. C] ckeek. l. 21. A, B and G] Thou thus steal'st downe. l. 22. A, B and G] Chaste kisse wrongs no. l. 26. A, B and G] The generous. l. 27. A, B and G] Nor need wee kill. l. 28. A, B and G *omit*] growing. Last line. A and B] subtile essence.

p. 298, l. 1. A, B and G] law warres. l. 2. A, B and G *omit*] walks ; &. l. 3. A, B and G] where our winds. A comma has been added after *stirr*. l. 4. A, B and G] And Fate's whole. A and B *add*]
> Her shafts, and shee fly farre above,
> And forrage in the fields of light, and love.

l. 6. A and B] where, or what. l. 10. C] antitode. l. 11. A, B and G] Temper'd 'twixt cold despaire. l. 15. A, B and G] And loves. G] fierce and fruitlesse. l. 16. G *omits*] all. l. 17. A and B] Huntresse. l. 18. A and B] field.

EPIGRAMMATA SACRA, 2nd Edn., 1670. Only those poems not in the 1st edition are here printed. I do not know what authority there may be for these additions, so long after Crawshaw's death, but they are probably genuine as two are in the Sancroft MS. (Improba turba tace *and* O ut ego, pp. 304 and 305). As the first of these differs somewhat from the Sancroft copy I have given the MS. form in its place on p. 318 (Tu mala turba tace).

p. 303, l. 2. σεὸs in text. l. 14. Ἤη in text.

p. 305, l. 4. E] ego ut. l. 8. E] error abegit. l. 12. E] Ex his quos. l. 13. E] Ex me.

p. 339, l. 18. Mr F. G. Plaistowe, M.A., Librarian of Queens' College, who has very kindly allowed me to refer to him in a few cases of difficulty in the reading of Abp Sancroft's transcript, suggests that ἀναίκην in the MS. is an error for ἀνάγκην.

p. 345, l. 13. E] forbid the.

p. 346. D gives the following variations in this poem. l. 1. Out of Petronius. l. 8. And dayntyest drake. The two following lines 'Though ...new' are not in D. l. 13. pretious Scarus. l. 17. The Barbill too is now. l. 18. And cloying.

p. 349, l. 6. E] from of.

p. 351, l. 9. A full stop has been supplied after *villanie*.

p. 356, l. 11. E] From of. l. 16. E] throwes of.

p. 359, l. 6. E] smile. for Chloe that.

p. 364, ll. 20 and 24. A colon has been supplied at the end of each line and also at the end of l. 19, p. 366.

386

INDEX OF TITLES

INDEX OF TITLES

388

INDEX· OF TITLES

INDEX OF TITLES

INDEX OF TITLES

INDEX OF TITLES

392

INDEX OF TITLES

INDEX OF FIRST LINES

INDEX OF FIRST LINES

INDEX OF FIRST LINES

396

INDEX OF FIRST LINES

INDEX OF FIRST LINES

INDEX OF FIRST 'LINES

400

INDEX OF FIRST LINES

INDEX OF FIRST LINES

CAMBRIDGE: PRINTED BY J AND C. F. CLAY AT THE UNIVERSITY PRESS.

Headpiece to the poem
'To the...Countesse of Denbigh.'

p. 190

Headpiece to the poem
'To the Name...of Jesus.'

p. 193

Ton Createur te faict voir sa naissance,
Daignant souffrir pour toy des son enfance.

Faces the full-page title of the poem
'In the Holy Nativity.'

Below the plate is printed

'Quem vidistis Pastores? &c.
Natum vidimus &c.'

p. 200

Headpiece to the poem

'In the Glorious Epiphanie.'

p. 208

Tradidit Semetipsum pro nobis oblationem, et hostiam Deo in odorem Suauitatis. ad Ephe. 5

On the reverse of the full-page title of

'The Office of the Holy Crosse.'

p. 216

Headpiece to

'The Recommendation.'

p. 230
See also p. 375

Headpiece to
'Sancta Maria Dolorum.'
p. 237

Ecce panis Angeloꝝ.

Headpiece to
'The Hymn of S. Thomas.'
p. 246

Full page, facing
'The Hymn...of the Day of Judgment.'
Below the plate is printed
'Dies Iræ Dies Illa.'

p. 251

S. MARIA MAIOR.
Dilectus meus mihi et ego illi,
qui pascitur inter lilia. Cant:

Headpiece to
'O Gloriosa Domina.'

p. 254

Headpiece to
'The Weeper.'
p. 259

Le Vray portraict de S.te Terese, Foudatrice
des Religieuses, & Religieux reformez de
l'ordre de N.Dame du mont Carmel Decedec
le 4.Octo. 1582. Canonisée le 12.Mars 1622.

On the reverse of the
full-page title to

' A Hymn to the Name
and Honor of...S.
Teresa.'

p. 266